Plural Temporality

Historical Materialism Book Series

The Historical Materialism Book Series is a major publishing initiative of the radical left. The capitalist crisis of the twenty-first century has been met by a resurgence of interest in critical Marxist theory. At the same time, the publishing institutions committed to Marxism have contracted markedly since the high point of the 1970s. The Historical Materialism Book Series is dedicated to addressing this situation by making available important works of Marxist theory. The aim of the series is to publish important theoretical contributions as the basis for vigorous intellectual debate and exchange on the left.

The peer-reviewed series publishes original monographs, translated texts, and reprints of classics across the bounds of academic disciplinary agendas and across the divisions of the left. The series is particularly concerned to encourage the internationalization of Marxist debate and aims to translate significant studies from beyond the English-speaking world.

For a full list of titles in the Historical Materialism Book Series
available in paperback from Haymarket Books, visit:
www.haymarketbooks.org/category/hm-series

Plural Temporality

*Transindividuality and the Aleatory
Between Spinoza and Althusser*

By
Vittorio Morfino

Haymarket Books
Chicago, IL

First published in 2014 by Brill Academic Publishers, The Netherlands
© 2014 Koninklijke Brill NV, Leiden, The Netherlands

Published in paperback in 2015 by
Haymarket Books
P.O. Box 180165
Chicago, IL 60618
773-583-7884
www.haymarketbooks.org

ISBN: 978-1-60846-480-7

Trade distribution:
In the US, Consortium Book Sales, www.cbsd.com
In Canada, Publishers Group Canada, www.pgcbooks.ca
In the UK, Turnaround Publisher Services, www.turnaround-uk.com
In all other countries, Publishers Group Worldwide, www.pgw.com

Cover design by Ragina Johnson.

This book was published with the generous support of
Lannan Foundation and the Wallace Global Fund.

Printed in Canada by union labor.

10 9 8 7 6 5 4 3 2 1

Library of Congress Cataloging-in-Publication data is available.

MIX
Paper from
responsible sources
FSC® C103567

Contents

Preface
The Multitude and the Moving Train

Jason E. Smith

The fundamental stakes of Louis Althusser's first interventions in the field of philosophy, represented by the texts gathered in his 1965 collection *Pour Marx*, were arguably to isolate the specificity of Marxist theory at the level of its method: the specificity of the Marxist dialectic with regard to the 'mystified' and idealist dialectical logic found in the philosophy of Hegel. Althusser's most important contribution to this project is his relatively short text from the summer of 1962, 'Contradiction and Overdetermination'.[1] This particular intervention is remarkable for many reasons, not least in the way it smuggles into the field of Marxist thought a term borrowed from Freud's analysis of the logic of dreams, a daring gesture in the airless confines of the PCF orthodoxy of the early 1960s. It is not, however, the Freudian contraband announced openly in the title that is the most surprising reference in this text, but its otherwise seemingly *de rigueur* reference to the texts of Lenin. Althusser's opening move in his attempt to formalise the logic of a properly Marxist dialecticity is to distance himself from Marx's own pronouncements regarding his relation to Hegel's thought: so many metaphors about extracting kernels from shells and setting thought back on its feet that have given rise to so many vague and inexact commentaries. And yet in having recourse to Lenin, Althusser does not, as does Mao in his 1937 essay 'On Contradiction', refer to the notes Lenin made on Hegel's *Science of Logic* during the first two years of the 'inter-imperialist' war (1914–15). It is not to Lenin's philosophical notes that Althusser's refers but to a series of texts written during or after 1917, with the most crucial reference being to a short intervention made in the early phases of the 1917 revolution: the first letter 'from afar', written in March of that year. The reconceptualisation of the specificity of the Marxist dialectic therefore occurs not through recourse to another *philosophical* text, but to a political one written in the heat of a revolutionary process whose emergence just months before could not have been foreseen, and whose subsequent leaps, turns and drifts remain entirely to come, unpredictable in their turn. It is not by chance, then, that in a curious text written in the 1980s Althusser sketched a 'portrait' of the materialist philosopher as someone who 'catches a moving train', as in the old American Westerns.

When Lenin speaks of the singularity of the Russian revolution – how was it possible that the revolution could occur in Russia rather than elsewhere, why now rather than later? – he underlines the way in which the trigger setting off the revolutionary

---

1   Althusser 1969, pp. 87–128.

process was not the surfacing of an always present but latent central contradiction (the conflictual relation between labour and capital) but the unexpected coming together of a host of seemingly secondary contradictions, factors, circumstances, pressures both internal to the Russian situation as well as those mustered by the inter-imperialist war raging in Europe. This situation, Althusser notes, produces an unprecedented historical moment in which Russia finds itself suspended between two times, at once the least developed country in Europe and yet at the forefront of the proletarian revolution. In his letter 'from afar' written on 7 March 1917, Lenin stresses that the rapid success of the revolutionary process in its early stages was due to the 'unique[ness]' of the historical situation, namely the improbable joining or fusing together of forces that are 'absolutely' at odds with one another:

> That the revolution succeeded so quickly and – seemingly, at the first superficial glance – so radically, is only due to the fact that, as a result of an extremely unique historical situation, *absolutely dissimilar currents, absolutely heterogeneous* class interests, *absolutely contrary* political and social strivings have *merged*, and in a strikingly 'harmonious' manner.[2]

Althusser uses this text and complementary ones from elsewhere in Lenin's post-1917 writings to argue that revolutionary situations by no means develop on the basis of exacerbation or intensification of a fundamental, core contradiction at the heart of capitalist society – what Marx once called the 'moving contradiction' of the capitalist class relation – but on the contrary through a process whereby any number of reputedly secondary contradictions in such societies *accumulate* in such a way that, at a given yet entirely contingent moment, they no longer simply lie side by side, but find themselves converging on and at a single point, fusing together in an explosive combination. But just as important as Althusser's staking out of this properly materialist dialectic in its difference from a Hegelian-idealist one is the relation it suggests between philosophy properly speaking and politics. Though Althusser does not thematise this question actively in his text, what is implicit in his use of these particular texts of Lenin is a new conception of the relation between the history, politics and philosophy. To seek the properly Marxist dialectic in Lenin's political interventions of 1917 is not to suggest a simple inversion of the classical philosophical subordination of politics to theory, in which philosophy would in some form deliver the 'essence' or 'truth' of the political. Rather than making philosophy a mere pendant to politics and history, Althusser suggests a more recursive structure of implication, in which revolutionary struggles in some way produce their own theory, a theory which must in turn produce profound modifications in philosophy. Put in different terms, philosophy is unable to

---

2   Lenin 2004, p. 21. Cited by Althusser 1969, p. 99 n19.

think *under its own power*, incapable of renewing itself by means of its own resources alone: it must be *forced* to think, through an unexpected or aleatory encounter with an historical reality structured by an array of conflictual forces that in certain determined circumstances come together to produce a properly revolutionary situation.

In Vittorio Morfino's remarkable 2000 book, *Il tempo e l'occasione: L'incontro Spinoza Machiavelli* [*Time and the Occasion: the Spinoza-Machiavelli encounter*],[3] a similar relationship between philosophical rationality and the contingency of political and historical ruptures is charted. At the centre of this book is the notion of the *encounter*, alluded to in the book's subtitle. The concept, which will be deployed in Morfino's work thereafter, does double duty here: it names both the rupture in Spinoza's metaphysics produced by his confrontation with Machiavelli's political thought, and designates the fundamental conceptual framework Spinoza appropriates and transforms in coming upon the Florentine's writings, namely history as a 'field of occasions, encounters . . . between virtue and fortune'.[4] It is after the publication of his early text, *Treatise on the Emendation of the Intellect*, that Spinoza began reading Machiavelli's texts with a view to addressing the question of history in his *Tractatus Theologico-Politicus*. What he discovered in his 'encounter with the historical and political theory of Machiavelli' produced, according to Morfino, a 'profound modification in Spinoza's metaphysics'.[5] While Machiavelli's conception of history as a broken sequence of encounters between virtue and fortune spurred or made possible, according to Morfino, Spinoza's 'deconstruction' of the Hebraic idea of election, the most important effect of Machiavelli's thought was in fact registered in Spinoza's properly metaphysical treatises.[6] Morfino identifies in particular the shift in the way Spinoza reconceptualises causality as the decisive impact of the encounter with Machiavelli: specifically, a conception of causality no longer as a linear, serial structure (as in *Treatise on the Emendation of the Intellect*) but as what Spinoza calls *connexio*, a term obviously evoking connection, but first and foremost the intricacy of the web, weave or *nexus*, a texture. And it is this philosophical reconceptualisation of causality on the basis of Machiavelli's historical reflections that will in turn give rise to what we can call a properly *materialist theory of time*, in which the 'eternity' of substance no longer names the gathering of the multiplicity of finite modal durations into the simultaneity of a living present, but rather the *necessarily contingent* nature of these finite modal times *and* of their relations: this eternity is not a present standing over above these many modes, but the uncertain knotting together of their multiplicity, the element in which they encounter and miss one another, the space of their clashes, alliances, and crossed paths.

---

3   Morfino 2002a.
4   Morfino 2002a, p. 158.
5   Morfino 2002a, p. 133.
6   Morfino 2002a, p. 157.

The organising scene of *Time and the Occasion* is Spinoza's encounter with Machiavelli's theory of time and history, and more generally *the way in which this encounter with the political thought of Machiavelli produced a transformation of Spinoza's metaphysics.* Morfino's reading of Spinoza therefore echoes both Althusser's recourse to Lenin's political writings in his reconceptualisation of the specificity of the Marxist dialectic as well as, importantly, Antonio Negri's strategy of reading Spinoza in *The Savage Anomaly.* In Negri's seminal book, we see an emphasis on the way political thought is folding back onto Spinoza's ontological considerations. But if a transformative encounter is at the heart of Morfino's *Time and the Occasion,* his own path to this field of research is marked instead by what we can call a *missed encounter,* namely *between Marx and Spinoza.* Morfino has remarked that his original philosophical work began with an interest in the relationship between Marx's philosophy and that of Spinoza, a relationship only hinted at – at crucial moments – in the work of Althusser and his circle. But in examining the notebooks Marx kept on Spinoza, Morfino came to the conclusion that, despite Althusser's oblique references to the continuity between Marx and Spinoza's thought in *Reading Capital,* Marx himself found in Spinoza neither an anticipation of his own thought nor even a radically materialist philosophy that could mobilised in the construction of properly Marxist dialectical materialism. It was in attempting to answer the question as to why Marx could *not* see in Spinoza a precursor – much less a vital link in what the later Althusser will call an underground, materialist 'current' in philosophy, stretching from Lucretius to Marx himself – that Morfino began to investigate the use made of Spinoza's philosophy in Germany in the late eighteenth century, culminating in Hegel's decisive *Auseindersetzung* with Spinoza's thought in, among other places, his *History of Philosophy* and in his *Science of Logic.* It is *this* reception of Spinoza, founded on a misprision or misrecognition of Spinoza's fundamental concepts (substance, cause, eternity, and so on) that Marx inherits whole cloth, and is unable or unwilling to challenge.[7]

That there is something about Spinoza's thought in particular that necessarily produces these types of misprision is a crucial question that Morfino's work investigates. In a very powerful text on the non-reception of Spinoza in Heidegger's tracing out of a 'history of being', Morfino examines one form of repression or exclusion Spinoza has been historically subject to.[8] It should be pointed out all the same that if Marx was unable to see a materialist philosophy that could rival and rupture with an ambient idealist-dialectical mode of philosophy, Althusser himself only rarely and cryptically alludes to Spinoza in his writing, even as he attributes the source or resource

---

7   See in particular Morfino 1997, which focuses on the role Spinoza's thought plays in Hegel's early writing, and which necessarily addresses Spinoza's reception in Germany in the late eighteenth century.

8   Morfino 2002c, pp. 31–46.

for thinking Marx's conceptual dialectical processes to Spinoza. It is true that it is the students (Balibar, Macherey, Moreau, Tosel) of Althusser who went on to produce the most consequential contemporary work on Spinoza, but in the work of Althusser himself there is, if not a missed encounter, nevertheless a *strategic play of allusion and avoidance* of Spinoza's text, as if a more frontal engagement would dissipate the power Spinoza's thought accrues as a hidden or latent force.[9] To these two forms of engagement with Spinoza – Heidegger's sheer omission, Althusser's strategic or oblique non-engagement – we can oppose an equally common form, namely the 'critical' forms of misrecognition found in Leibniz and Hegel, in which an imaginary Spinoza is produced in order to then be characterised as either incoherent (Leibniz) or as a powerful but limited forebear, one who cannot think the necessity of the becoming-spirit of substance (Hegel).

The philosophical strategy undertaken by Louis Althusser in the 1960s, in his polemical interventions against the humanist deviations and drifts within the PCF in the early 1960s, consisted in purifying the rigour of Marx's dialectical method of its Hegelian idealist dregs. This operation's objective was the drawing of a line of demarcation between Marx's and Hegel's dialectical logics, and with it, their concepts of causality, of totality, the forms and types of contradictions that are articulated in their respective concepts of totality or the structured whole. Now, the paradoxical aspect of this strategy, and one that remained encrypted within the readings Althusser produced, or left to circulate in an *esoteric* manner within the circles at the ENS, was that this *return* to Marx required a passage *outside* of the Marxist tradition altogether, a reaching back past Hegel himself towards Spinoza. The latter's most profound achievement is the production of a concept of immanent causality that is divorced from every figure of teleology and finalism, and it is with this figure of immanent or structural causality that Althusser is able to successfully pry apart Marx and Hegel. If it is only today, through the work of Morfino (along with Warren Montag, among others) that we are beginning to understand the exact trajectory of Althusser's return to Spinoza, we must also recognise a different strategy, the one specifically taken by Morfino, who emphasises that the recourse to Spinoza in the Marxist tradition is in fact hardly exceptional and rarely done behind closed doors. Indeed, Spinoza – in the Western (Labriola, Mondolfo) or in the Soviet context (Plekhanov, teacher of Lenin, and Ilyenkov's *Dialectical Logic*) – has been a common and decisive reference in what might be called the most ambitious aspect of the Marxist project, the production of a properly Marxist philosophy, a dialectical materialism.[10]

If Marx was incapable of having a properly transformative encounter with the thought of Spinoza, we must assign the origin of this tradition of Marxist 'Spinozism'

---

9   See in particular Macherey 1979.
10   See in particular Morfino's 'Introduction' to this volume.

to Engels's aborted *Dialectics of Nature*. It is to Engels that Morfino often turns in these pages, not in order to complete or correct Engels's often derided ambitions, but to put his finger on the precise point at which Engels's project goes off the rails, with real theoretical and practical consequences: the assimilation of Spinoza's concept of *causa sui*, his definition of substance, with Hegel's own treatment of that concept in his *Science of Logic*, where it is developed in the concept of reciprocal action [*Wechselwirkung*]. The term reciprocal action, located at the hinge between Hegel's objective and subjective logic, allows Engels to transform Spinoza's affirmation of the *strict equality and irreducibility* of matter to thought and vice versa, into a narrative of the passage from nature to history, from matter to thought, and from substance to subject.

Engels's project is not only sensitive to recent discoveries in the biological sciences and in evolutionary theory – Darwin is a decisive reference, and Morfino will also consider Marx and Engels's reception of Darwin's theory in another essay in *Plural Temporalities* – but is to some extended founded on the results of their scientific practice. Where Althusser refounds the Marxist dialectical method through recourse to the political interventions and practices of Lenin in 1917 and beyond, Engels turns instead to scientific practice. If Engels understands dialectical materialism to be, in its most rigorous formulation, a 'science of interconnections' – a term Morfino notes resonates with the *connexio* of Spinoza's immanent causality – this weave of interconnections is proposed as an antidote to and overcoming of the system of binary categories inherited from the idealist tradition, categories whose reciprocal exclusion claims to organise the very intelligibility of the real: cause and effect, efficient and final cause, necessity and contingency, whole and part. Even the most primitive phenomena of the natural world, Engels notes, and *a fortiori* the world of history and of class struggle, reveal the inability of such concepts to unravel the complexity of these real processes.

Engels is therefore quick to seize upon the Spinozan definition of substance as *causa sui* as a way to wedge one's way out of the closure of these metaphysical categories, for the very notion of substance defined as cause of itself was meant to demolish the categories inherited from the tradition, namely cause and effect and necessity and contingency. Spinoza defines substance as an *actuosa essentia* in a manner that collapses essence and existence, power and act, free and necessary cause; and in the strategic collapsing of these terms, in the identification of substance with the contingency of material connections and with real processes of history, he is able, paradoxically, to stave off any narrative or historical reconstruction of the relation between the attributes of extension and thought, between matter and the mind. Morfino's reading of Engels's treatment of Spinoza through the lens of Hegel's *Science of Logic* identifies this as the point where Engels loses the properly materialist thread: it is here that he assimilates the radical *connexio* of Spinoza's field of immanent causality to Hegel's concept of *Wechselwirkung* or reciprocal action, and therefore the irreducibility of the attribute matter to mind to the becoming-subject of substance. This concept is seductive for Engels insofar as the category of reciprocal action most rigorously articulates the nature of the 'interconnections' that are the very stuff of dialectical materialism. It replaces the seriality of cause and effect with a weave or web of nodes and nexuses; it names not a relation between individuals substances but the *efficacy* of the whole over and in its elements, the whole being here simply the weave of interconnections that articulate those elements. But in this assimilation of Spinoza's weave of interconnections to Hegel's category of reciprocity or reciprocal action – the category that, constituting the final moment of the second phase of the book of *Wesen*, necessarily prepares the passage from the objective to the subjective logic, from being to the concept, and from substance to subject and necessity to freedom – Engels is compelled to introduce a hierarchical relation between the attributes of extension and thought that simply does not exist in Spinoza's thought, and in doing so violates the axiom of anti-finalism that is the correlate of his theory of substance as *connexio*. Engels, while speaking of the eternity of matter and movement, finds himself all the same positing the necessary *emergence* of more 'complex' forms of matter out of this eternity, the historical emergence of thought or consciousness out of matter, and the subsequent domination of that very same matter by thought – in short, a matter organised in such a way that it necessarily gives rise to a form of matter that will come to master it in turn, in view of the construction of freedom.

For Spinoza, as has already been underlined, the postulate of the so-called parallelism of the attributes means that neither can develop into the other, both because each attribute is merely the same thing viewed from a different 'angle', and more decisively *because neither develops at all*. Each attribute is eternal, as is substance. This eternity, however, takes a strange form. It does not refer to the eternity of 'fixed and immutable' essences that could be distinguished from the existence of singular things in the contingency of their relations and in the modal *duration* that characterises them. As I have already mentioned, Morfino stresses the definition of substance proposed in the *Ethics*: substance is *actuosa essentia*, that is, an actuosity in which essence is absolutely immanent to both existence and to potentiality. The essence of the thing, as Morfino has it, 'is indistinguishable from the singular thing's capacity to enter into relations with the outside (and the more complex the relations, the more powerful the individual)'.[11] The thing is now conceived – adequate knowledge of the thing in a 'science of connections', to use Engels's term for materialist, dialectical ontology – from the point of view of its existence and its power to act. Because Spinoza's conception of substance abolishes the distinction between essence and existence and necessity and contingency, Spinoza's eternity must be conceived of not as a form of being, and

---

11   See in this volume, p. 68.

time, that exists apart from the web of finite, modal durations – from the space of encounters between individual modes – but *as simply this weave itself*, as 'the infinity of necessary relations between contingent existences'.[12] What this means, then, is that eternity is not the name for a separate place of essential things immune from the slings and arrows of fortune; it simply means that 'there is no temporality of the totality' and that 'there is no history of the whole'.[13] What it means is that *there is no essence*, or rather that substance does not stand outside of and unaffected by the jolts and surprises of fortune; it means that *there are only* durations and their convergence, overlap, alliance and reciprocal cancellation. To say that there is no history of the whole does not mean that the time of the whole is the time of presence, of simultaneity; it does not mean that the whole is nothing more than the element of contemporaneity in which all of the modal differences and their durations are gathered together in a single glance that can traverse the entire series of existences in a timeless blink. It means quite simply that there is *no such thing as history*, understood as a single time in which a single, fundamental contradiction unfolds in view of a final reconciliation of times and their conflicts, of durations and their contrapuntal rhythms, dissonances, vibrations. There are only durations, times and moments that endure, take hold, and organise themselves according to a conflictual consistency; encounters with other times against which they adhere, bounce off, interpenetrate or are repelled. A duration, a time with its own consistency, its own conatus, its own drive to reproduce itself, can only appear against the ground of other durations with which it moves into and out of phase, with which it forms constellations of compounded force or by which it is, to the contrary, disarmed, broken or destroyed.

In his 'Introduction' to this volume, Morfino situates his own project squarely within the Marxist tradition that has, at certain moments of theoretical crisis, needed to reactivate Spinoza's philosophy to renew itself. Indeed, it was a crisis within Althusser's own theoretical production – one that coincided, it cannot be ignored, with a more general political crisis not only within the PCF but within the communist movement as a whole – that led him, in his *Elements of Self-Criticism*, to refer once again to Spinoza's metaphysics in order to rebuild a properly Marxist theoretical framework, with Spinoza's thought making possible the renewal or clarification of Marx's theories of knowledge, causality, and ideology. But it is Morfino's inclusion of Antonio Negri in this tradition of recourse to Spinoza in moments of theoretical crisis that draws out the true *political* stakes of Morfino's own project, and situates his project decisively within our own current theoretical conjuncture.

The importance of Negri's *Savage Anomaly* for Morfino's approach to Spinoza is undeniable, as Morfino often notes. It is the strategy Negri deploys in reading the

---

12   See pp. 22–50 in this volume.

13   Ibid.

different parts of Spinoza's work that is particularly decisive, namely the manner in which Negri places particular emphasis on the political works – and especially on the concept of the *multitudo* from *The Political Treatise* – to reread the *Ethics*, as well as the way in which *The Savage Anomaly* assimilates and integrates more generally Spinoza's political and metaphysical thought. But where Morfino's examination of the encounter between Spinoza and Machiavelli leads him to see Machiavelli's theory of time – of history as the encounter between virtue and fortune – as a crucial factor in Spinoza's rewriting of his own theory of causality and time, Negri will instead identify the political concept of the multitude with what Morfino calls the 'eternal present of ontology', or what Negri himself calls a 'living God' whose temporal mode is that of a eternal present set off against the contingency of historical intersections, events, and accidents. The difference between Negri and Morfino's positions could not be clearer. If Negri positions the multitude as a potentiality or *Potenza* that is the foundation of a historico-political power while itself structurally exceeding these always contingent historical configurations, he must make a clear, non-dialectical separation between the living present of the multitude as pure potentiality and the forever contingent form this potentiality assumes historically. Such a stratification, or separation, between ontology and history, between the invariant communist potentiality of multitude – communism as eternal, as always now, not even a mere possibility, but always present beneath the deforming skin of its historical manifestation – is dependent ultimately on a separation between two figures of the present and two interpretations of the 'eternity' of Spinoza's substance: the multitude as ontologically always-already present, standing over and above, or lurking beneath the maze of historical accidents and overdetermined lurches, and the multitude of finite modes and the contingency of their durations.

It is precisely at this level, in turn, that Morfino reconceives of the multitude: not as an eternal potentiality separate from its own historical happening, but rather as nothing more than the weave itself of finite temporalities, a weave that, in its very texture, forces us to conceive of the multitude not in the temporal mode of the present – whether the eternity of the living present of *Geist* or in the mere self-coincidence of a given historical moment – but as a form of non-contemporaneity, a mode of historical existence that never coincides with itself, that is always at odds and out of joint with itself. Making this claim requires a reworking not only of the relation between eternity and duration, or between substance and finite modes, but a reconceptualisation of the nature of eternity itself. Eternity is, in Morfino's reading, not a timeless time transcending the conflictual weave of the multitude's many times, gathering their temporal differentiation into the bosom of a simultaneity (whether in the form of 'pre-established harmony' or as a 'ruse' of reason), but simply the structural necessity *that there be* finite modes that encounter one another – or do not – as well as the structural necessity that these encounters can always produce new, ruptural configurations that can stick together or that can vanish, taking on an historical shape or separating as soon as they intersect, leaving behind no trace of their meeting up.

It can be argued that, in the most simple terms, what separates Althusser's recourse to Spinoza from Negri's is that where both thinkers, in moments of theoretical crisis, reach back toward Spinoza in view of separating Marxism from the residues of Hegelianism, Negri wants to use in Spinoza in order to found a non-dialectical Marxism, whereas Althusser's fundamental project is oriented towards locating the specificity of the Marxist dialectic itself. Though Morfino rarely frames his own project as an attempt to renew the resources of dialectical thought, it is clear that his critique of Negri's reading of Spinoza rests on his sizing up of Negri's non-dialectical separation between eternity and history, between ontology and the historical 'encounter'. And yet what is most powerful about Morfino's analysis of Negri is not, perhaps, the way in which arguably Morfino develops a more powerful theory of the relation between eternity and time – that is, an intra-philosophical critique – but the way Morfino gestures at *an historicisation of Negri's reading itself*, coming as it does on the heels of the defeat not only of the Italian Autonomia movement of the 1970s (and more generally, of the worker struggles that first crystallised in the late 1960s), but at the tail-end of the complete decomposition of the historical workers' movement, and at the beginning of the 'winter' years of the 1980s. At stake in the separation between the eternity of the multitude as living God and the historical forms this potentiality might assume is the denial – if not the denegation – of that very failure and that very defeat: the affirmation that communism is always now and not a hazy horizon, the affirmation that every defeat is in fact a victory, one more step closer to the final, preordained coincidence of ontology and history. Against the various forms of communist ontology that have emerged in the dark light of these last few decades, whether in the form of an eternal, always triumphant multitude or in the invariant, eternal presence of a minimal communist hypothesis or Idea, Morfino's work proposes a different way of conceiving and measuring success or failure: failure is no longer understood either as the wearing out of an historical form that is inadequate to the deep content or potentiality lurking beneath it, nor as a finite sequence triggered by an event that can only reactivate, inadequately, an omni-temporal idea. Success or failure are instead simply the names we assign the coming together of forces that either take hold in a determined historical conjuncture, opening a new history, a new world, and a new field of possible encounters, or in the inability of these same encounters to find their point of fusion. And history is in turn not the eventual realisation of an eternal substance but so many moving trains, to be caught or missed.

Stella sperduta,
nella luce dell'alba
cigolío della brezza,
tepore, respiro –
è finita la notte.

Sei la luce e il mattino

a Béatrice

⠒

Introduction

Entweder Spinozismus oder keine Philosophie

G.W.F. HEGEL, *Vorlesungen über Spinoza*

∴

When in his *Essays in Self-Criticism* Louis Althusser openly confesses the philosophical sin he committed in his so-called 'theoreticist' works, he repeats, consciously or not, a move that has been often made in the history of Marxism. That is, he has recourse to Spinoza, at least for some of his key concepts, in order to discover the philosophy of Marx and in order to have a clearer idea of those ten pages on the materialist dialectic that Marx never had the time to write.

This gesture is as old as Marxism itself. Engels proposed it when he exclaimed, in a conversation with Plekhanov, that 'old Spinoza was right' concerning the conception of nature. And against Bernstein, who contested the philosophical self-sufficiency of Marxism by dividing it into a evolutionist sociology and an ethics of Kantian inspiration, Lenin's teacher Plekhanov proposed the genealogy Spinoza-Feuerbach-Marx in view of providing a true ontological foundation for historical materialism, in the sense of a strict monism unifying the sciences of nature with the sciences of history. In those same years, Labriola also referred to Spinoza, but in opposed terms, with the precise aim of refusing the naturalisation of history and in order to found the specificity of history with regard to nature. In the Soviet Union of the 1920s, the two principal currents of an emerging Soviet Marxism, i.e. the 'Deborinites' and the 'Mechanists', confronted each other over the name of Spinoza: the former understanding substance as matter, the latter understanding it as a universal conformity to laws. A few years later, in Fascist Italy, Rodolfo Mondolfo, before being forced to take refuge in Argentina due to the racial laws, proposed the genealogy Spinoza-Marx with the aim of overturning Gentile's actualism into a philosophy of praxis. In the 1970s, Evald Ilyenkov sketched a dialectical and materialist Spinoza in one of the main chapters of his *Dialectical Logic*. Last but not least, at the beginning of the 1980s, we once again find a still different Spinoza at the heart of the Italian workerist tradition, for which Spinoza was supposed to provide an ontological foundation: namely, Antonio Negri's Spinoza. Negri, like Althusser, uses Spinoza in order to found a non-Hegelian, non-dialectical Marxism, placing the accent on the political Spinoza while identifying the concepts of 'potentia' and 'multitude' as tools for thinking a new revolutionary subjectivity.

Spinoza has been invoked throughout the history of Marxism in different theoretical and political conjunctures, in order to take up different, sometimes even opposed, positions.[1] We therefore need to reconstruct briefly the meaning of Althusser's own invocation of Spinoza, in order to locate it precisely both with respect to the history of Marxism and to the use made of Spinoza in the Marxism of the present.

In his 1972 *Essays in Self-Criticism*, when Althusser refers to his writings of the 1960s, *For Marx* and *Reading Capital*, he rejects the accusation of structuralism levelled against them with the following words:

> If we never were structuralists, we can now explain why: why we seemed to be, even though we were not, why there came about this strange misunderstanding on the basis of which books were written. We were guilty of an equally powerful and compromising passion: *we were Spinozists.* In our own way, of course, which was not Brunschvicg's! And by attributing to the author of the *Tractatus Theologico-Politicus* and the *Ethics* a number of theses that he would surely never have acknowledged, though they did not actually contradict him. But to be a heretical Spinozist is almost orthodox Spinozism, if Spinozism can be said to be one of the greatest lessons in heresy that the world has seen! In any case, with very few exceptions our blessed critics, imbued with conviction and swayed by fashion, never suspected any of this. They took the easy road: it was so simple to join the crowd and shout 'structuralism'! Structuralism was all the rage, and you did not have to read about it in books to be able to talk about it. But you have to read Spinoza and know that he exists: that he still exists today. To recognize him, you must at least have heard of him.[2]

The meaning of this reference to Spinoza is clarified in a text published in 1975, 'Is it simple to be a Marxist in philosophy?'. Althusser affirms that a philosophy 'only exists in so far as it occupies a position, and it only occupies this position in so far as it has conquered it in the thick of an already occupied world'. In other words, it 'only exists in so far as this conflict has made it something distinct, and this distinctive character can only be won and imposed in an indirect way, by a detour involving ceaseless study of other, existing positions':

---

1   Tosel 1993, pp. 515–25.
2   Althusser 1976, p. 132.

To prove it, I need only refer, aside from the whole of philosophical history, to Marx himself, who was only able to define himself by reference to Hegel and by marking himself off from Hegel. And I think that, from afar, I have followed his example, by allowing myself to refer back to Spinoza in order to understand why Marx had to refer back to Hegel.[3]

Spinoza therefore provides Althusser with the conceptual tools to think Marxism outside the tradition of Hegel, *en matérialiste*. The reference to Spinoza in this sense is fundamental with respect to three decisive questions in the Althusserian re-reading of Marxism: the process of knowledge, structural causality, and ideology. Regarding the process of knowledge, Althusser maintains that Spinoza develops a theory that rejects any question regarding 'the Origin, the Subject and the Rights of knowledge', that is, he rejects the juridical problem of classical epistemology:

What does Spinoza in fact mean when he writes, in a famous phrase, '*Habemus enim ideam veram . . .*'? That we have a true idea? No: the weight of the phrase lies on the '*enim*'. It is *in fact* because and only because we have a true idea that we can produce others, according to its norm. And it is *in fact* because and only because we have a true idea that we can know that it is true, because it is '*index sui*' . . . Thus Spinoza *in advance* makes every theory of knowledge, which reasons about the *justification* of knowledge, dependent on the *fact* of the knowledge which we already possess.[4]

This conception of the true as *index sui* allows Spinoza to think the scientific status of a concept not on the basis of its presumed correspondence with a real object, but on the basis of the function it has within the problematic in which it is situated. Spinoza's theory of knowledge therefore breaks with a religious reading that would be made possible by an imaginary complicity between the *logos* and being. As a consequence, it breaks with what Althusser considered to be the fundamental philosophical variant of such a reading, i.e., empiricist-idealist ideology. According to Althusser, Spinoza – repeating in advance the argumentation of Marx's famous 1857 Introduction – affirmed that knowledge goes from the abstract to the concrete (against empiricism) while also affirming that the real object that gives rise to the process remains outside of knowledge (against idealism): 'the idea of a circle is not the circle, the concept of a dog

3 Althusser 1976, p. 166.
4 Althusser 1976, pp. 187–8.

does not bark – in short, you must not confuse the real thing and its concept'.[5]
Knowledge therefore is neither the production nor the reflection of the real
object; it is the production (in the double sense of the term of 'fabricating' and
'bringing to light') of a concrete-in-thought, starting from the transformation
of an imaginary material which is always-already given as structured, then generating a radical discontinuity with it: 'Between the first and the second kind
of knowledge which, in its immediacy (abstracting from the totality in God),
presupposed precisely a radical *discontinuity*. Although the second kind makes
possible the understanding of the first, it is not *its truth*'.[6]

    In Althusser's eyes, Spinoza deposes the categories of Subject, Object and
Truth by showing how they constitute a vicious circle of criteria:

> Whether the criterion is external (relation of adequacy between mind
> and thing, in the Aristotelian tradition) or internal (Cartesian self-
> evidence), in either case the criterion can be rejected: for it only rep-
> resents a form of Jurisdiction, a Judge to authenticate and guarantee
> the validity of what is True. And at the same time Spinoza avoids the
> temptation of talking about the Truth: as a good nominalist (nominal-
> ism, as Marx recognized, could then be the antechamber of materialism)
> Spinoza only talks about what is 'true'. In fact the idea of Truth and the
> idea of the Jurisdiction of a Criterion always go together, because the
> function of the criterion is to identify the Truth of what is true.[7]

The process of knowledge cannot be subordinated to the forms of the subject
and of criterion, but must be conceived by means of a new logic in which the
relation between result and conditions is a productive rather than an expressive relation: 'Therefore as what, in a phrase that clashes with the classical
system of categories and demands the *replacement* of those categories themselves, we can call the *necessity of its contingency*'.[8]

    Concerning causality, Spinoza produces a theory through which he is able to
think the efficacy of the structure on its elements, by introducing 'an unprecedented theoretical revolution in the history of philosophy, probably the great-
est philosophical revolution of all time, insofar as we can regard Spinoza as
Marx's only direct ancestor, from the philosophical standpoint'.[9] This theory

---

5 Althusser 1976, p. 192.
6 Althusser 1979, p. 78.
7 Althusser 1976, p. 137.
8 Althusser 1970, p. 45.
9 Althusser 1970, p. 102.

breaks with two conceptions of causality that have endured throughout modern philosophy right down to our day: the mechanist conception of causality, of Cartesian origin, 'which reduced causality to a transitive and analytical efficacy'; and the expressive conception of causality, of Leibnizian origin, which conceived each part of a whole as *pars totalis*, or as the form of phenomenal expression of an inner essence.[10] This revolutionary theory of causality, precisely expressed in the Spinozan assertion that God is an immanent and not a transcendent cause, theorises a form of efficacy that can be described, in Althusser's words, as the efficacy of an absent cause, that is, as structural causality or metonymical causality. Such a model of causality transforms every foundation, every original or primary cause, into a necessary structure of contingent effects:

> Spinoza for his part begins with God, but in order to deny Him as a Being (Subject) in the universality of His *only* infinite power (*Deus* = *Natura*). Thus Spinoza, like Hegel, rejects every thesis of Origin, Transcendence or an Unknowable World, even disguised within the absolute interiority of the Essence.[11]

The negation of a transcendent foundation, of an origin of reality, entails the absorption of any imaginary hierarchy of being, be it even the transcendental one of the Kantian *I think*, into the infinite processuality of the real, without sense, centre or end. Spinoza in this sense is 'a first and almost unique guide' in seeking a causality able to provide an account of 'the action of the Whole on its parts, and of the parts on the Whole – an Whole without closure'.[12]

And yet Althusser also maintains that Spinoza, far from falling into the intellectualism of the century of the Enlightenment, not only theorises the necessity of ideological illusion, centred on the metaphysical category of the Subject, but also constructs a theory of the mode of production, thereby founding a new *materialism of the imaginary*:

> Is it necessary to add that Spinoza refused to use the notion of the Goal, but explained it as a necessary and therefore well-founded illusion? In the Appendix to Book I of the *Ethics*, and in the *Tractatus Theologico-Politicus*, we find in fact what is undoubtedly the first theory of *ideology*

---

10   Althusser 1970, p. 187.

11   Althusser 1976, p. 135.

12   Althusser 1976, p. 142 (translation modified).

ever thought out, with its three characteristics: (1) its *imaginary* 'reality';
(2) its internal *inversion*; (3) its 'centre': the illusion of the *subject*.[13]

Ideology therefore is neither simple error nor naked ignorance, insofar as
Spinoza has founded 'the system of this imaginary phenomenon on the relation of men to the world "expressed" by the state of their bodies';[14] the first
type of knowledge is therefore not simply an epistemological stage. It is, on the
contrary, 'the material world of men *as they live it*, that of their concrete and
historical existence'.[15]

We should say immediately and clearly that Althusser's reference to Spinoza
with regard to the critique of the theory of knowledge, the theory of structural causality and the theory of ideology constitute the implicit premise of
this book. Furthermore, the results of the inquiries developed on the plane of
ontology by Pierre Macherey in his *Hegel ou Spinoza*,[16] and by Etienne Balibar
in his writings on Spinoza's political theory, are here taken for granted.[17] In this
book, it is a matter of moving beyond these claims, a matter of thinking with as
much precision as possible the conceptual system of this philosophy between
Spinoza and Althusser.

If we were to summarise in a few words the fundamental move motivating
this philosophical gesture, we might say that it consists in the establishment of
a sort of hermeneutical circle between the texts of Spinoza and of Althusser.
In other words, it is a case of interrogating Spinoza's text through Althusser
and vice versa regarding the question of materialism. I have here tried to propose a comprehensive interpretation of Spinoza's philosophy that takes up
Althusser's fragmentary intuitions, doing so in such a way that this interpretation may either clarify some of the cryptic aspects of Althusser's philosophy in
its turn or, where necessary, help produce new concepts.

Whether this circle is vicious or virtuous will be judged by the reader on the
basis of the results produced, that is, on the basis of the internal rigour of the
conceptual reconstruction. But the initial move is openly declared: *on com-
mence toujours quelque part...* In any case, it is clear that the circle between
Spinoza-Althusser is not a closed one, a talmudic deciphering of the word of
God. From time to time, different theoretical characters, some who do not

---

13   Althusser 1976, p. 135.
14   Althusser 1976, p. 136.
15   Ibid.
16   Macherey 1979.
17   I refer, in particular, to Balibar 1982.

even belong to philosophical fields of knowledge, will be called on stage, following a double strategy:

On the one hand, genealogical paths from Spinoza to Machiavelli to Lucretius, from Althusser to Simondon and Darwin, are traced. Here, genealogy means that the author who is chronologically prior never plays the role of a simple origin, but is a strategic element in a complex theoretical apparatus.

On the other hand, lines of demarcation are drawn and radical alternatives within modernity are posed: in this context, causality, totality, temporality, relationality, form, contingency and violence are what is at stake in the conflict between the philosophy of Spinoza and the great German philosophical tradition of immanence, from Leibniz to Husserl and from Hegel to Engels.

In the preface to a recent edition of Althusser's *Machiavelli and Us,* Balibar has written:

> [I] understood (or thought I understood, for I am proposing this only as a hypothesis to be confronted by others) that a tension has always inhabited Althusser's thought, as a reflection on the articulation of history and politics based on the reading and transformation of the work of Marx. It's what I have happened to refer to since as the difference between the 'Althusserianism of structure' centred on the efficacy of *social relations,* economic as well as ideological, and the 'Althusserianism of the conjuncture,' centred on the expected *historical encounters* between circumstances and political forces, revolutionary or counter-revolutionary. Of course, the idea of such a tension has sense and interest only if it corresponds to a single problem ... and not to an ontological dualism (nature and freedom, the real and the virtual, being and event, praxis and the practico-inert, the constituent and the constituted).[18]

The attempt to stay within this tension between structure and conjuncture, between Althusser and Spinoza, without indulging in any form of dualism, constitutes the centre of the problematic treated in this book. At the same time, it also constitutes the point of differentiation with respect to some contemporary attempts that explicitly link themselves to Spinoza, the most important of which is certainly Negri's work. Between the *Savage Anomaly* (1981) and *Insurgencies* (1992), Negri constructs the fundamental theoretical framework that will remain unchanged in the more popular works he has written together with Michael Hardt (*Empire, Multitude, Commonwealth*). The cornerstone of

---

18   Balibar 2009, p. 19.

this entire project is Spinoza's concept of *multitudo*, the ontological collective subject whose *potentia* is at once the basis of, and against, power. If we take into consideration Negri's conceptual apparatus from the point of view of the question of temporality, we can see that two very distinct forms of time appear: the time of power, which is the time of illusion and repression of life, and the time of *potentia*, which instead is the time of life, time turned to the future, toward becoming. The first is void, a mere exterior existence without reality; the second is full, it is the time of free necessity, of the fusion of duration and eternity:

> Power (*potestas*) is contingency. The process of being, the always-more-complex affirmation of subjective power, and the construction of the necessity of being all excavate the basis of Power, to demolish it. Power (*potestas*) is superstition, the organisation of fear, nonbeing; power opposes it by constituting itself collectively.[19]

The implicit effect of Negri's affirmation that there is a metaphysics of time at work in Spinoza, constituting the *potentia multitudinis*, is a genuine disarticulation of ontology and history, a disarticulation that is not only at the basis of Negri's book on Spinoza but of all of Negri's mature work.[20] On the one hand, there is the time of history, which is the time of constituted power; on the other hand, there is the time of ontology, of being, of collective praxis, of *potentia*, of constituent power. Certainly, *potentia multitudinis* founds power; and yet in Negri's reading, *potentia* and power maintain two separate realities insofar, as Negri explicitly says, as there are ontological transitions of the *potentia* of the multitude (from *cupiditas* to *generositas*, to *amor* and finally to *democratia*) that are not historical transitions, for if they were Negri's thesis would run the risk of falling into a form of philosophy of history of a dialectical type that Negri clearly refuses.[21] These transitions happen, rather, in the eternal present of ontology. The time of the multitude is the present, a full

---

19   Negri 1991, p. 226.
20   I refer, in particular, to Negri 1991 and Negri and Hardt 2000.
21   'The plot: of the constitution of the political here is sustained by the unstoppable and progressive expansion of *cupiditas* [desire], which is the determinant force of the constitution of the social, determinate in the formation of the political institutions resulting from the interweaving of the multitude of singularities, and surpassed and exalted by the absoluteness of democratic synthesis. It is the moment of full interpenetration of the will of all and sovereignty' (Negri 1999, p. 304).

present projected towards the future. It is the present of democracy as 'living God', of communism as the 'real movement that abolishes the present state of things', as a never-tamed revolution. However, it is a present that does not coincide with the historical present despite being its ontological foundation. Faced with defeats on the terrain of politics and history, there is in Negri all the same an emphatic proclamation of the omnipotence of the multitude, of the expansive *potentia* of communism in the *turris eburnea* of ontology. Naturally, what is at stake here is not simply Negri's reading, but a strong tendency within Marxism in the theoretical conjuncture of the beginning of the twenty-first century: i.e., an 'ontologism' that tends to produce a genuine split between ontology and history, and that produces a short-circuit between ontology and politics by making the latter the specular and immediate reflection of the former.

My own proposition is diametrically opposed to this tendency. In my view, it is necessary to try to hold together ontology and history, structure and conjuncture, rather than separate them. This attempt can be articulated by means of three theses:

- the primacy of the relation over the elements, or the thesis of trans-individuality;
- the primacy of the encounter over form, or the thesis of the aleatory;
- the primacy of the temporal intertwining on the line, or the thesis of plural temporality.

The simple proclamation of these theses, however, is not enough. The hierarchical relation among these theses needs to be made more precise in order for each of them to be correctly thought.

Transindividual. In the first place, we are concerned with thinking, with Spinoza and by following a certain Althusserian interpretation of Marx, an *ontology of relation* (an expression I take from Balibar). I want to draw out the tension within this paradoxical formulation, in the sense in which the discourse of ontology traditionally has been the discourse of the primacy of substance over relation. We are concerned here with inverting the relation between substance-relation, not simply by highlighting the importance of relations, but by highlighting their constitutiveness. In other words, this thesis affirms, to repeat a famous expression of Hegel's *Science of Logic*, that 'nowhere, neither in the sky nor on the earth' is there an element or essence that is not only not influenced by a set of relations, but, more radically, there is no element or essence that is not *constituted* by this set of relations (this thesis should draw a clear line of demarcation with respect to those Marxist positions that are grounded on the essentialism of the *Gattungswesen* or of the *multitude*). The more difficult theoretical problem that must be addressed in order to arrive at the correct position on this thesis requires drawing a precise line of demarcation between the idealist theory of relation as it is formulated in the tradition that goes from Leibniz to Hegel and the materialist one.

We must, then, begin by analysing the different meanings of the term 'relation'; second, define with precision a concept of relation that can be based on Spinoza's philosophy; finally, we must rigorously draw out the difference between the Spinozan and the idealist position. This work of the construction of an ontology of relation is the same project as the clarification of the concept of the transindividual, a term that Balibar took from Simondon with the aim of inducing a sort of chemical reaction in Spinoza's as well as in Marx's work. The model of transindividuality is here counterposed to the individualist model of intersubjectivity that presupposes the subject and poses it at the foundation of both ontological and social relations, insofar as it thinks the subject as pre-existing relations and not constituted by them. In this sense, a brief comparison between Spinoza and Leibniz's philosophy on the issue of relation may be clarifying.

In Leibniz, thanks to the theory of pre-established harmony, every extrinsic determination is in reality founded on an intrinsic determination; each external relation is founded on a property of the monad; it is an internal state of the monad. In Spinoza, on the other hand, each intrinsic determination is in reality founded on a complex play of extrinsic determinations; each property of an individual is produced by the complex play of relations that has constituted its individuality. And if we move the level of comparison from Leibniz's metaphysical intersubjectivity to that of Husserl's transcendental variant, we can highlight the way in which phenomenology, formerly closed in the solipsistic island of consciousness, can constitute a bridge between the *ego* and the *alter ego*, a bridge that allows the establishment of the objectivity of worldly time – but only at the price of betraying the entire program of transcendental philosophy, by hypostasising an essential contemporaneity between monads that must necessarily have a metaphysical and transcendent character.

In this sense, by posing the Husserlian question to Spinoza, it is possible to catch the question off guard, precisely because Spinoza does not start from the *cogito* as a space of interiority, but from the mode, an *esse in alio* which is structurally constituted by relations. In Spinoza, then, the opposition between *ego* and *alter ego* turns out to be purely fictitious, or better, imaginary, because the *alter* is not what is external to the space of interiority of the *ego*, something originally excluded from it. Rather, it is what always-already traverses or crosses through it, what constitutes it as a complex weave of bodies, practices, passions, ideas, words; a complex weave of temporality which cannot be reduced to the essential contemporaneity of the Husserlian intersubjective community.

Aleatory. Second, the thesis of the primacy of the relation over the elements has to be placed under the tutelage of the second thesis, namely the thesis of the primacy of the encounter over form. What does tutelage mean? It means that the first thesis can be thought in a correct way only if it is subordinated to the second one. Leibniz as well as Hegel posed the question of relationality in radical terms, but both ended up subordinating relationality to teleology. *On the one hand*, the theory of pre-established harmony enables Leibniz to posit substance in terms of relations only if substance is understood as a form of possible essence in the divine intellect, thereby making these relations nothing more than the combinatory play of the world built by a sovereign God, a game of the world which is always-already decided by the tending of the divine will towards the good. *On the other hand*, the theory of the ruse of reason as the activity that weaves the grand tapestry of universal history allows Hegel to dominate the meaning of the play of relations. Pre-established harmony and the ruse of reason, therefore, put relationality in the service of teleology. In order to make the comparison clearer, we could say that both have formulated the thesis of the primacy of teleology over relationality. If, then, the thesis of the primacy of relation can be found in the idealist tradition, as Althusser himself emphasised, we need to find a formula able to express this conception with a force that is equal and opposed to this tradition of expressive causality. The primacy of the aleatory over relationality? In my view, the clearest formula is instead: the primacy of the encounter over form.

I borrow this expression from an Althusserian text posthumously published with a strong editorial intervention by its editor, François Matheron: 'The Underground Current of the Materialism of the Encounter'. In this text, the expression 'primacy of the encounter over form' is not literally present. Nevertheless, I would risk saying that it is present in its effects, insofar as here a complex theory of the encounter is built with the precise aim of providing Marxism with a model that differs from the classical one found in Hegel's *Phenomenology of Spirit*, which affirms the relation of co-essentiality of genesis and structure. However, Althusser's text is not without ambiguity. Therefore I have worked less on elucidating the text itself than on performing a genuine conceptual construction, in the literal sense that I have attempted to provide a solid conceptual structure for some fascinating formulations that were not sufficiently developed by Althusser on the theoretical level. In this sense, *détours* have been fundamental – on one hand through Aristotle and

Darwin, on the other hand through Lucretius and Spinoza – in order to make sure that the 'void', the most powerful term from the rhetorical point of view in this Althusserian text, is not dissociated from its strict interdependence with the concept of encounter, in which case it can be interpreted as a sort of mystical abyss into which any and all rationalism collapses in favour of a philosophy of chance, of the event or, *even worse*, of freedom.

In particular, it is Darwin who provides a precise model in the field of the natural sciences for the application of the primacy of the encounter over form. The fundamental nucleus of his theory does not lie, as has long been believed, in the thesis of the evolution of forms (against notions of fixity), but rather in the primacy of the encounter over form, that is, in the affirmation not of the contingency of the world (contingency which would be the consequence of the collapse of the world into the mystical abyss of the void, one of the many metamorphoses divinity can assume), but rather in the contingency of each form as the result of a complex intertwining of encounters. Each of these encounters is necessary, though of a necessity that, if I may be permitted this oxymoron, is entirely aleatory; that is, without a project or a *telos*. The elements that take hold in a form all have their own histories which are in turn the effect of an intertwining of encounters, an effect as much of encounters that have taken place as those that were missed. In this sense, that is, if we agree that both *telos* and project are rejected (as well as the correlative concept of nature as order), Darwin seems to provide a model that is perfectly compatible with the thesis of the primacy of the encounter over form and of the relation over the elements. The complex weave of relations that constitutes the stable face of nature in a given period is not an order and guarantee of stability, but a complex weave of encounters, where the very fact that one of them is missing or takes place can reconfigure the entire ensemble of encounters, as Darwin writes, 'in circles of increasing complexity'.

Plural temporality. Third, precisely in order to avoid making our reference to aleatory materialism a sort of evocation of a philosophy of the event, of chance, of freedom, or a philosophy of radical discontinuity, it is necessary to place the thesis of the primacy of the encounter over form in turn under the tutelage of the primacy of a temporal braiding or weaving over the time of the line, over linear temporality. In order to highlight the fundamental philosophical *enjeu* of this thesis, it is necessary to go back briefly to Kant's antinomies of reason, in particular the either/or which is established between causality according to laws and causality according to freedom in the attempt, illegitimate according to Kant, to apply the categories of relation not to phenomena but to the idea of the world understood as a totality of external phenomena:

Thesis. Causality in accordance with the [mechanical] laws of nature is not the only causality from which the appearances of the world can one and all be derived. To explain these appearances it is necessary to assume that there is also another causality, that of freedom. Antithesis. There is no freedom; everything in the world takes place solely in accordance with the laws of nature.[22]

It would not be difficult to reconstruct, from the medieval period to modernity, the historical referents for the Kantian antinomies. On the one hand, the scholastic tradition of special and general metaphysics and Cartesianism. On the other hand, Ockham and the tradition of English empiricism. However, this antinomy, far from being a dusty chapter in the history of philosophy, will constitute a sort of watershed for the future, by drawing the border that will separate the great philosophies of history centred on a subject (humanity, spirit, class) – a subject that follows an ascending line of time along which its power and perfection grow – from the anti-historicist and nihilist philosophies that replace this ascending serial line of time with the eruption of the discontinuous instant: on the one hand, Lessing, Hegel, Hegelian-Marxism and the early Lukács; on the other hand, Kierkegaard, Nietzsche, Benjamin, Schmitt, the early Heidegger and the last Derrida.

Against Hegelian historicism and Hegelian Marxism which affirm, as does the antithesis in Kant's antinomy, that 'an experience having thoroughgoing coherence' is possible only when the 'guidance of rules' is maintained, the Kantian thesis of 'causality according to freedom' (which is contrary to Kant's philosophy of history itself, which is fundamentally Leibinizian, theorising progress and the infinite perfectibility of man as a regulative idea of reason) tears the instant from the linear series of worldly events and fills it with a meaning that transcends the series of phenomenon. Thus, Kierkegaard, Nietzsche, Benjamin, Schmitt, Heidegger and Derrida can be read according to this interpretative model. Each of them gives the contingent instant that frees itself from the necessary series of events a different meaning: they fill it with sense (namely, God), life, purifying revolution, the void of the decision, authenticity, or messianism without messiah.[23]

Each of them thinks contingency, whether intended or not, as the effect of causality according to freedom. Derrida, in his Benjaminian book on Marx, spoke *apertis verbis* of an *eskaton* which is not prepared by a *telos*, namely, in

---

22   Kant 1996, A 444–5, p. 409.
23   For an analysis in this sense of Derrida's philosophy, see Morfino 2010.

terms of an eschatology without teleology.[24] When we look closely, these two great schemas for reading historical time, which we could call in shorthand continuist and discontinuist, can be read as the secularisation of the two great models of Christian temporality, that of Joachim of Fiore's tripartite division of the line of time into the successive epochs of humanity,[25] and that of Paul of Tarsus, according to whom God 'so cometh as a thief in the night'.[26]

To affirm the primacy of the weave of time over its straightening out into a line means to go beyond continuism and discontinuism, or rather, in a Spinozan fashion, to denounce both as imaginary simplifications of the complexity of the real. This operation sets out from what are perhaps the densest pages of *Reading Capital* – 'An Outline for a Concept of Historical Time' – in order to return to Spinoza's theory of temporality. The cornerstone of this operation is the lodging of the category of the *non-contemporaneous* at the heart of Spinoza's thought. This challenges in the first instance the powerful acosmic interpretation of Spinoza magnificently expressed in the following lines by Bloch:

> *The world stands here as a crystal, with the sun at its peak, so that nothing throws a shadow...* Time is missing, history is missing, development is missing and especially any concrete multiplicity in the one ocean of substance... Spinozism stands there as if there was eternal noon in the necessity of the world, in the determinism of its geometry and of its both carefree and situationless crystal – *sub specie aeternitatis.*[27]

To posit the equation eternity = non-contemporaneity means to give ontological consistency back to time, not understood according to its traditional image of a circle or line, but as a plurality of durations, a complex and articulated intertwining. Its structure *is* the non-contemporaneous, understood not in the sense of survival of archaic forms in a contemporaneity which is given as a term of comparison, but rather as the radical impossibility of any absolute contemporaneity, as the impossibility on the ontological level of positing one rhythm as an absolute measure for others. Again, it is Althusser who guides us through Spinoza's text:

24   Derrida 1993.
25   See Löwith 1949.
26   I Thessalonians 5:2.
27   Bloch 1986, p. 853.

What the synchrony aims at has nothing to do with the *temporal* presence of the object as a *real object*, but on the contrary, concerns a different
type of presence, and the presence of a *different object*: not the temporal
presence of the concrete object, not the historical time of the historical presence of the historical object, but the presence (or the 'time') *of
the object of knowledge of the theoretical analysis itself,* the presence of
knowledge. The synchronic is then nothing but *the conception* of the specific relations that exist between the different elements and the different
structures of the structure of the whole, it is the knowledge of the relations of dependence and articulation which make it an organic whole,
a system. *The synchronic is eternity in Spinoza's sense [Le synchronique,
c'est l'éternité au sens spinoziste]*, or the adequate knowledge of a complex
object by the adequate knowledge of its complexity.[28]

Thus, Spinozan substance has no content – that is, compared with the existence
of finite modes it is nothing but a schema of non-linear causality (whether we
want to call it overdetermination or modulation). It is not the ladder to be got
rid of once it has been used, but the categorical lens through which alone it is
possible to correctly read modal reality. In the same way, eternity also has no
content, does not possess the secret of time as it is contracted in an instant.
Rather, it is the articulation of a plurality of durations and at the same time
the guarantee of the impossibility of hypostatisation of one rhythm in relation to the others (in Spinoza, time exists as an hypostatisation, understood as
auxilium imaginationis). It is, in a certain sense, the guarantee that time has no
secret, that its fundamental structure is that of *non-contemporaneity*.

If we now return to the confrontation with Negri and with his description of the time of the *potentia multitudinis* in terms of *presence*, the political sense of the three theses will become clear. Presence, *parousia*, is in the
history of Western thought the temporal metaphor of spirit, of the interpenetration of the I and We, that bars all thought of the profound materialistic
implications of the concept of multitude. *Multitude*, in the reading I propose,
is not a full subject, an absolute presence, which it is sufficient to evoke in the
imaginary dimension of ontology in order to win at the roulette table against
power; it is a weaving, an articulation of times that cannot be reduced to an
essential contemporaneity and that constitutes the ineluctable horizon of all
political action. The *multitude* is a Lucretian *textura* or, to use the more properly Spinozan term, a *connexio* of bodies, traces, images, ideas, words, practices,
passions, usages and customs, habits, beliefs, rituals, apparatuses, institutions,

---

28   Althusser 1970, p. 107.

conflicts and resistances, a *connexio* with respect to which power, violence and ideology are not opposed as an other, the empty shell that imprisons them, but the form itself of the necessity of their intertwining. This *connexio*, however, must not be thought as given once and for all, like a Parmenidian structure: its taking hold, its historicity, is founded on a weave of encounters that have occurred or have been missed, that were short or durable, and that all take place precisely on the basis of the existence of different temporal rhythms.

Thus, to return to the question of the short-circuiting of ontology and politics that is produced by the disarticulation of ontology and history, we must emphasise strongly and in explicitly polemical terms that the *multitudo* is a card that we cannot play twice. In other words: once its *potentia* is posited as the basis of the existing order, we cannot tell ourselves that this order is nothing but an empty shell, thus dissociating its *potentia* from this order, so as to imaginarily produce another one which, obviously, precisely as imaginary, can take the form of a sort of 'Bacchanalian revel'. This discourse on the *multitudo* (that presents itself in reality in the rhetorical form as the discourse *of* the *multitudo*) seems to me to be similar to Schopenhauer's discourse of/on the 'water':

> I can form high waves (as in a storm at sea); I can rush down a hill (as in the bed of a torrent); I can dash down foaming and splashing (as in the waterfall); I can rise freely as a jet into the air (as in a fountain); finally, I can even boil away and disappear (as at 212 degrees Fahrenheit). However, I do none of these things now, but voluntarily remain calm and clear in the mirroring pond.[29]

To think the *multitudo* as *connexio* means taking leave of this imaginary, omnipotent, revolutionary subject, the revolutionary force of which seems to consist, in the last analysis, in its very existence itself, because its existence is *against* power. What is gained instead is, perhaps, a sort of 'critique of pure political reason', namely the formulation of the conditions of possibility for thinking the political horizon or the problematic starting out from which it is possible to produce an analysis of the relations of force within which political action can be inscribed. In other words, the task of a philosophy for Marxism does not lie in the imaginary dissolution of power through the affirmation of an omnipotent subject, which abandons the empty shell of historical reality in order to give rise to a Bacchanalian revel in some other ontological order whose present never coincides with the historical present. Rather, the task of a

---

29   Schopenhauer 1999, p. 37.

philosophy for Marxism lies in thinking the non-contemporaneity of the *multi-tudo* in all its radicality, the articulation of its many times, through an archaeology of the present on whose basis we can devise a complex strategy capable of intervening in and on all the planes and levels of the real.

Translated by Sara Farris

CHAPTER 1

Causa Sui or *Wechselwirkung*: Engels between Hegel and Spinoza

1   Monod and Dialectical Materialism

Jacques Monod dedicates the second chapter of *Chance and Necessity* to the analysis of vitalist and animist theories, among which he also discusses the dialectical materialism of Engels. Introducing the theme, Monod affirms that the only hypothesis that modern science can accept regarding the relation between invariance and teleonomy is 'that invariance necessarily precedes teleonomy'.[1] All the other conceptions, according to Monod, presuppose the opposite hypothesis, 'that is, that *invariance* [*is*] *protected, ontogenesis guided, evolution oriented* by a teleonomic initial principle of which all these phenomena (living beings) would be manifestations'.[2] Implicit in this inversion is the renunciation of the principle of objectivity.[3] Among the conceptions that invert the relation between invariance and teleonomy, Monod distinguishes two groups: vitalism, which admits an intervention of the teleonomic principle into the environment of the biosphere, and animism, which 'appeals to a *universal* teleonomic principle, responsible both for cosmic evolution and for the evolution of the biosphere, within which it is expressed only in a most precise and intense way'.[4] The animist conceptions stabilise a profound alliance between man and nature: they project onto animals, plants, minerals, meteorological phenomena and celestial bodies 'man's awareness of the intensely

---

1   Monod 1997, p. 25 (translation modified). For a comprehensive evaluation of Monod's theory, see the magisterial analysis in Althusser 1974, pp. 145–65.

2   Monod 1997, p. 26 (translation modified).

3   The cornerstone of scientific method is the postulate of the objectivity of nature, that is, 'the *systematic* denial that "true" knowledge can be got at by interpreting phenomena in terms of final causes – that is to say, of "purpose"' (Monod 1997, p. 21).

4   Monod 1997, p. 27. Monod concludes: 'Such theories see in living beings the most elaborated, perfected products of an evolution oriented in the entire universe and leading, because it *must*, to man and to humanity. These conceptions, which I will call animist, are in many respects more interesting than the vitalist ones, to which I will dedicate only a brief mention' (Monod 1997, pp. 27–28 [translation modified]).

teleonomic functioning of his own central nervous system'[5] ('the project gives the reason of being and being has sense only in virtue of the project').[6]

These conceptions, Monod warns, far from being the distant memory of an age now definitively superseded, 'still send down deep and strong [*vivaces*] roots into the soul of modern man'.[7] This is attested by the efforts made in modern culture from the seventeenth century onwards to reconstruct the ancient alliance: 'It is enough to think, for example, of the great attempts of Leibniz or of the enormous and powerful [*pesant*] monument raised by Hegel'.[8]

Arriving at the heart of the matter with an analysis of some of the theories of the nineteenth century, Monod maintains that such a conception can be found in Teilhard de Chardin, in the evolutionism of Spencer and even in Marx and Engels. It was 'the central idea of the ideology of scientific progress in the nineteenth century'.[9] When considering dialectical materialism, Monod explicitly refers almost exclusively to two classic texts of Engels on the philosophy of nature, that is, *Anti-Dühring* and the fragments published posthumously under the title of *Dialectics of Nature*. After having summarised dialectical materialism in a few schematic points,[10] Monod emphasises that making 'dialectical

---

5   Monod 1997, p. 30.

6   Ibid.

7   Monod 1997, p. 29.

8   Monod 1997, p. 30.

9   Monod 1997, p. 32.

10   Monod enumerates the following points: '1) the mode of existence of matter is movement. 2) The universe, defined as the totality of matter, the only existing totality, is in a state of perpetual [*perpétuelle*] evolution. 3) Any true knowledge of the universe is such in so far as it contributes to the intelligence of this evolution. 4) But such knowledge is not attained other than in interaction, itself evolutionary and the cause of evolution, between man and matter (or more exactly, the "remainder" of matter). Any true knowledge is therefore "practical". 5) Consciousness is related [*se rapporte*] to this cognitive interaction. Conscious thought reflects, consequently, the movement of the universe itself. 6) As, therefore, thought is a part and reflex of universal movement, and as its movement is dialectical, the evolutionary laws of the universe also must be dialectical. That explains and justifies the use of terms like contradiction, affirmation and negation in relation to natural phenomena. 7) Dialectics is constructive (above all [*notamment*]), thanks to the third "law"): consequently, the evolution of the universe is also ascending and constructive. Its highest expression is human society, consciousness, thought, necessary products of this evolution. 8) Due to the accent placed on the evolutionary essence of the structure of the universe, dialectical materialism superannuates radically the materialism of the eighteenth century which, founded on classic logic, was able to recognise only mechanical interactions between objects supposed to be classical; it was therefore not able to think evolution' (Monod 1997, p. 34 [translation modified]).

CHAPTER 1

had as an effect the systemisation 'of a subjective interpretation of nature, in
which an ascendant, constructive, creative project can be discovered'.[11] This
therefore led to the weakening of the principle of objectivity. The anthropocentric illusion is here presented in new clothes: the theory of evolution makes
man no longer the immovable centre of creation but, rather, 'the natural, long-
awaited inheritor of the entire universe'.[12] As confirmation of this statement,
Monod cites a passage from *Dialectics of Nature* that promises 'if not to the
human species, at least to the thinking brain, an eternal return'.[13]

But however often, and however relentlessly, this cycle [*Kreislauf*] is
completed in time and space [Engels is referring to the eternal cycle of
matter – V.M.], however many millions of suns and earths may arise and
pass away, however long it may last before the conditions for organic life
develop, however innumerable the organic beings that have to arise and
to pass away before animals with a brain capable of thought are developed
from their midst, and for a short span of time find conditions suitable for

---

11   Monod 1997, p. 38.

12   Monod 1997, p. 40. Balibar notes that if it is true that in Engels there is 'the tendency to
      conceive the proletariat not only as "the inheritor of classical German philosophy" ... [but
      as] the inheritor of evolution in its entirety, in short, the Son of Man (certainly, not
      theological man, but "natural", Darwinian man)', there is also present in Engels the
      counter-tendency: 'It is paradoxical to discover it in the same manner in which he
      "refinds" Hegel and turns to his dialectic, a dialectic which is certainly "evolutionary",
      but irreducible to the model of biological evolutionism ... The idea of history, conceived
      as a law of evolution, though full of consequences, furnishes Engels only provisionally
      with the matrix of his "materialist dialectic" by means of the relation to a determinate
      conception or image of the world, the "fixism" [doctrine of fixity] or the mechanicist
      ideology of natural science, of political philosophy and metaphysics of the seventeenth
      and eighteenth centuries. But the criticism reverses immediately its arms: after having
      combated fixism with the arms of evolutionism, it passes to combating, by means of
      Hegelian references (and also, on occasions, Fourierist, following an old predilection of
      Engels), the transformation, in turn, of evolutionism into a metaphysics, into a system.
      The idea of a law of evolution never means of contradiction (precisely that which
      evolutionism ignores completely – including Darwin and, at any rate, Häckel). The
      importance of the thought of Hegel derives from the fact that, according to Engels, though
      completely incapable of discovering determinant laws, it posits the entire world (natural
      and social) as a process and identifies immediately this process with the immanent event,
      with the entire concatenation of a totality of contradictions. ... In short, we see Engels
      here putting in play one teleology against another' (Balibar 1984, pp. 245–246).

13   Monod 1997, p. 41.

life, only to be exterminated later without mercy, we have the certainty
[*Gewissheit*] that matter remains eternally the same in all its transformations [*Wandlungen*], that none of its attributes [*Attribute*] can ever be lost,
and therefore, also, that with the same iron necessity that it will exterminate on the earth its highest creation, the thinking mind [*denkender
Geist*], it must somewhere else and at another time again produce it.[14]

It is precisely this passage, used by Monod to illustrate Engels's animist projection, which leads us into the heart of our present argument: for a conception
of matter remaining eternally equal to itself in the infinite change of its modes
and unable to lose any of its attributes refers us to the theoretical horizon of
Spinoza.

However, it is not so much this reference that is surprising, since it is also
confirmed by a story of Plekhanov according to which Engels was supposed to
have responded to a precise question about the Spinozist conception of nature
in the following terms: 'He was entirely correct, the old Spinoza'. Nor does such
a reference constitute an exception within German materialism of the second
half of the nineteenth century. It is enough to think of Häckel and Dietzgen.[15]
What is surprising is that this reference should lead to Engels being accused
of anthropocentrism and, therefore, of animism. The philosophy of Spinoza,
'Copernican thought *par excellence*',[16] seems to be constructed in such a way

---

14   Marx and Engels 1975–2005, vol. 25, p. 335. The passage is cited in Monod 1997, p. 30 et
      sq. See the following passage: 'The old teleology has gone to the devil, but the certainty
      [*Gewissheit*] is now firmly established that matter in its eternal cycle moves according
      to laws which at a definite stage – now here, now there – necessarily give rise to the
      thinking mind in organic beings' (Marx and Engels 1975–2005, vol. 25, pp. 475–476); or the
      following: 'it is the nature of matter to advance to the evolution of thinking beings, hence
      this always necessarily occurs wherever the conditions for it...are present' (Marx and
      Engels 1975–2005, vol. 25, p. 490).
15   See Dietzgen 1984; Häckel 1883; see also Plekhanov 1969. Engels's knowledge of Spinoza
      seems to be decisively mediated by Hegel, as appears from the few passages in which
      Spinoza is cited. For example, in *Anti-Dühring* (Marx and Engels 1975–2005, vol. 25, p. 18);
      in the same work he recalls the appendix of Book I of the *Ethics* with the motto, dear
      to Marx, '*Ignorantia non est argumentum*' (Marx and Engels 1975–2005, vol. 25, p. 102).
      And further, evidently relying upon Hegel's *Logic*, the proposition '*Omnis determinatio est
      negatio*' (Marx and Engels 1975–2005, vol. 25, p. 131).
16   Sini 1991, p. 91. Sini continues: 'Now, following these considerations and upsetting a
      commonplace of philosophical historiography, it would be necessary to say that Kant
      didn't in any way realise the Copernican revolution (Kant's revolution was very timid):
      the true Copernican revolution was accomplished by Spinoza; he is the Copernicus of
      Philosophy, not Kant' (ibid.).

as to prohibit any form of anthropomorphism and teleology. In order to explicate the theoretical reasons for which Engels, despite his reference to Spinoza's
philosophy, can be accused of animism (a judgment which, we should say from
the start, we share), it will be necessary to make a detour via the texts of Engels,
of Spinoza and, finally, of Hegel.

2   'Causa Sui' as 'Wechselwirkung'

Firstly, however, let us dwell for a moment on Engels's reference to Spinoza's
theory; this reference is explicitly confirmed by Engels himself, though in
general terms, in a passage in the 'Introduction' to *Dialectics of Nature*. After
having underlined how modern science was still profoundly immersed in theology, he writes:

> It is to the highest credit of the philosophy of the time that it did not let
> itself be led astray by the restricted state of contemporary natural knowl-
> edge, and that – from Spinoza right to the great French materialists – it
> insisted on explaining the world from the world itself and left the justifi-
> cation in detail to the natural science of the future.[17]

Spinoza, that is, has the merit of explaining the world in terms of itself and
not through recourse to a transcendent being, as in the case of Descartes and
Newton who point to a first impulse external to matter. Movement constitutes
for Spinoza, just as for Engels, the very mode of being of matter.[18] Matter without movement, therefore, is unthinkable. Engels writes:

---

17   Marx and Engels 1975–2005, vol. 25, p. 320 (translation modified).
18   This is Engels's definition: 'Motion in the most general sense, conceived as the mode
      of existence [*Daseinsweise*], the inherent attribute of matter, comprehends all changes
      and processes [*Prozesse*] occurring in the universe, from mere change of place right to
      thinking' ('Basic Forms of Motion', in *Dialectics of Nature* [Marx and Engels 1975–2005,
      vol. 25, p. 362]). Engels maintains that attraction and repulsion are the two '*simple forms
      of movement*' (Engels rejects the concept of *Kraft* because it is founded on the analogy of
      the action of the human organism on the environment) and that 'all movement consists
      in the interchange of attraction and repulsion' (Marx and Engels 1975–2005, vol. 25,
      p. 364). See the following passage from *Anti-Dühring*: '*Movement is the mode of existence
      [Daseinsweise] of matter*. Never anywhere has there been matter without movement,
      nor can there be. Movement in cosmic space, mechanical movement of smaller masses
      on the various celestial bodies, the vibration of molecules as heat or as electrical or
      magnetic currents, chemical disintegration and combination, organic life – at each given

The whole of nature accessible to us forms a system, an interconnected totality [*Gesamtzusammenhang*] of bodies, and by bodies we understand here all material existence extending from stars to atoms, indeed right to ether particles, in so far as one grants the existence of the last named. In the fact that these bodies are interconnected [*in einem Zusammenhang*] is already included that they react on one another [*aufeinander einwirken*], and it is precisely this mutual reaction [*gegenseitige Einwirkung*] that constitutes motion. It already becomes evident here that matter is unthinkable without motion. And if, in addition, matter confronts us as something given, equally uncreatable as indestructible, it follows that motion also is as uncreatable as indestructible. It became impossible to reject this conclusion [*Folgerungen*] as soon as it was recognised that the universe is a system, an interconnection [*Zusammenhang*] of bodies.[19]

Engels, therefore, like Spinoza, holds that nature is a universal interconnected totality, the parts of which cannot be separated from the whole other than by abstraction:

In nature nothing takes place in isolation. Everything affects and is affected by every other thing, and it is mostly because this manifold motion and interaction [*dieser allseitigen Bewegung und Wechselwirkung*] is forgotten that our natural scientists are prevented from gaining a clear insight into the simplest things.[20]

Knowledge of reality is possible on the condition of thinking this same reality as an infinite interrelation of events.[21] These can be explained in their individuality only by the connections that each of them establishes with the totality – connections which constitute the very nature of their individual

---

moment each individual atom of matter in the world is in one or other of these forms of movement, or in several forms at once' (Marx and Engels 1975–2005, vol. 25, p. 56 [translation modified]). For Spinoza, movement and rest constitute the infinite mode of extension: Spinoza thinks movement as a mode and not as an attribute precisely in order to deconstruct the theory of the first impulse of Descartes.

19   Marx and Engels 1975–2005, vol. 25, p. 362.
20   Marx and Engels 1975–2005, vol. 25, p. 458.
21   Interesting in this regard are the reflections developed by Whitehead regarding the concept of the event in his attempt to think the philosophical results of Einstein's theory of relativity.

becoming [*evenire*].[22] Therefore, in nature there are no isolated facts, except in the imaginary laboratory of the natural and social scientists (the example of the billiard table in mechanics and the Robinsonades in political economy). It is precisely for this reason that Engels maintains that science has need of dialectics, stripped of its mystical shell, in order to impede the sclerosis of the findings of scientific research

> in the rigid oppositions [*fixen Gegensätze*] of principle and consequence [*Grund und Folge*], cause and effect, identity and difference, appearance and essence [*Schein und Wesen*].[23]
>
> Chemistry – atomistics. The abstract divisibility in physics – bad [*schlechte*] infinity. Physiology – the cell (the organic process of development, both of the individual and of species, by differentiation, the most striking test of rational dialectics), and finally the identity of the forces of nature and their mutual convertibility [*gegenseitige Verwandlung*], which put an end to all fixity of categories. Nevertheless, the bulk of natural scientists are still held fast in the old metaphysical categories and helpless when these modern facts [*Tatsachen*], which so to say prove the dialectics in nature, have to be rationally explained and brought into relation [*Zusammenhang*] with one another. And here *thinking* is necessary [*Und hier musste gedacht werden*]: atoms and molecules, etc., cannot be observed under the microscope, but only by the process of thought. Compare the chemists (except for Schorlemmer, who is acquainted with Hegel) and Virchow's *Cellularpathologie*, where in the end the helplessness has to be concealed by general phrases. Dialectics divested of mysticism becomes an absolute necessity for natural science, which has forsaken the field where rigid categories sufficed, which represent as it were the lower mathematics of logic, its everyday weapons.[24]

Dialectics as conceived by Engels is thus 'to be developed as the science of interconnections, in contrast to metaphysics'.[25] This explains the reference to

---

22 See the following passage: 'When we consider and reflect upon nature at large or the history of mankind or our own intellectual activity, at first we see the picture of an endless entanglement of relations [*von Zusammenhänngen*] and interactions [*Wechselwirkungen*], in which nothing remains what, where and as it was, but everything moves, changes, comes into being and passes away' (Marx and Engels 1975–2005, vol. 25, p. 19 [translation modified]).

23 Marx and Engels 1975–2005, vol. 25, p. 485.

24 Marx and Engels 1975–2005, vol. 25, p. 486.

25 Marx and Engels 1975–2005, vol. 25, p. 356.

Spinozist theory, the first and perhaps the most pure attempt in the history of Western thought to think the primacy of the relation over the individual as opposed to traditional metaphysics, which thinks the relation in the form of subject-predicate.[26] Dialectics thinks reality, therefore, not as 'a complex of things', but as 'a complex of processes'. It is the stage reached by scientific knowledge, in particular with Darwin, which demands such an effort.[27] Whereas metaphysics thinks a hierarchy of ordered and separate substances by means of the concepts of genus and species, dialectics thinks a complex of interrelated process in which individuals are constituted in their infinite variety.

> For a stage in the outlook on nature where all differences become merged in intermediate steps, and all opposites pass into one another through intermediate links, the old metaphysical method of thought no longer suffices. Dialectics, which likewise knows no *hard and fast lines*, no unconditional, universally valid 'either-or' and which bridges the fixed metaphysical differences, and besides 'either-or' recognises also in the right place 'both this and that' and reconciles the opposites, is the sole method of thought appropriate in the highest degree to this stage. Of course, for everyday use, for the small change of science, the metaphysical categories retain their validity.[28]

In the same fragment, Engels shows, on the basis of Hegelian logic and indirectly on Spinozist arguments, how the old metaphysical categories become obsolete when thinking the results of modern science. For example, in the animal world the concept of an individual is not definable in a strict way: 'Not only as to whether a particular animal is an individual or a colony, but also where in development one individual ceases and the other begins (nurses)'.[29]

---

26   The theory of Leibniz constitutes perhaps a paradigmatic model of the difficulty encountered by a logic of the proposition that is founded on the form of subject-predicate regarding the problem of the relations. In this respect, see Russell's interpretation of Leibniz's philosophy regarding the problem of the relations (Russell 1900, p. 139) and the lucid criticism in Mugnai 1976, pp. 159–82.

27   Engels writes: 'Natural scientists ... are still under the domination of philosophy. It is only a question whether they want to be dominated by a bad, fashionable philosophy or by a form of theoretical thought which rests on acquaintance with the history of thought and its achievements' (Marx and Engels 1975–2005, vol. 25, p. 491).

28   Marx and Engels 1975–2005, vol. 25, pp. 493–494 (translation modified).

29   Marx and Engels 1975–2005, vol. 25, p. 493. In another fragment, Engels writes: 'The *individual.* This concept also has been dissolved into something purely relative. Cormus, colony, tapeworm – on the other hand, cell and metamere as individuals in a certain sense (*Anthropogenie* and *Morphologie*)' (Marx and Engels 1975–2005, vol. 25, p. 581).

Thus, in the organic world, the rigid opposition of categories like the whole and parts becomes insufficient.[30] In the same way, the opposition of categories like simple and compound 'already becomes inadequate in organic nature'.[31] Furthermore, for knowledge of the organic world just as for that of the inorganic world, the rigid opposition of identity and difference turns out to be of no service:

> The old abstract formal identity standpoint, that an organic being is to be treated as something simply identical with itself, as something constant, becomes out of date. Nevertheless, the mode of thought based thereon, together with its categories, persists. But even in inorganic nature identity as such is in reality non-existent. Every body is continually exposed to mechanical, physical, and chemical influences, which are always changing it and modifying its identity. Abstract identity, with its opposition to difference, is in place only in mathematics – an abstract science which is concerned with creations of thought, even though they are reflections of reality – and even there it is continually being sublated.[32]

---

30   Engels adds later on as an example: 'The ejection of seeds – the embryo – and the newborn animal are not to be conceived as a "part" that is separated from the "whole"; that would give a distorted treatment. It becomes a part only in a dead body. *Encyclopädie*, I, p. 268' (Marx and Engels 1975–2005, vol. 25, p. 494).

31   Marx and Engels 1975–2005, vol. 25, p. 494. 'An animal is expressed neither by its mechanical composition from bones, blood, gristle, muscles, tissues, etc., nor by its chemical composition from the elements. Hegel, *Encyclopädie*, I, 256. The organism is *neither* simple *nor* compound, however complex it may be' (Marx and Engels 1975–2005, vol. 25, p. 495).

32   Ibid. Further on, Engels writes: 'The law of identity in the old metaphysical sense is the fundamental law of the old outlook: A=A, each thing is equal to itself. Everything was permanent, the solar system, stars, organisms. This law has been refuted by natural science bit by bit in each separate case, but theoretically it still prevails and is still put forward by the supporters of the old in opposition to the new: a thing cannot simultaneously be itself and something else. And yet the fact that true, concrete identity includes difference, change, has recently been shown in detail by natural science' (Marx and Engels 1975–2005, vol. 25, p. 496). See the following passage from *Anti-Dühring*: 'Every organic being is every moment the same and not the same; every moment it assimilates matter supplied from without, and gets rid of other matter; every moment some cells of its body die and others build themselves anew; in a longer or shorter time the matter of its body is completely renewed, and is replaced by other atoms of matter, so that every organic being is always itself, and yet something other than itself ' (Marx and Engels 1975–2005, vol. 25, p. 23).

Furthermore, the rigid metaphysical opposition between contingency and necessity has become unusable regarding knowledge of natural processes. This sense, in fact, includes conceptions that, on the one hand, imagine that nature contains contingent processes next to necessary processes and that indicate exclusively the knowledge of the latter as the objective of science; and, on the other, the determinism which, transferred to science from French material-ism, simply negates the existence of the contingent. In both cases, they remain imprisoned in a theological conception of nature.

> In contrast to both conceptions, Hegel came forward with the hitherto quite unheard-of propositions that the accidental has a cause [*Grund*] because it is accidental, and just as much also has no cause [*Grund*] because it is accidental; that the accidental is necessary, that neces-sity determines itself as chance, and, on the other hand, this chance is rather absolute necessity (*Logik*, II, Book III, 2: *Die Wirklichkeit*). Natural Science has simply ignored these propositions as paradoxical trifling, as self-contradictory nonsense, and, as regards theory, has persisted on the one hand in the barren thought of Wolffian metaphysics, according to which a thing is *either* accidental *or* necessary, but not both at once; or, on the other hand, in the hardly less thoughtless mechanical determinism which in words denies chance in general only to recognise it in practice in each particular case.[33]

Finally, Engels emphasises that the rigidity of the metaphysical opposi-tion of cause and effect needs to be replaced by the category of interaction [*Wechselwirkung*]:

> *Reciprocal action* is the first thing that we encounter when we consider matter in motion as a whole from the standpoint of modern natural sci-ence. We see a series of forms of motion, mechanical motion, heat, light, electricity, magnetism, chemical compound and decomposition, transi-tions of states of aggregation, organic life, all of which, if *at present* we *still* make an exception of organic life, pass into one another, mutually determine one another, are in one place cause and in another effect, the sum-total of the motion in all its changing forms remaining the same... [W]e cannot go back further than to knowledge of this reciprocal action,

---

33   Marx and Engels 1975–2005, vol. 25, p. 501 (translation modified). Fleischmann shows with precision how Hegel is thinking here of the Spinozist modes (Fleischmann 1968, pp. 176–206). See also Fleischmann 1964, pp. 3–29.

for the very reason that there is nothing behind to know. If we know the forms of motion of matter (for which it is true there is still very much lacking, in view of the short time that natural science has existed), then we know matter itself, and therewith our knowledge is complete.... [O]nly from this universal reciprocal action do we arrive at the real causal relation. In order to understand the separate phenomena, we have to tear them out of the general inter-connection and consider them in isolation, and *then* the changing motions appear, one as cause and the other as effect.[34]

Thus, just as the concept of interaction demonstrates the uselessness of the rigid opposition of cause and effect, in the same way it shows the uselessness of the opposition of efficient cause and final cause:

> for the modern standpoint the whole hopeless rubbish about this anti-thesis is put to an end because we *know* from experience and from theory that both matter and its mode of existence, motion, are uncreatable and are, therefore, *their own final cause*; while to give the name effective causes to the individual causes which momentarily and locally become isolated in the mutual interaction of the motion of the universe, or which are isolated by our reflecting mind, adds absolutely no new determination but only a confusing element. A cause that is not effective is no cause.[35]

Engels shows, therefore, how the developments of scientific knowledge render the formulation of new philosophical categories necessary: this new order of philosophical discourse appears to be commanded by the category of *Wechselwirkung*, thought not as the reciprocal action of two substances but as the efficacy of the totality on its elements in as much as it is the interrelation between the action of these elements. The position itself of such a category confines the classical metaphysical oppositions – between individual

---

34   Marx and Engels 1975–2005, vol. 25, pp. 511–12. See the following passage from *Anti-Dühring*: 'Cause and effect are conceptions which only hold good in their application to each individual case [*einzelnen Fall*]; but as soon as we consider the individual cases in their general connection with the universe as a whole [*allgemeinen Zusammenhang mit dem Weltganzen*], they run into each other, and they become confounded in the contemplation [*Anschauung*] of that universal interaction [*Wechselwirkung*] in which causes and effects are eternally changing places, so that what is effect here and now will be cause there and then, and vice versa' (Marx and Engels 1975–2005, vol. 25, p. 22 [translation modified]).

35   Marx and Engels 1975–2005, vol. 25, p. 533 (emphasis added, translation modified).

and totality, whole and parts, identity and difference, simple and compound, quantity and quality, contingent and necessary, cause and effect, final cause and efficient cause – to the terrain of 'common sense' [*senso comune*].[36]

3   The Implications of the '*Causa Sui*'

The first theorist who had the *unprecedented audacity* to think this category in all of its anti-metaphysical implications was, according to Engels, Spinoza: 'Spinoza: *substance is causa sui* strikingly expresses the reciprocal action [*Wechselwirkung*]'.[37] The circle closes. Spinoza was, according to Engels, the first theorist of the modern age to think nature in itself. Although he did not have the opportunity to know more than a minimal part of the discoveries of natural science, he was the first to formulate the only philosophical category that is able to accord with these same discoveries: the category of *Wechselwirkung*.

Let us now briefly examine the Spinozist concept of *causa sui*, as it is formulated in the *Ethics*. By means of the theory of substance as *causa sui*, Spinoza thinks the self-production of the infinite substance as a production of the totality of modes,[38] in order thereby to understand the immanent (infinite) causality of proposition XVIII[39] and the transitive (finite) causality of proposition XXVIII[40] not as two distinct activities, but as a single and contemporaneous process.[41] In this way the concept of immanent causality, in its negation

---

36   See Marx and Engels 1975–2005, vol. 25, p. 527.

37   Marx and Engels 1975–2005, vol. 25, p. 511.

38   'God must be called the cause of all things in the same sense in which he is called the cause of himself' (Spinoza 2002, *Ethics* I, pr. XXV, schol, p. 232).

39   'God is the immanent, not the transitive, cause of all things' (Spinoza 2002, *Ethics* I, pr. XVIII, p. 229).

40   'Every singular thing, or any thing which is finite and has a determinate existence, can neither exist nor be determined to produce an effect unless it is determined to exist and produce an effect by another cause, which is also finite and has a determinate existence; and again, this cause also can neither exist nor be determined to produce an effect unless it is determined to exist and produce an effect by another, which is also finite and has a determinate existence, and so on, to infinity' (Spinoza 2002, *Ethics* I, pr. XXVIII, p. 233).

41   Macherey writes: 'Immanent causality and transitive causality therefore do not define two independent levels of causality, at the intersection of which finite things would themselves be produced. Rather, they constitute a single order which, synthetically considered in its entirety, acts absolutely in itself, and considered analytically, *partes extra partes*, distributes its operations according to determinate relations which have no autonomy because they do not possess their reason in themselves' (Macherey 1992, p. 101).

of any originary givenness of sense and of movement (the first impulse of Descartes) to the being of the world, reabsorbs in the absoluteness of the surface the imaginary double level of being.

The negation of a first cause understood as transient causality necessitates the rethinking of the model of transitive, finite causality, because that which is *causa sui* is also necessarily *effectus sui*. Thus every single existence is not the effect of a given cause, but of the infinite necessary relations that such existence maintains with all of the others. The concepts of cause and effect thus lose the anthropomorphic simplicity of the relation of juridical imputation, becoming instead a structural, processual multiplicity: every reality, every power, exists as infinite and definite, and is traversed by the multiple relations which constitute it as such.

Such a conception of causality carries with it a redefinition of the concept of the individual. Every individual is in fact whole and parts, simple and compound, because the individual is not understood as a *subjectum* always identical with itself, but as a constant relation between elements that can vary without transforming the form of the individual, if the proportion of the relation of movement and rest between the elements does not change.

Finally, the concept of *causa sui* led Spinoza to rethink the classical antithesis between the necessary and the contingent. Substance, in as much as it is *effectus sui*, has a cause and therefore its existence is dependent on another, that is, it is contingent. However, in as much as it is *causa sui*, it does not have a cause and therefore its existence is necessary. In other words, the mode which, if isolated from the totality, is contingent,[42] does not exist if not in its reference to another, to the absolutely necessary, that is, to substance. However, this same substance does not exist other than as the necessity of the modal contingency,[43] or as the infinity of necessary relations which maintain between them the contingent existences. The reason why Spinoza considers the concepts of genus and species to be useless is now clear: such concepts are useful within a hierarchical ontology like that of Aristotle in which each substance-individual occupies a definite space in the universal order on the basis of coordinates furnished by genus and species, but become useless within a horizon like that

---

42 Spinoza writes: 'By mode I understand the affections of a substance, or that which is in another through which it is also conceived' (Spinoza 2002, *Ethics* I, def. III, p. 217). In this sense the mode is contingent in as much as its essence does not entail existence: it is not, that is, cause of itself, but refers to substance which is the cause of itself and of the modes.

43 'In nature there is nothing contingent, but all things have been determined from the necessity of the divine nature to exist and produce an effect in a certain way' (Spinoza 2002, *Ethics* I, pr. XXIX, p. 234).

of Spinoza which dissolves every fixity and every hierarchy in the radical processuality of being.[44] Spinoza writes in Letter XXXII to Oldenburg:

> all bodies are surrounded by others, and are mutually determined to exist
> and operate in a fixed and definite manner [*ratione*], observed together
> by all constantly in every circumstance; hence it follows that each body,
> in so far as it exists as modified in a particular manner, must be consid-
> ered as a part of the whole universe, as agreeing with the whole, and
> associated with the remaining parts. As the nature of the universe is not
> limited ..., but is absolutely infinite, its parts are by this nature of infinite
> power infinitely modified, and compelled to undergo infinite variations.[45]

4   Genealogy of *Wechselwirkung*

Let us return now to Engels's statement that the concept of *causa sui* effectively expresses the concept of *Wechselwirkung*. The translation is not neutral
(admitting that neutral translation is impossible). The term *Wechselwirkung*
in fact relates to a theoretical history completely foreign to both Spinozan
philosophy and to the tradition of interpretation of Spinoza in Germany. It
is with Kant that the term *Wechselwirkung* acquires importance for the pur-
poses of our study. He poses *Wechselwirkung* as the third category of relation,[46]
deducing it from disjunctive judgments.[47] The application of such a category

---

44   Spinoza writes in the *Short Treatise*: 'For if we can only know a thing perfectly through
     a definition consisting of genus and difference, then we can never know perfectly the
     highest genus, which has no genus above it' (Spinoza 2002, *Short Treatise*, I, 7, p. 57).

45   Spinoza 2002, Letter XXXII, p. 848.

46   The position of *Wechselwirkung* as the third category is not unimportant, because, as Kant
     notes, 'the third category in each class always arises from the combination of the second
     category with the first' (Kant 1996, B183–4 A 144, p. 185); thus 'community [*Gemeinschaft*]
     or reciprocity is the causality of substances reciprocally [*wechselseitig*] determining one
     another' (Ibid.).

47   Kant 1996, B95 A70, p. 107. Regarding precisely such a deduction, Kant adds an observation:
     'in the case of one category, namely, that of *community*, which is found in the third group,
     its accordance with the form of a disjunctive judgment – the form which corresponds
     to it in the table of logical functions – is not as evident as in the case of the others. To
     gain assurance that they do actually accord, we must observe that in all disjunctive
     judgments the sphere ... is represented as a whole divided into parts ... and that since
     no one of them can be contained under any other, they are thought as co-ordinated with,
     not subordinated to, each other, and so as determining each other, not in one direction

to appearances [*Erscheinungen*] is rendered possible, according to Kant, by the transcendental schema which 'by means of the transcendental determination of time ... mediates the subsumption of the appearances under the category'.[48] The schema of *Wechselwirkung*, or of the reciprocal causality of substances in respect of their accidents is, therefore, 'the co-existence, according to a universal rule, of the determinations of the one substance with those of the other'.[49] On the basis of this schema, Kant formulates the third of the analogies of experience (the rule of all temporal relations which precede experience and render it possible for the first time):[50] 'All substances, in so far as they can be perceived to coexist in space, are in thorough-going reciprocity [*Wechselwirkung*]'.[51]

The idealistic re-conceptualisation of Kantian critique had as its epicentre precisely the redefinition of the transcendental schematism or of the imagination, the site of the encounter of appearance and the category. German idealism, against Kant, thought this imagination as productive, as the site of the original constitution of reality itself. In the *System of Transcendental Idealism*, Schelling affirms that

> the first category underlying all the others, the only one whereby the object is already determined in production, is, as we know, that of relation, which, since it is the sole category of intuition, will be alone in presenting inner and outer sense as still united.[52]

---

only, as in a series, but reciprocally, as in an aggregate – if one member of the division is posited, all the rest are excluded, and conversely. Now in a whole which is made up of things, a similar combination is being thought; for one thing is not subordinated, as effect, to another, as cause of its existence, but, simultaneously and reciprocally, is co-ordinated with it, as cause of the determination of the other... This is a quite different kind of connection from that which is found in the mere relation of cause to effect (of ground to consequence), for in the latter relation the consequence does not in its turn reciprocally determine the ground, and therefore does not constitute with it a whole – thus the world, for instance, does not with its Creator serve to constitute a whole' (Kant 1996, B112, p. 117).

48   Kant 1996, B178 A139, p. 181.
49   Kant 1996, B183–4 A144, p. 185.
50   Kant 1996, B218 A177, p. 208.
51   Kant 1996, B257 A211, p. 233. Kant specifies his discourse in the following passage thus: 'The word community is in the German language ambiguous. It may mean either *communio* or *commercium*. We here employ it in the latter sense, as signifying a dynamical community, without which even local community (*communio spatii*) could never be empirically known' (Kant 1996, B260 A213, p. 235).
52   Schelling 1978, p. 145.

The category of *Wechselwirkung* (the above mentioned third category of rela-tion) is posited by Schelling as the synthesis of the categories of substance and cause, from which he deduces it in the following way:

> Hence the first category as such is intuitable only through the second, as has been shown at the proper juncture; the ground of this, which appears here, is that only through the second do we add the transcen-dental schema of time. Substance is intuitable as such only by being intuited as persisting in time, but it cannot be intuited as persistent unless time, which has so far designated only the absolute boundary, flows (extends itself in one dimension), which in fact comes about only through the succession of the casual sequence [*Causalzusammenhang*]. But conversely, too, that any succession occurs in time is intuitable only in contrast to something that persists therein, or, since time arrested in its flow=space, that persists in space, and this is in fact substance. Hence these two categories are possible only mutually through one another [*Wechselseitigdurcheinander*], that is, they are possible only in a third, which is reciprocity [*Wechselwirkung*].[53]

Nevertheless, without wishing to play down the importance of Kant's and Schelling's thought, it is not difficult to recognise in Engels's equation 'causa sui = Wechselwirkung' the direct effect of his reading of the concluding pages of Hegel's 'Doctrine of Essence'.[54] (Engels himself alluded to this on numerous occasions).[55] Engels repeatedly uses the argumentation found in these pages,

---

53   Schelling 1978, p. 146.

54   Hegel, criticising Jacobi's interpretation of Spinoza's concept of *causa sui*, exclaims: 'causa sui (*effectus sui* is the same), which is the absolute truth of the cause' (Hegel 1975, p. 216).

55   In formulating the second law of dialectics, 'the law of the interpenetration of opposites', Engels affirms that Hegel's treatment of it in the 'Doctrine of Essence' is 'by far the most important part' of the system ('Dialectics' in *Dialectics of Nature* (Marx and Engels 1975–2005, vol. 25, p. 357). See also the following letter of Engels to Marx: 'I am deeply immersed in the doctrine of essence. Back from Jersey, I found Tyndall's and Huxley's speeches in Belfast waiting for me, which once again reveal the plight of these people, and the way they are stuck fast in the thing in-itself and their cry of anguish for a philosophy to rescue them. This brought me back again, after all manner of interruptions during the first week, to the theme of dialectics. In view of the feeble mind of the natural scientists, the great *Logic* can only be used sparingly, although as far as dialectics are concerned, it goes much more nearly to the heart of the matter. But the account of it in the *Encyclopaedia*, on the other hand, could have been tailor-made for these people, the illustrations are taken largely from their own subject and are striking, they are freer of idealism. Now, since I

as we have also seen above, in his polemics against the categorical couples of traditional metaphysics. *Wechselwirkung* occupies a fundamental strategic position in the Hegelian system. It constitutes the supreme development of objective logic, or of substance; at the same time, it is also the bridge thrown up by substance or objective logic toward subjective logic, the concept. In other words, it is objectivity that, having become transparent to itself, allows the pure rays of subjectivity (of the idea) to shine within itself.[56]

Hegel treats *Wechselwirkung* in the third chapter of the third section of the 'Doctrine of Essence' in the *Science of Logic*.[57] This third section, whose title is 'Reality' [*Wirklichkeit*], is posited as a unity of existence and essence.[58] Nevertheless, the unity of reality cannot be the immediate unity of being, but must be a unity mindful of the duality that has tormented it, a mediated unity. As Béatrice Longuenesse writes, 'there is no hidden world to oppose to the thought world, to the world transformed in thought'.[59] In the first chapter, the third section of the 'Doctrine of Essence' develops a speculative exposition of the Spinozan categories of the absolute, attribute and mode;[60] in the second, a speculative exposition of the Kantian modal categories;[61] and in the third, an

---

neither can nor will exempt these gentlemen from the punishment of having to learn from Hegel, it is clear that there is a veritable treasure-trove here, all the more so since even today the old fellow can give them a number of tough nuts to crack' (Marx and Engels 1975–2005, vol. 45, p. 50).

56   Although Hegel modified the architectonic of his system throughout the years, it should be noted that the category of *Wechselwirkung* always had a key role as a moment of passage from the objective to the subjective, from being to thought. In the *Logic of Jena*, *Wechselwirkung* constitutes the moment of passage from the relation of being to the relation of thought (See *Jenaer Systementwürfe II*, in Hegel 1968, vol. 7, pp. 65–75). In the course of Logic from 1810/11 for the middle school just as in the course of the philosophical encyclopaedia from 1808 for the superior class, *Wechselwirkung* constitutes the moment of passage from essence to the concept (*Philosophische Propädeutik*, in Hegel 1927, pp. 129–38, p. 180).

57   Hegel 2004 p. 529; *Wissenschaft der Logik*, in Hegel 1968, vol. 11, p. 369. I have consulted the following commentaries on the 'Doctrine of Essence': Biard 1983, 279–375; Findlay 1958; Fleischmann 1968, pp. 176–206; Opiela 1983, pp. 195–205, 329–34; Yamane 1983; Doz 1987, pp. 125–75; Longuenesse 1981, pp. 138–204; Belaval 1976, pp. 253–378. Regarding the logic of the *Encyclopaedia*, the following commentaries have been useful: Harris 1983; Léonard 1974, 240–314; Lakebrink 1979, pp. 329 et sq.

58   'Reality [*Wirklichkeit*] is the unity of essence and existence' (Hegel 2004, p. 529).

59   Longuenesse 1981, p. 142.

60   Hegel 2004, pp. 530–40.

61   Hegel 2004, pp. 541–53.

exposition of the dialectic of the Kantian categories of relation.[62] The general lines of dialectical movement of such a speculative exposition are exhibited in the beginning of this third chapter entitled 'the absolute relation':

> This relation [*Verhältniss*] in its immediate concept is the relation of *substance* and *accidents*, the immediate disappearance [*Verschwinden*] and becoming of absolute appearance in itself. By determining itself as a *being for itself* against another, or the absolute relation as real, it is the *relation of causality*. Finally, by passing over to interaction [*Wechselwirkung*] as relating to itself [*als sich auf sich Beziehendes*], the absolute relation according to the determinations which it contains is also posited; this, its *posited unity* in its *determinations, which are posited* precisely *as* the whole itself and with that also as determinations, is thus the *concept* [*Begriff*].[63]

Interaction is, therefore, posited by Hegel as a synthesis of substantiality and causality. In interaction, the duality still present in the relations of substance-accident and cause-effect is dispensed with; reflection as infinite substance absorbs every immediacy within itself in such a way that in *Wechselwirkung* the alterity and the multiplicity of the presupposed given are all reabsorbed in the immanence of reflexive unity (determinate reflection).[64]

Through the moments of formal causality [*die formelle Causalität*], determined causality [*das bestimmte Causalitätsverhältniss*], and of action and reaction [*Wirkung und Gegenwirkung*], one finally attains with *Wechselwirkung* to thinking the truth of the concept of cause and substance understood as an infinite totality:

> *Interaction* is therefore only causality itself; the cause not only does not have an effect, but, in the effect, it is in relation with itself *as cause*. ... Causality is this posited *passing* from originary being, that is, of *cause*,

---

62   Hegel 2004, pp. 554–72.

63   Hegel 2004, pp. 554–5 (translation modified).

64   Hegel writes in the conclusion to the paragraph on *determinate reflection*: 'determination of reflection, on the contrary, has taken back into itself its being other. It is posited being, negation, which however bends back into itself its relation to the other, and is negation which is equal to itself, the unity of itself and its other and only insofar is it essentiality [*Wesenheit*]. It is therefore posited being, negation; but as reflection into itself it is also at the same time [*zugleich*] the sublated being [*Aufgehobenseyn*] of this posited being, it is the infinite relation to itself' (Hegel 2004, p. 408 [translation modified]).

into appearance or into mere *posited being*, and vice versa of posited being into originality; but the identity itself of being and appearance is still inner necessity. This *interiority* or this being in itself sublates the movement of causality; with that, the substantiality of the sides that are in relation is lost, and necessity is revealed. Necessity does not become *freedom* by disappearing, but rather, only through the *manifestation* of its still inner identity; a manifestation that is the identical movement of the distinct in itself, the reflection into itself of appearance as appearance. – On the other hand, contingency [*Zufälligkeit*] thus becomes at the same time *freedom*, in so far as the sides of necessity which have the form of realities for themselves, which do not appear [*scheinen*] in each other, are now *posited as identity*, so that these totalities of reflection into self, in their difference, now *appear* [*scheinen*] also *as identical*, or are posited only as one and the same reflection.[65]

In the *Encyclopaedia*, the 'hard craggy melody' becomes more accessible:

In interaction . . ., the progress of cause and effect to infinity is really sub- lated [*aufgehoben*] as progress, as the linear proceeding from cause to effect and from effect to cause is folded back and turned back into itself [*in sich um- und zurückgebogen ist*]. This folding back of infinite progress into a relation *closed in itself* [my italics] is, as everywhere, simple reflec- tion that is one and the same in any thoughtless repetition, that is, *one cause* and *another cause* and their relationship to each other. The devel- opment of this relationship, interaction [*das Wechselwirken*], is however itself the alternation of *the differentiating*, not of causes, however, but of moments *in each of which* the *other* moment is posited also as *for itself*, according to the identity that cause in effect is cause and vice versa, that is, according to the inseparability of both.[66]

65   Hegel 2004, pp. 570–1 (translation modified).
66   Hegel 1975, pp. 217–18. A. Doz comments: 'We noted above that reciprocal action, to the extent that at first it is nothing but the indefinite continuation of the couple action- reaction, does not cancel out the existence of linkages in rectilinear series. We may now note that there are also linkages in closed, circular series; but these linkages in turn are subordinate to a new relation, and with respect to them freedom appears as an infinite spontaneity which they themselves presuppose and which surpasses them by integrating them' (Doz 1987, p. 174).

A few lines later, Hegel adds:

> The course [*Verlauf*] of substance through causality and interaction is therefore only in positing that independence [*Selbständigkeit*] is the infinite *negative relation* to itself – actually *negative*, in which differentiation and mediation becomes an originality of opposed, *independent real* elements, – *infinite relation to itself*, as the independence of them is precisely only their identity.[67]

By means of the category of *Wechselwirkung* Hegel thinks the identity of thought as thinking and thought as that which is thought, of form and matter, the sensible given and intellectual category. We are now ready, following the programme of the *Phenomenology of Spirit*, to think the true not only as substance, but also as subject:

> In the *concept* [*Begriff*], therefore, the kingdom [*Reich*] of freedom is opened. The concept is the free, because *identity in and for itself*, which constitutes the necessity of substance, is at the same time [*zugleich*] sublated [*aufgehoben*] or is *posited being*, and this posited being, as relating itself to itself, is precisely that identity. The obscurity of the substances which are in a causal relation to each other is lost, for the originality of their existence for themselves [*Selbstbestehen*] is overcome in posited being, and has thus become *clarity* transparent to itself. The *original thing* is *this*, in so far as it is only the cause of itself, and this is *substance liberated into the concept* . . . the concept, insofar as it has attained to such an *existence*, which is precisely free, is nothing other than the 'I' or the pure self-consciousness.[68]

The concept of *causa sui* and the concept of *Wechselwirkung* are not, therefore, the same concept. The second is marked, as an indelible inheritance of Kantianism, by a reference to a principle of interiority – although this interiority in Hegel 'has made itself a world'[69] – and an implicit teleology in the process of substance becoming subject (or in its becoming that which it always-already is). The concept of *Wechselwirkung* in fact implies temporality as the

67   Hegel 1975, pp. 219–20 (translation modified).
68   Hegel 2004, p. 582.
69   Bloch 1971, pp. 271–94.

simultaneity of the totality with respect to itself,[70] a temporality that is the synchronic foundation (the interpenetration of opposites, that is, contradiction) of the diachronic development of the totality itself (the negation of the negation). It is thus the conservation of all of the suppressed contradictions in the highest phase of the diachronic development (*Erinnerung* as the simultaneous consciousness of succession).[71] In the simultaneity of each phase of the

---

70 In Hegel's early text *Glauben und Wissen*, he defines the eternity of the totality as *absolute Zugleich* (see Hegel 1968, vol. 4, pp. 352–6). It should be noted here that in the *Critique of Pure Reason* Kant defines the concept of the 'present [*Gegenwart*]' as one of the derived (able to be predicated) concepts of the original concept of 'community' or 'interaction': the absolute simultaneity of the Hegelian totality is therefore absolute presence of the totality to itself. We thus find ourselves in this case close to Heidegger's criticism of 'the Hegelian conception of time' as 'the most radical ... conceptual elaboration of the ordinary comprehension of time' (see Heidegger 1996, p. 392 [translation modified]).

71 'But the other side of its Becoming, *History*, is a *conscious*, self-*mediating* process – Spirit emptied out into Time; but this externalization, this kenosis, is equally an externalization of itself; the negative is the negative of itself. This becoming presents a slow-moving succession of Spirits, a gallery of images, each of which, endowed with all the riches of Spirit, moves thus slowly just because the Self has to penetrate and digest this entire wealth of its substance. As its fulfilment consists in perfectly *knowing* what *it is*, in knowing its substance, this knowing is its *withdrawal into itself* in which it abandons its outer existence [*Dasein*] and gives its existential shape over to recollection. Thus absorbed in itself, it is sunk in the night of its self-consciousness; but in that night its vanished outer existence is preserved, and this transformed existence – the former one, but now reborn of the Spirit's knowledge – is the new existence, a new world and a new shape of Spirit. In the immediacy of this new existence the Spirit has to start afresh to bring itself to maturity as if, for it, all that preceded were lost and it had learned nothing from the experience of the earlier Spirits. But recollection [*Er-Innerung*], the *inwardizing*, of that experience, has preserved it and is the inner being, and in fact the higher form of the substance. So although this Spirit starts afresh and apparently from its own resources to bring itself to maturity, it is none the less on a higher level that it starts. The realm of Spirits which is formed in this way in the outer world constitutes a succession in Time in which one Spirit relieved another of its charge and each took over the empire of the world from its predecessor. Their goal is the revelation of the depth of Spirit, and this is *the absolute Notion*. This revelation is, therefore, the raising-up of its depth, or its *extension*, the negativity of this withdrawn "I", a negativity which is its externalization or its substance; and this revelation is also the Notion's Time, in that this externalization is in its own self externalized, and just as it is in its extension, so it is equally in its depth, in the Self. The *goal*, Absolute Knowing, or Spirit that knows itself as Spirit, has for its path the recollection of the Spirits as they are in themselves and as they accomplish the organization of their realm. Their preservation, regarded from the side of their free

history of the totality, therefore, every preceding phase is conserved, as sublated, until attaining to the consciousness of itself which is the transparency of the totality with respect to itself. This consciousness, however, was present *ab origine* in the concept of simultaneity, because the simultaneous is such only with respect to the experience of a consciousness which hypostasises its own temporality and measures the phenomena of the external world on this basis. Thus the misrecognition of the difference between the concepts of *causa sui* and *Wechselwirkung* cannot be without consequences. Let us now try to determine the significance of this for Engels.

5   Hegel or Spinoza

The question of the relation between the rational dialectic and the mystified dialectic in Hegel are well known. It was Marx who, in the 'Afterword' to the second edition of *Capital*, determined the terms of such question:

> Fundamentally, my dialectic method is not only different from the Hegelian, but is its direct opposite. To Hegel, the life-process of the human brain, i.e., the process of thinking, which, under the name of 'the Idea', he even transforms into an independent subject, is the demiurgos of the real [*das Wirkliche*], and the real is only the external, phenomenal form [*Erscheinung*] of 'the Idea'. With me, on the contrary, the ideal is nothing else than the material element reflected by the human mind, and translated into forms of thought ... The mystification which dialectic suffers in Hegel's hands by no means prevents him from being the first to present its general form of working in a comprehensive and conscious manner. With him it is standing on its head [*sie steht bei ihm auf dem Kopf*]. It must be turned right side up [*umstülpen*], if you would discover the rational kernel within the mystical shell.[72]

---

existence appearing in the form of contingency, is History; but regarded from the side of their [philosophically] comprehended organization, it is the Science of Knowing in the sphere of appearance: the two together, comprehended history, form alike the inwardizing and the Calvary of absolute Spirit, the actuality, truth, and certainty of his throne, without which he would be lifeless and alone. "Only from the Chalice of this realm of spirits foams forth for Him his own infinitude"' (Hegel 1977, pp. 492–3).

72   Marx and Engels 1975–2005, vol. 35, p. 22.

In expounding the same problem, Engels seems to accept Marx's definition:

> First of all it must be established that here it is not at all a question of
> defending Hegel's point of departure: that spirit, mind, the idea, is
> primary and that the real world is only a poor copy [*Abklatsch*] of the
> idea. Already Feuerbach abandoned that. We all agree that in every field
> of science ... one must proceed from the given facts [*Tatsachen*], in natu-
> ral science, therefore from the various objective forms and the various
> forms of motion of matter; that therefore in theoretical natural science
> too the inner-connections are not to be built into the facts but to be dis-
> covered in them, and when discovered to be verified as far as possible by
> experiment.[73]

The relation between materialist and idealist dialectics is therefore one of polar
opposition: the former posits matter as cause and thought as effect; the latter
poses thought as cause and matter as effect. Nevertheless, the fundamental
structures of dialectical movement that Hegel had correctly described remain
the same in both. The frame of the problematic within which such an alternative
is rendered possible is unequivocally that proposed by Fichte in *The Vocation
of the Scholar* and in the *Doctrine of Scientific Knowledge* [*Wissenschaftslehre*]:
the alternative, that is, between thinking the I as a production of the non-I – a
thesis which would be the expression of a transcendental materialism devoid
of any rationality – and thinking the non-I as a product of the I, a thesis of idealism. The Hegelian system, now thought within this problematic, needs to be
set again on its feet, as Feuerbach suggested, that is, by applying to speculative
philosophy the model of the subject/predicate inversion.

But is it really possible to turn Hegel upside down, or rather, is his system, as
Hegel himself had said of Spinoza, fluctuating in the free ether without either
height or depth?[74] Can a category like that of *Wechselwirkung* have a rational
kernel and thus be liberated from its mystical shell simply by making it the
modality of the action of matter?

The category of *Wechselwirkung* allows Hegel to make the transition from
objective logic to subjective logic, from substance to subject (that is, to the I),
from blind necessity to the kingdom of freedom. Engels inverts this category,
or turns it into a reflex in the mind 'of the forms of movement of the world

---

73   Marx and Engels 1975–2005, vol. 25, pp. 342–3 (translation modified).
74   Hegel 1968, vol. 4, p. 392.

of nature just as of History'.[75] He attains the same result, because the general interaction of matter reaches, via intermediate stages,[76] to 'its highest fruit':

---

75   Marx and Engels 1975–2005, vol. 25, p. 458.

76   In the addendum to paragraph 156 of the *Encyclopaedia Logic*, after having affirmed that interaction is the relation of causality posited in its complete development, Hegel demonstrates its application to the field of history: 'Thus, for example, in observations on history, the question treated at first is the question of whether the character and the habits of a people are the cause of their constitution and of their laws, or whether, on the other hand, they are effects of them. Further, an advance is made in so far as they both, character and habits, on the one hand, and constitutions and laws, on the other, are conceived from the point of view of reciprocal action, so the cause is the whole effect in the same relation in which it is cause, and the effect is the whole cause in the same relation in which it is effect. The same thing occurs, further, also in observation of nature, and particularly of the living organism, whose single organs and whose single functions show equally to be the one with respect to the other in a relation of reciprocal action' (Hegel 1975, pp. 21–9). Nevertheless, a few lines later, he adds: 'The unsatisfying aspect of the application of the relation of reciprocal action consists in the fact that this relation, instead of being able to function as an equivalent of the concept, must, rather, in its turn, above all be conceived, and this occurs if it is not limited to leave its two aspects as something given immediately but, as has been demonstrated in the two preceding paragraphs, if they are recognised here as moments of a third, higher term which is, precisely, the concept. If, for example, we consider the habits of the Spartan people as an effect of their constitution, and, vice versa, their constitution as an effect of their habits, this observation can certainly be correct, but this mode of comprehending things is, all things considered, not satisfying, because, in effect, it does not allow us to comprehend conceptually either the constitution or the habits of this people. That occurs only when both of those aspects, as well as all of the remaining sides of life and of history of the Spartan people, are recognised as founded in this concept' (Hegel 1975, p. 219). We have already analysed how Engels uses the category of *Wechselwirkung* in the theory of nature. We should emphasise that it is a category just as central in the definition of the theory of history. Engels writes to Bloch: 'The economic situation [*Lage*] is the basis, but the various elements of the superstructure [*Überbau*] – political forms of the class struggle and its results, to wit: constitutions established by the victorious class after a successful battle, etc., juridical forms, and even the reflexes of all these actual struggles in the brains of the participants, political, juristic, philosophical theories, religious views and their further development into systems of dogmas [*Dogmensystemen*] – also exercise their influence [*Einwirkung*] upon the course [*Verlauf*] of the historical struggles and in many cases preponderate in determining their *form*. There is an interaction [*Wechselwirkung*] of all these elements in which, amid all the endless host of accidents [*Zufälligkeiten*] (that is, of things and events whose inner interconnection is so remote or so impossible of proof that we can regard it as non-existent, as negligible), the economic movement finally asserts itself as necessary' (Engels to J. Bloch, 21/22 September 1890, Marx and Engels 1975–2005,

the consciousness that in communist society auto-transparency of the natural
and social totality must come to pass (that is, where natural and social matter
is organised according to its nature), thus opening the kingdom of freedom:[77]

---

vol. 49, p. 33). Engels writes to Schmidt: 'What these gentlemen all lack is dialectic. They
never see anything but here cause and there effect. That this is a hollow abstraction,
that such metaphysical polar opposites only exist in the real world during crises, while
the whole vast process [*der ganze frosse Verlauf*] proceeds in the form of interaction
[*Wechselwirkung*] (though of very unequal [*ungleicher*] forces, the economic movement
being by far the strongest, most originary [*ursprünglichste*] and most decisive) and that
here everything is relative and nothing is absolute – this they never begin to see. Hegel has
never existed for them' (Engels to C. Schmidt, 27 October 1890, Marx and Engels 1975 2005,
vol. 49, p. 64 [translation modified]). Again, to Mehring: 'Hanging together with this too
is the fatuous notion of the ideologists that because we deny an independent historical
development to the various ideological spheres which play a part in history we also deny
them any historical efficacy [*Wirksamkeit*]. The basis of this is the common undialectical
conception of cause and effect as rigidly opposite poles, the total disregarding of
interaction [*Wechselwirkung*]; these gentlemen often almost deliberately forget that
once an historic element [*Moment*] has been brought into the world [*in die Welt gesetzt*]
by other elements, ultimately by economic facts, it also reacts in its turn and may react
on its environment [*Umgebung*] and even on its own causes' (Engels to F. Mehring,
14 July 1893, Marx and Engels 1975–2005, vol. 50, p. 163 [translation modified]). Finally,
to Borgius: 'Political, juridical, philosophical, religious, literary, artistic, etc., development
is based on economic development. But all these react upon one another and also
upon the economic base [*Basis*]. It is not that the economic position is the *cause and
alone active*, while everything else only has a passive effect. There is, rather, interaction
[*Wechselwirkung*] on the basis [*auf Grundlage*] of the economic necessity, which in the
last instance [*in letzter Instanz*] always asserts itself' (Engels to W. Borgius, 25 January
1894, Marx and Engels 1975–2005, vol. 50, p. 294 [translation modified]). It turns out that
for Engels just as for Hegel the reciprocal action of historical elements has a *telos*, that is,
a necessary direction, imposed, in Hegel, by the concept, in Engels, by the economic base:
such a *telos* emerges from the immanence of interaction as the destined point of arrival
of the historical process.

77   'Hegel was the first to state correctly the relation between freedom and necessity. To
him, freedom is the insight into necessity [*die Einsicht in die Notwendigkeit*], "necessity
is blind only in so far as it is not understood [*begriffen*]". Freedom does not consist in
any dreamt-of independence from natural laws, but in the knowledge of these laws, and
in the possibility this gives of systematically making them work towards definite ends
[*bestimmten Zwecken*]. This holds good in relation both to the laws of external nature
and to those which govern the bodily and mental existence of men themselves – two
classes of laws which we can separate from each other at most only in thought but not in
reality. Freedom of the will therefore means nothing but the capacity to make decisions
with knowledge of the subject [*Sachkenntnis*]. Therefore the freer a man's judgement is
in relation to a definite question, the greater is the necessity with which the content of

[In communism] man, in a certain sense, is finally marked off from the rest of the animal kingdom, and emerges from mere animal conditions of existence into really human ones. The whole sphere of the conditions of life which environ man, and which have hitherto ruled man, now comes under the dominion [*Herrschaft*] and control of man, who for the first time becomes the real, conscious lord [*Herren*] of nature because he has now become master of his own social organisation [*Vergesellschaftung*]. The laws of his own social action [*Tun*], hitherto standing face to face with man as laws of nature foreign to and dominating him, will then be used with full understanding [*Sachkenntnis*], and so mastered by him. Man's own social organisation, hitherto confronting him as a necessity imposed by nature and history, now becomes the result of his own free action [*Tat*]. The extraneous objective forces that have hitherto governed history pass under the control of man himself... Only from that time will the social causes set in movement by him have, in the main and in a constantly growing measure, the results intended by him. It is humanity's leap from the kingdom of necessity to the kingdom of freedom.[78]

Et voilà, the leap from necessity to liberty, from substance to subject, is inscribed in Engels's thought by the philosophical memory of the concept of *Wechselwirkung* and by its necessary correlate, the concept of consciousness as reflection (the progression from in-itself to for-itself).

But why, then, have we seen, in the passage cited by Monod, a reference to the theory of Spinoza? Let us take up again the concluding passage of this citation:

we have the certainty that matter remains eternally the same in all its transformations, that none of its attributes can ever be lost, and therefore, also, that with the same iron necessity that it will exterminate on the

---

this judgement will be determined; while the uncertainty, founded on ignorance, which apparently [*scheinbar*] makes an arbitrary choice among many different and conflicting possible decisions, shows precisely by this that it is not free, that it is controlled by the very object it should itself control. Freedom therefore consists in the control over ourselves and over external nature, a control founded on knowledge of natural necessity; it is therefore necessarily a product of historical development' (Marx and Engels 1975–2005, vol. 25, pp. 105–6 [translation modified]).

78   Marx and Engels 1975–2005, vol. 25, p. 266.

earth its highest creation, the thinking mind, it must somewhere else and at another time again produce it.[79]

For Engels, thought is the highest attribute of matter, the most complex form of movement, which the eternal cycle [*Kreislauf*] of matter must return to create. Spinoza, on the other hand, in the VI Definition of the first part of the *Ethics*, writes: 'By God I understand a being absolutely infinite, that is, a substance consisting of an infinity of attributes, of which each one expresses an eternal and infinite essence'.[80] The essence of every attribute is in Spinoza eternal and infinite. This means that thought cannot be understood as the highest form of extension, just as, on the other hand, extension cannot be considered as the lowest form of thought (as in the neo-Platonic model). There is no hierarchy between the attributes: they are eternal and infinite, and therefore cannot be subordinated either the one to the other nor to any form of temporality. The asymmetry of Engels's thought with respect to the symmetry of Spinoza's produces a radical difference in the two systems: the dialectical materialism of Engels, like Hegel's idealism, understands the process of the becoming subject of substance as the becoming liberty of necessity, while the Spinozist theory of substance as *causa sui* – identifying *ab origine* in the absoluteness of substance the concepts of essence and existence, of power and act, of free cause and necessary cause, of *in se esse* and *per se concipi* – bars any conception of nature and of history as a *Bildungsroman* of a subject (Hegel's Idea; Engels's humanity). Thought and extension, understood as attributes of the eternal substance, are posited outside of duration, though they are the conditions of existence of any modal duration. This means that there is no temporality of the totality or history of the totality; neither can its eternity be understood as an absolute simultaneity in which the modal temporality is immersed; neither, finally, can it be understood as a *Kreislauf* in Engels's sense, that is, as identity of succession and simultaneity. On the contrary, in every singular existence (of things and of ideas) the necessary contingency of duration is inscribed *ab origine*; its persevering is the open and aleatory effect of a field of encounters and clashes between powers (that is, between other durations) that can never become destined.

If therefore the concept of *Wechselwirkung* implies a totality present to itself as simultaneity, a simultaneity that constitutes the track which permits the flow of a linear, homogenous and empty time, which can be filled by the chronology of stages of development, then the concept of *causa sui* implies a total-

---

79   Marx and Engels 1975–2005, vol. 25, p. 335.
80   Spinoza 2002, *Ethics* I, def. VI, p. 217.

ity without closure, a totality whose eternity is identified with the necessary and infinite network of modal durations. This means that freedom cannot be understood, as in Engels, as a conscious reflection of necessity,[81] as a finally attained transparency of nature and of history to thought, but as a degree of power of necessity in the aleatory space of the conjuncture.

Translated by Peter Thomas

---

81 Timpanaro speaks of the 'Spinozist and Hegelian formulation of freedom as "consciousness of necessity"' (Timpanaro 1975, p. 106), thus suppressing almost intentionally the difference between the two theories. In reality, Hegelian necessity is a rational necessity, that is, a bestowing of meaning for the elements that are here concatenated, while Spinoza's necessity, though intelligible, is a-rational, that is, chance without meaning. Furthermore, Timpanaro seem to mistake radically Spinoza's thought when he affirms that this 'insists that man not only recognize necessity, but also glory and efface himself in it' and therefore belongs to a whole 'conception of philosophy as asceticism and self-repression . . . which Marxism utterly rejects' in as much as it is not eudaimonistic (ibid.).

Spinoza: An Ontology of Relation?

For over a century after it appeared on the modern philosophical scene, Spinoza's philosophy was considered surprising and even scandalous for its assertion of the oneness or singularity of substance. From Bayle's early *Dictionary* article to Hegel's *Lectures on the History of Philosophy*, the core of Spinoza's philosophy was said to be its unheard-of gesture of making God the sole *res* that could be thought through the concept of substance (substance, according to Definition 3 of the first part of the *Ethics*, is 'that which is in itself and is conceived through itself').[1] The enormous emphasis placed on this move by the interpretative tradition (almost into the twentieth century) managed, however, to obscure every other dimension of Spinoza's thought: Spinoza's thought was simply a metaphysics or ontology of the oneness of substance. It is this coupling of Spinozism and the metaphysics of substance that I want to undo. In line with a whole series of interpretative developments in France over the last thirty years, I want to disperse this identification by employing a paradoxical formulation. Far from being a metaphysics of substance, I contend that Spinoza's philosophy is instead an ontology of relation. By emphasising his negation of the substantiality of what he calls *res singulares*, we can locate Spinoza's originality less in having posited the existence of a single substance (in fact, Letter 50 suggests that substance can only 'improperly' be called 'single' or 'one') than his laying out the foundation for this ontology of relation.

1   The Expression 'Ontology of Relation'

We should begin with a consideration of the terms in play in the expression 'ontology of relation'. Contrary to what one might think, the term ontology is fairly new. It was probably initially coined by Goclenius and Calovius, and was canonised only with the appearance, in 1728, of Christian Wolff's *Philosophia prima sive Ontologia metodo scientifica pertracta*. But if the word itself is relatively young, the concept it refers to can be traced all the way back to the Aristotelian science of being as being. Such a science examines the fundamental characteristics of all beings; as a result, this science can be said to precede every specific science or knowledge. At the root of the discourse of

---

1   Spinoza 2002, *Ethics* I, def. III, p. 217.

ontology – this discourse ranging from Aristotle to Thomas Aquinas and from the sixteenth-century scholastics to Christian Wolff – lies the concept of substance. The undisputed primacy of substance over all other characteristics of being is constitutive of the Western tradition. Within this tradition, the hierarchy between substance and these other traits is structured and governed by the rule of inherence. The first principle of ontology is therefore the principle of non-contradiction, and it is this principle that assures both the unity of substance with itself and opens the possibility of predication. The discourse on being – onto-logy – has therefore historically been a discourse on substance (it is perhaps not useless to recall that *ousia* is derived from *ousa*, the feminine present participle of *einai*).

As for the problem of relation, the richest and most extended treatment of it is found in the Aristotelian tradition. There are two privileged passages in the *corpus aristotelicum* where this problem is addressed: the *Categories* and the *Metaphysics*. In the *Categories*, Aristotle offers a very thorough analysis of the category of relation, and this analysis is all the more remarkable insofar as it tends to spill over the bounds of the category of relation in order to re-emerge in a latent or explicit way in the discussion of other categories as well. This is how Aristotle defines relative notions: 'We call *relatives* all such things as are said to be *of* something else or *related to* something else, are explained with reference to that other being'.[2] As the Scholastics would later put it, what is specific to the category of relation is that its *in esse* is at the same time an *esse ad*; that is, its inherence in one substance is simultaneously a reference to another substance. This reference or referral to another substance will, however, pose a problem for a subject-predicate logic: a relation cannot be an accident in two substances at one time. From Avicenna to Leibniz we witness an unwavering prohibition on thinking that 'unum accidens sit in duobus subjectis';[3] as a result, relation came to be thought of as the inherence of two accidents to two related substances.[4] This problem will not be solved until the end of the nineteenth century with the logical innovations developed by De Morgan, Peirce, Russell and Whitehead.

If we now take a look at another passage, this time from the *Metaphysics*, we find a very precise distinction between various types of relations:

---

2 Aristotle 1984, vol. 1, p. 10 (translation modified).

3 Avicenna 1977, p. 177.

4 Leibniz 1970, p. 609: 'I do not believe that you will admit an accident that is in two subjects at the same time'.

Things are relative (1) as double to half and treble to a third, and in general that which contains something else many times to that which is contained many times in something else, and that which exceeds to that which is exceeded; (2) as that which can heat to that which can be heated, and that which can cut to that which can be cut, and in general the active to the passive; (3) as the measurable to the measure and the knowable to knowledge and the sensible to sensation.[5]

In a study devoted to the question of relations in the Middle Ages, M.G. Henninger suggests we translate this division into mathematical, causal and psychological terms. Despite the risks such a translation implies, we can sub-scribe to them provided they are only employed in a general and schematic fashion.[6]

The ancient and medieval response to the problematic status of relations was based on these passages from Aristotle. This series of responses, stretch-ing from Thomas Aquinas to Duns Scotus and from Ockham to Peter Auriol, presents most of the fundamental variants of the question.[7] But this tradition was, nevertheless, incapable of addressing another possibility: *that relations could be purely mental*. This possibility, which is fundamentally foreign to the Aristotelian tradition, seems to have its oldest, Greek, source in the Stoics, and will reappear in the Middle Ages with the Mutakallimum.[8]

We can therefore hear the formula 'ontology of relations' in two different ways. The first way would understand it to be a discourse on being that would simply emphasise the question of relations. But another more forceful and rad-ical way to understand the expression would be to let the discordant note this paradox emits resonate; it would be to understand it to be a discourse on being in which the traditional articulation of substance and relation is inverted. It is this second path that I want to head down, to see where – if anywhere – it leads.

2   The Category of Relation: Intrinsic or Extrinsic Determination

Before confronting the difficult question of whether it is possible to reverse the traditional hierarchical articulation of the categories of substance and

---

5   Aristotle 1984, vol. 2, p. 1612 (translation modified).
6   Henninger 1989, p. 6.
7   Henninger provides a useful schema of the different variants on p. 180 of *Relations*.
8   'Despite the variety of theories, no one held that real relations are completely mind depen-
     dent' (Henninger 1989, p. 174).

relation, we should pinpoint the spot where the two fundamental theoretical tendencies concerning relation – relations understood as mental or real – diverge. This alternative was first posed in all its radicality at the dawn of modernity, in the figures of Locke and Leibniz. A whole series of intermediate positions, both ancient and medieval, had been explored prior to the posing of this alternative. There is no room here to go back over this long history – a history that at points intersects with the Christian question of the Trinity.[9] But the opposition between Locke and Leibniz has a theoretical autonomy with respect to this historical arc. It is an opposition that poses a radical alternative and, because of this, it is paradigmatic: either the objectivity of relations is founded on their ontological reality or, conversely, these relations are arbitrary to the extent that their being is purely mental.

In *An Essay on Human Understanding*, Locke distinguished both between complex ideas and the idea of modes and between substances and relations. Locke writes that 'Besides the Ideas, whether simple or complex, that the Mind had of Things, as they are in themselves, there are others it gets from their comparison with one another'.[10] From here we get the definition of relation: 'When the Mind so considers one thing, that it does, as it were, bring it to, and set it by another, and carry its view from one to t'other: This is, as the Words import, *Relation* and *Respect* . . .'[11] Locke continues:

> *The nature* therefore *of Relation*, consists in the referring, or comparing two things, one to another; from which comparison, one or both comes to be denominated. And if either of those things be removed, or cease to be, the Relation ceases, and the Denomination consequent to it, though the other receive in it self no alteration at all, *v.g. Cajus*, whom I consider to day as a Father, ceases to be so to morrow, only by the death of his Son, without any alteration made in himself. Nay, barely by the Mind's changing the Object, to which it compares any thing, the same thing is capable of having contrary Denominations, at the same time. *v.g. Cajus*, compared to several persons, may truly be said to be Older, and Younger; Stronger and Weaker, *etc.*[12]

---

9   'Christian thinkers followed Augustine in speaking of three persons as constituted in some way by their relations to one another. As the writings of Aristotle became available to the West in the thirteenth century, many sought to understand more clearly the doctrine of the Trinity by adapting some of Aristotle's thoughts on relations' (Henninger 1989, p. 1).

10   Locke 1975, p. 319.

11   Ibid.

12   Locke 1975, p. 321.

As a consequence of this analysis, Locke can conclude that:

1)   There are an infinite number of relations for each thing, since the ways each thing can be compared is infinite;
2)   Although the relation is not 'contained in the real existence of things', the ideas of relation are often clearer than the ideas of substance to which they refer;
3)   The ideas of relation can be reduced to the simple ideas of sensation and reflection that constitute the primary materials of all knowledge.[13]

Locke is therefore able to conclude that relations are relative arbitrary to the extent that, if they are the result of exterior comparisons, they are nevertheless rooted in the materials given to our perceptual or reflective consciousness.

When we first turn to Leibniz's thesis on relation, he seems to agree with Locke: there is relation when two things are thought at the same time, or, more precisely, relation is the thinking together of two objects. In this sense, relation is nothing other than the co-presence of a series of objects in the mind of a given subject.[14] It is only in his commentary on Locke's theory of relation that Leibniz spells out their differences. In the *New Essays*, Leibniz reproduces Locke's position in the guise of Philalethes ('However, a change of relation can occur without there having been any change in the subject: Titius, "whom I consider to day as a father, ceases to be so to morrow, only by the death of his son, without any alteration made in himself" ')[15] in order to contest it through the figure of Theophilus: 'That can very well be said if we are guided by the things of which we are aware; but in metaphysical strictness there is no wholly extrinsic denomination (*denominatio pure extrinseca*), because of the real connections amongst all things'.[16] If, then, we manage to look more deeply into extrinsic denominations, if we are able to move beyond the limited set of connections we are conscious of, we find that there are no extrinsic

---

13   Locke also provides a classification of relations: 1) the most comprehensive relation is that of cause and effect, then identity and diversity (comparisons of time, place and causality); 2) proportional relations (whiter, sweeter, equal, etc.); 3) natural relations (father-son/cousins/fellow countrymen=from the circumstances of origin); 4) instituted or voluntary relations (general-army/citizen-privileges in a given place); 5) moral relations (conformity or disagreement of an action with a norm).

14   See Mugnai 1976, pp. 139–58.

15   Leibniz 1981, p. 227.

16   Ibid.

denominations that are not founded on an intrinsic denomination.[17] From this metaphysical perspective, there are no exterior relations because every relation is ultimately grounded in the interiority of substance. The theory of pre-established harmony contends that every form of change in a substance witnesses a corresponding change – be it conscious or not – in every other substance. The exemplary site of this omnirelationality of the real is Leibniz's theory of space and time. Far from being co-ordinates that pre-exist objects, space and time are relations structuring the order of things. In his famous correspondence with the Newtonian Clarke, Leibniz writes: 'As for my opinion, I have said more than once that I hold space to be something merely relative, as time is; that I hold it to be an order of co-existences as times is an order of successions'.[18] This relational theory of time and space requires the articulation of a new concept: the 'situation'. For Leibniz, each thing exists in a situation and therefore in a network of relations, and it is within this network that space, time and the actions and passions of things take shape.

3   The Category of Substance as Relation

Modern philosophy offers two different solutions to the problem of relations: relations are either purely mental (Locke) or they constitute the order of space-time (Leibniz). Neither solution, however, questions the limits initially posed by Aristotle in the *Categories*: the impossibility of conceiving substance as a relation. Let us look at the passage where Aristotle discusses the possibility of thinking substance as a relative concept:

> It is a problem whether (as one would think) no substance is spoken of as a relative, or whether this is possible with regard to some secondary

---

17   Sven Knebel has succinctly reconstructed Leibniz's break with the Scholastic theory of intrinsic and extrinsic determination. For the Scholastics, an intrinsic determination inheres in the subject ('est per inhaerentiam'), while the extrinsic 'non est per inhaerentiam vel per aliquid quod faciat unum suppositum cum eo, de quo dicitur'. An example of the first is 'the wall is white', an example of the second is 'the wall is seen'. This implies that the extrinsic determination of one thing is always intrinsic to another ('est ... advertendum, semper eam rem, quae extrinseca aliam denominat, esse intrinsece in aliqua re'). Leibniz's break consists in the fact that the extrinsic determination is intrinsic not to another subject, but to the same subject: 'Sequitur etiam nullas dari denominationes pure extrinsecas, quae nullum prorsus habeant fundamentum in ipsa re denominata' (see Knebel 2001, pp. 615–19).

18   Leibniz 1970, p. 682.

substances. In the case of primary substances it is true; neither wholes nor parts are spoken of in relation to anything. An individual man is not called someone's individual man . . . Similarly with parts; an individual hand is not called someone's individual hand . . . Similarly with second-ary substances, at any rate most of them. For example, a man is not called someone's man . . . With such cases, then, it is obvious that they are not relatives, but with some secondary substances there is room for dispute. For example, a head is called someone's head and a hand is called some-one's hand . . .[19]

Aristotle is quite clear here: he excludes all primary substances and most secondary substances from the field of relations. But because he has doubts about some secondary substances, he is compelled to be more precise in his definition of the relative. Relation cannot be understood, he argues, as relative *secundum dici* (in this case, the head is the man's head), but only as *secundum esse*. If we restrict the definition of 'relative' to those 'terms in which to be con-sists in nothing other than to be affected by a certain relation', then Aristotle's doubt can be overcome. Since terms are only relative when the knowledge of one implies the knowledge of the other, and because the hand, head, etc. can be known without knowing what object they refer to, Aristotle can conclude that 'no substance is a relative'.[20]

Aristotle's prohibition against thinking substance itself as a relation is of course respected in the medieval debates concerning relations; but it is also respected in the opposing modern solutions we have already discussed. Locke and Leibniz do not transgress this fundamental limit. Locke clearly separates the ideas of substance and relation: substances are aggregates of qualities, while relations only emerge through the comparison of ideas. And even though Leibniz sees the spatio-temporal order as constituted by relations, he still toes the Aristotelian line. These relations of space-time and action-passion are ulti-mately rooted in substance and, as Aristotle dictated, substance cannot be a relation. Relations are instead understood as predicates inherent in a subject: being in a certain place, at a certain moment, undertaking a specific action. It is the ordered relations between these predicates (or events) that constitute the single spatio-temporal and causal order of history – and these ordered and ordering relations have their first and final foundation in substance. The unity of substance is, therefore, the ultimate guarantee of this spatio-temporal and

---

19   Aristotle 1984, vol. 1, p. 13.
20   Aristotle 1984, vol. 1, p. 140.

causal order, since each individual predicate-event envelops the totality of all present, past and future predicate-events.

The first author who seems to have had enough daring to violate the Aristotelian order is Immanuel Kant – even if his discourse is, as will become clear, highly ambivalent. On the one hand, Kant's metaphysical deduction of the categories from the table of judgments allows him to situate the category substance-accident among the categories of relation (alongside the relations of cause-effect and reciprocal actions).[21] The category of substance should therefore be thought in relation to the category of accidents: the schemata synthesising the given and category is that of permanence for substance and change for accidents. The permanence of substance, therefore, will always be relative. According to Enzo Paci, 'substantiality constitutes itself in finite forms characterized by their relative permanence'.[22] But if Kant had the intuition that substances 'are not closed realities, but moments of a process dependent upon this very process', these forms tend nevertheless to become static forms, unrelated to anything else.[23] This tendency is a direct result of Kant's absolutisation and substantialisation of the principle of inertia. If we take the *Critique of Pure Reason* and in particular the analogies of experience – those fundamental propositions considering the existence of phenomena and their reciprocal relation – we can confirm this. In the first analogy, which deals with substance, Kant writes: 'PRINCIPLE OF THE PERMANENCE OF SUBSTANCE. In all variation by appearances [*Erscheinungen*] substance is permanent, and its quantum in nature is neither increased nor decreased'.[24] Kant therefore sees permanence as the substrate of the empirical representation of time – without permanence, it would not be possible to conceive of simultaneity and succession:

> I find that in all ages not just philosophers but even the common understanding have presupposed this permanence as a substratum of all variation of appearances [*Erscheinungen*]; and they probably always assume it, moreover, as indubitable. The only difference is that the philosopher expresses himself somewhat more determinately on this point than does the common understanding, by saying that in all changes in the world *substance* endures and only the *accidents* vary.[25]

---

21 See Paci 1959, p. 194.
22 Paci 1959, p. 195.
23 Ibid.
24 Kant 1996, A 182 B 224, p. 212.
25 Kant 1996, A184 B 227, p. 214.

Here Kant's ambivalence is out in the open. Kant posits the category of substance as a temporal relation (a permanence in relation to change) and places it among the categories of relation; but he also makes substance the foundation of relations and the condition of possibility for determining the temporal relations of succession and simultaneity. This becomes quite clear in the following passage: 'And hence this category has indeed been put under the heading of the relations, but more as the condition of relations than as itself containing a relation'.[26] The relations of causality and reciprocal action are therefore thinkable through the schemata of succession and simultaneity. The analogies of experience dealing with successive connection and interconnection are in turn only thinkable thanks to the fact that a permanent substrate of experience has been presupposed: substance and permanence are presupposed as the condition of temporality itself. As a result, Kant seems to respect the Aristotelian limit after all, since for Kant substance is still a permanent temporal substrate founding both relation and the very thinkability of succession and simultaneity. Paci again: 'on the one hand, Kant tends to dissolve substance into relational forms of relative temporal permanence; but on the other hand, he does not manage to stay on the plane of relationality, returning instead to the old logic of subject and predicate'.[27] Kant, then, like Locke and Leibniz, still seems to respect the Aristotelian taboo forbidding the thinking of substance as relation.

If for Kant substance is both relation and the foundation of relations, we must wait for Hegel to finally cross the line drawn by Aristotle. Here the obligatory reference is a passage from Hegel's *Science of Logic* called 'The Absolute Relation [*Das absolute Verhältnis*]' from the third chapter of the 'Doctrine of Essence'. In this chapter, Hegel posits substance as the final unification of being and essence: it is the being of all being that should be conceived neither as 1) immediate reflection nor as 2) an abstraction lurking behind existence and phenomena. Substance is the totality that appears: accidentality. The movement of accidentality is the '*actuosity* [*Aktuosität*] of substance, as a tranquil coming forth of itself'.[28] Substance is therefore nothing other than a 'relational unity in process'.[29] Hegel expresses this clearly:

> Substance, as this identity of the reflective movement, is the totality of the whole and embraces accidentality within it, and accidentality is the

---

26 Kant 1996, A187 B230, p. 216.
27 Paci 1959, pp. 195–6.
28 Hegel 1989, p. 556.
29 Biard et al. 1983, p. 346.

whole substance itself. The differentiation of itself into *the simple identity of being* and the *flux of accidents* in it is a form of its *appearing* [*eine Form ihres* Scheins].[30]

Here Hegel presents an extremely important thesis: this 'simple identity of being' is nothing other than the formless substance of the 'imagination' [*Vorstellung*], of representation. Appearance or illusion [*Schein*] is therefore not determined as such, and pulls up short at 'indeterminate identity' as if it were an absolute. But in reality, substance is absolute power [*absolute Macht*]:

Substance manifests itself through actuality with its content into which it translates the possible, as *creative* power, and through the possibility to which it reduces the actual, as *destructive* power. But the two are identical, the creation is destructive and the destruction is creative . . .[31]

Accidents have no power over one another. They are things endowed with multiple properties, things composed entirely of independent parts and forces. But when it seems as if something accidental exercises some power over another accident, it is in fact substance that is acting. Substance as 'power' is precisely what mediates between substance as being identical for itself and substance understood as the totality of accidents: 'this *middle term* is thus the unity of substantiality and accidentality themselves and its *extremes* have no subsistence of their own. Substantiality is, therefore, merely the relation as immediately vanishing . . .'[32]

Once Hegel dissolves substance into a vertical relationality (there are no relations between accidents), he can then think substance as a purely horizontal relation. He does this through the 'dialecticisation' of cause and reciprocal action, and it is from out of this relationality that the Concept, at last, will emerge. To gauge the importance of this rethinking of the concept of substance, we can look at how it comes to function on the level of Hegel's philosophy of Right. Hegel there deploys this concept of substance in the context of a critique of contractualism:

A social or political community cannot, as contract theorists imply, consist only of subjects, of individuals who are constantly reflective in their thoughts and deeds. It presupposes a background of unreflective

---

30   Hegel 1989, p. 556 (translation modified).
31   Ibid.
32   Hegel 1989, p. 557.

relationships and activities, in which people do not stand out as individual subjects ... This background is '(the) ethical substance', that which underlies.[33]

4   Reality of Relations and Primacy of Relations: An Idealist Position?

Having outlined (somewhat arbitrarily, to be sure) these two trajectories within the philosophical tradition, we are now at a point where we can finally isolate in the positions of Leibniz and Hegel some of the tools necessary for constructing an ontology of relation. Leibniz holds that relations constitute reality insofar as they order the spatio-temporal structure of phenomena. But if these relations structure the world such as it appears, they nevertheless require two foundations: both a spiritual substance not constituted by relations (and therefore beyond all relation) and a divine intellect, without which, according to Leibniz, 'nothing would be true'.[34] Hegel, in turn, dissolves all substantiality into the most radical relationality. But this relationality is not, however, the pure, unqualified play of action and reaction. It is instead conceived of as the presence of an all-pervading time that orders relations rather than being constituted by them. This presence is understood to be the contemporaneity of a principle that is immanent to the play of relations (the beautiful individuality, the abstract juridical person, and so on), a power that decides in advance what developments the play of relation can give rise to. The obscurity at the heart of the *Wechselwirkung* necessarily tends toward the light of the concept: this tension and tendency is lodged *ab initio* in the schema of simultaneity, the great temporal metaphor of *Geist*.

It seems, then, that both Leibniz and Hegel were able to pose the question of relations in the most radical way; and yet they both seem to have fled in the face of the extreme consequences these positions imply. Leibniz's theory of pre-established harmony, for example, permits substance to enter into the play of relations only when it still has the form of a possible essence in the divine intellect. Leibniz therefore reduces relation to the combinatory game of a God cast as both architect and sovereign, a game always-already decided in advance by the divine will's tendency toward the good. In the same way, Hegel's theory of the ruse of reason is said to weave the great tapestry of universal history, a tapestry whose warp and woof is the Idea and whose passions are the individual woven threads. Both pre-established harmony and the ruse of reason make relationality serve the ends of teleology.

---

33   Inwood 1992, p. 287.
34   Leibniz 1960, vol. 5, p. 210.

It is necessary, then, to separate relationality from both teleology and idealism. This was, in fact, the explicit philosophical programme of the Italian philosopher Enzo Paci. Paci understood idealism to be nothing other than the closure of relationality and, working with and on the philosophy of Whitehead, he proposed a 'relationist' philosophy that would be resolutely non-idealist.[35] Paci suggests that such a relationism would be a veritable general ontology; but he makes a point of stressing that the very term 'ontology' is used in this instance in a metaphorical manner. Properly speaking, the term 'ontology' refers to philosophical knowledge taken to be the *discourse on beings or on being*,[36] and it is precisely this type of knowledge that has been undone through the emergence of the theory of relativity: what ontology calls 'being' has now been dispersed in time or, better, into spatio-temporal situations. This process *events* does not, therefore, settle into things or substances, but determines itself in spatio-temporal situations. An individual thing is never a substance that is 'immobile and closed in on itself, but instead ... a more or less organized complex of processes, of events'.[37] A relation never comes between 'two or more [pre-existing] terms' but exists, 'to use a figurative language, *before* its terms'.[38]

Paci plots out the border between relation and idealism along three points: relationism '1) excludes the closed identity of the universe; 2) whereas the closed and identical universe identifies each moment with the whole such that no moment is discernible, relationism determines the nodes of universal relations as distinct spatio-temporal moments, and actualizes them as existential situations that are discernible from one another; 3) relationism insists upon the non-exhaustibility of relations ... an always open relationality'.[39]

5   Spinoza: An Ontology of Relation?

Throughout his 'relationist' manifesto, Paci opposes the philosophy of relation to the philosophy of substance: while the latter holds that 'reality is substance which is in itself and for itself, and needs nothing else to exist', the philosophy

---

35   Paci writes: 'The Hegelian vanity of returning [to the foundation] must be opposed by the impossibility of such a return, that is, opposed to the necessity of the irreversible' (Paci 1959, p. 117).

36   Paci 1959, p. 17.

37   Paci 1959, p. 30.

38   Paci 1959, p. 90. Paci maintains that if, for Russell, reality is constituted by elements independent of the relations they can enter into, for Whitehead, 'on the basis of the principle of irreversibility ... reality should be considered to be already in relation, in the form of spatio-temporal structures' (Paci 1959, p. 105).

39   Paci 1959, p. 63.

of relation maintains that 'real existence [is] always in some other and for some other'.[40] Paci replaces the traditional concept of substance with the concept of the event: 'substance', he writes, 'is what exists in itself, whereas the event is what exists for an other and in relation to some other'.[41] At this point we should point out that Paci always opposed his relationist metaphysics to the metaphysics of substance he claims is found in Aristotle and Spinoza.[42] But we can ask: is Spinoza's philosophy truly a philosophy of substance in the sense Paci draws out? To be sure, the unprecedented theoretical gesture of Part One of the *Ethics* is its presentation of infinite substance as the sole *in se esse*. But this same gesture produces an important consequence: singular things are now known as modes, that is, as *esse in alio*. The mode understood as *id quod in alio est* is precisely what Paci calls an 'event'; the mode's existence is always in and for some other. Spinoza's substance is, in turn, nothing other than the immanent *structure* of this reference to some other – it is in no way a permanent substance in which modifications inhere.

Is it possible to speak, then, not of Spinoza's ontology of substance but his ontology of relation? Or can we at the very least locate in Spinoza the conceptual tools necessary for thinking the primacy of relation over substance – that is, to really think relationality in all its radicality? The primary difficulty this programme poses is found in the fact Spinoza's work offers no veritable thematisation of the problem of relation.

There is in fact a brief allusion to the question in his *Appendix Containing Metaphysical Thoughts*:

> From our comparing things with one another there arise certain notions that are nevertheless nothing outside things themselves but modes of thinking. This is shown by the fact that if we wish to consider them as things having a place outside thought, we immediately render confused the otherwise clear conception we have of them. Such notions are opposition, order, agreement, difference, subject, adjunct, and any others like these. These notions, I say, are quite clearly perceived by us insofar as we conceive them not as something different from the essences of things that are opposed, ordered, etc., but merely as modes of thinking whereby we more easily retain or imagine the things themselves.[43]

---

40   Ibid.

41   Paci 1959, p. 53.

42   Paci 1959, p. 105.

43   Spinoza 2002, *Metaphysical Thoughts*, I, 5, p. 186.

The concept is already clearly articulated in the *Short Treatise*: 'Some things are in our understanding and not in Nature, and so they are also only our creation, and their purpose is to understand things distinctly: among these we include all relations, which have reference to different things, and these we call *Entia Rationis* [things of reason]'.[44]

There are seventeen occurrences of the word *relatio* in the *Ethics*, but there is no definition of relation as such.[45] In the majority of cases, the word is used in connection with verbs like *considerari, imaginari, concipi* and *contemplari* and with the prepositions *cum, absque, sine*. This set of terms implies that relations have a purely mental status: we can 'consider' things both in relation and outside relations. There is only one case where the word takes on an ontological value, namely when Spinoza denies that eternity can be defined in time and can have a relation to time.[46] And there is one case where the term 'relation' is used in the technical sense, at the moment Spinoza provides definitions of the affects in Part Three. It is useful to read the passage in its entirety:

> The definitions of jealousy and of other waverings of the mind I pass over in silence, both because they arise from the combination of the emotions which I have already defined, and also because most of them have no names, which shows that it is enough for practical purposes just to know them in general. For the rest it is clear, from the definitions of the emotions I have explained, that all the emotions spring from desire, pleasure, or pain [*Cupiditas, Laetitia* or *Tristitia*]; or rather, that there are no emotions apart from these three, which are customarily called by various names on account of their relations and extrinsic denominations.[47]

Relations are therefore extrinsic denominations. This is the only use of the formula 'extrinsic denominations' in the entirety of the *Ethics*. But we do find one occurrence of the expression 'intrinsic denominations', where they are explicitly identified with *proprietates*.[48] It seems then that Spinoza clearly separates the characteristics constituting the essence of the thing from those that depend on the thing's interaction with something else: that is, he clearly separates *proprietates* from *relationes*.

---

44   Spinoza 2002, *Short Treatise*, I, X, p. 59.
45   Robinet et al. 1977, p. 287.
46   Spinoza 2002, *Ethics* V, pr. 23 schol, p. 374.
47   Spinoza 2002, *Ethics* III, aff. def. 48 exp, p. 318.
48   Spinoza 2002, *Ethics* II, def. 4, p. 244.

But the *Ethics* nowhere theorises this distinction in any explicit way. To find this theorisation *avant la lettre*, we must backtrack to the *Tractatus de intellectus emendatione*. In outlining the properties of what he calls knowledge of the fourth type, Spinoza asserts that 'all the properties of the thing, when regarded by itself and not in conjunction with other things, can be deduced from it'.[49] To reproduce the order of nature, we must know the series through which these things concatenate *secundum seriem causarum*; this series is not, however, the series of singular and mutable things [*series rerum singularium mutabilium*] but the series of fixed and eternal things [*series rerum fixarum aeternarumque*]. Knowledge therefore tries to reproduce the order of fixed and eternal things. In the *essentia intima* of these eternal things we discover the laws 'which govern the coming into existence and the ordering of all singular things', not the series or order of the existence of singular and mutable things which only ever provide 'extrinsic denominations, their relations, or, at the most, their circumstances'.[50] Spinoza's distinctions would authorise us to say that the concept of 'property' is tied to the interiority of an essence, while the concept of 'relation' is linked to the exteriority of existence. In other words, it would permit us to say that there is one ontological plane where things are ordered by essential properties (and by the exclusive logical relations between these properties) and another plane where this order is disturbed by existential relations and circumstances. Such is, it seems, the ontological framework within which we find the sole technical usage of the word *relatio* in the *Ethics*. But does the ontological framework of the *Ethics* as a whole permit such a usage?

When we compare the *Ethics* with the *TIE*, certain problems arise:

1) The *Ethics* forbids any distinction of levels between fixed and eternal things and singular and mutable things;
2) The term 'series' disappears in the *Ethics* in favour of *connexio*; instead of a linear series, we find a weave, an intrication, a braiding;
3) In the *Ethics*, Spinoza never speaks of *essentia intima*, preferring instead *actuosa essentia*. Moreover, from the theoretical point of view, the identification of the concept of *essentia* with that of *existentia* and *potentia* is fundamental.

All of these differences seem to result from the theoretical gesture of positing God not simply as a first cause, but as immanent cause as well. The radical

---

49   Spinoza 2002, *Treatise of the Emendation of the Intellect*, p. 26.
50   Spinoza 2002, *Treatise of the Emendation of the Intellect*, p. 27.

thought of immanent causality forbids any serial conception of finite causality, since it brings with it a theoretical constellation that destroys all of the elements necessary for the functioning of transitive causality. The concept of the individual or singular thing has now lost the simplicity and unity that in the *TIE* constituted its inmost essence, i.e., an inwardness sheltered from exterior relations and existential circumstances. Now the singular thing is characterised by the complexity and complications of a proportioned relation in which essence is indistinguishable from power or potential, that is, indistinguishable from the singular thing's capacity to enter into relations with the outside (the more complex the relations, the more powerful the individual). The cause no longer has the form of a juridical imputation and becomes instead a structural plurality of complex relations with the outside. In the *TIE*, all of these things were considered inessential and therefore excluded from the adequate knowledge of the singular thing. It is therefore perfectly legitimate to state that the *Ethics* reverses the relation between essence and existence found in the *TIE*: the essence of things is now the *fait accompli* of relations and circumstances that have produced and continue to reproduce this existence. That is, the essence of the thing is now conceived *post festum*, starting from the fact of its existence; it is now conceived only starting from its power to act, its potential for action, which alone reveals its true interiority. The *Ethics* demolishes the barrier between inside [*essentia intima*] and outside [*circumstantia*, what 'lies around']; power is now understood to be the regulated relation of an outside with an inside that is constituted in this very relation.

When in Letter 60 Tschirnhaus asks if there is a way to choose between the multiple adequate ideas from which it is possible to deduce the property of a thing, Spinoza responds:

> [I]n order that I may know which out of many ideas of a thing will enable all the properties of the object to be deduced, I follow this one rule, that the idea or definition of the thing should express its efficient cause. For example, in order to investigate the properties of a circle, I ask whether from the following idea of a circle, namely, that it consists in an infinite number of rectangles, I can deduce all its properties; that is to say, I ask whether this idea involves the efficient cause of a circle. Since this is not so, I look for another cause, namely, that a circle is the space described by a line of which one point is fixed and the other moveable. Since this definition now expresses the efficient cause, I know that I can deduce from all the properties of a circle, etc. So, too, when I define God as a supremely perfect Being, since this definition does not express the efficient cause (for I take it that an efficient cause can be internal as well

as external), I shall not be able to extract therefrom all the properties of God, as I can do when I define God as a Being, etc.[51]

It is not by chance that, at the very moment he is asked to provide an example of an idea from which it is possible to deduce the properties of a subject [*proprietates subjecti*], Spinoza proposes the circle and God, that is, an *ens rationis* and an infinite being. Neither of these examples belong to the sphere of *connexiones singulares*, whose adequate idea should bring to light a tissue of *relationes*, not *proprietates*. This is why, when Tschirnhaus asks 'how can we deduce a priori the many and various forms [things] can assume…[if] extension when conceived through itself is indivisible, immutable, etc.?', Spinoza dodges the question.[52] This is because, in my opinion, Spinoza thinks the perspective of the question is mistaken. The variety of things is not a priori deducible from extension, since the essence of real things is constituted in and by relations and connections; the essence of things can therefore in no way logically precede these relations and connections.[53]

The privileged example of this is to be found in the theory of the passions. In the famous 'Preface' to Part Three of the *Ethics*, Spinoza says he will discuss 'human actions and appetites just as if the inquiry concerned lines, planes, or bodies'.[54] The affects, like God and the soul that are dealt with in the first two Parts, will be treated *more geometrico*: that is, they will be considered to be 'properties' of human nature, as Spinoza explicitly puts it in the *TP*.[55] Properties or intrinsic denominations – that is, the affects will be treated as characteristics of the *essentia intima* of a human nature taken apart from everything else. But should Spinoza's expression be read in this way? Perhaps we should instead stress Spinoza's anti-theological polemic (*proprietates contra vitia*) and avoid identifying *proprietas* with what is *proprium* to an *essentia*, i.e. as what precedes existential relations and circumstances. In the Italian translation of the *Tractatus Politicus*, Paolo Cristofolini provides an extremely rich and suggestive translation of an expression that we often find in Spinoza's

51   Spinoza 2002, *Letter* LX, p. 913. See *Ethics* I, def. 6.

52   Spinoza 2002, *Letter* LIX, p. 911 (translation modified).

53   See Balibar 1997.

54   Spinoza 2002, *Ethics* III, praef. p. 278.

55   'I have regarded human emotions…not as vices of human nature but as properties pertaining to it…[*humanos affectus…non ut humane naturae vitia, sed ut proprietates contemplatus sum*]' (Spinoza 2002, *Political Treatise*, I, 4, p. 681).

texts: *passionibus obnoxius*.[56] This formula should be literally translated as 'subjugated to, submitted to, dominated by the passions'. But Cristofolini notes that 'the Latin term *obnoxius* bears... two values, [designating both] what is harmful and what invades or pervades'. Invoking Leopardi's translation of Epictetus, Cristofolini therefore proposes that we translate *passionibus obnoxius* as 'attraversati dalle passioni' – in English, 'traversed by, shot through with, crossed through by the passions'. Such a translation could be considered a stylistic refinement. But it might be worth the effort to emphasise the interpretative possibilities it opens up. It allows us to argue that the passions are not the *proprietates* of the human species, of a human nature, but relations that *traverse* and *cross through* the individual, relations that constitute both its self-image and its image of the world. Likewise, an analogous expression found in the 'Preface' to the *TTP* – *superstitionibus obnoxii*[57] – shows with perfect clarity the indissociability of the emotive and cognitive aspects of the weave of relations constituting the *social being* of the individual.

It hardly needs to be repeated that for Spinoza the individual is neither substance nor subject (neither *ousia* nor *hypokeimenon*): the individual is a relation between an outside and an inside paradoxically constituted by this very relation (for Spinoza, there is no absolute interiority of the *cogito* opposed to the absolute exteriority of a world in which my own body is included).[58] This relation constitutes the essence of the individual, which is now nothing other than its existence-power. The individual is a power that is not, however, given

---

56 See Spinoza 1999. There are fourteen occurrences of this locution (*passionibus* or *affectibus obnoxius*) in the *Ethics*.

57 Spinoza 2002, *Theologico-Political Treatise*, praef, p. 388.

58 Descartes presupposes two subjects, the soul and the body, such that 'whatever takes place or occurs is generally called... a "passion" with regard to the subject to which it happens and an "action" with regard to that which makes it happen' (Descartes 1985, vol. 1, p. 328). The actions of the soul are voluntary acts, while the passions are perceptions or cognitions derived from the representation of external things: it is therefore clear that in Descartes the metaphysical nucleus of the 'I', the soul as *res cogitans*, precedes the multiple encounters with and of the body. The principal effect of the passions 'is that they move and dispose the soul to want [*volere*] the things for which they prepare the body' (Descartes 1985, vol. 1, p. 343). The passions therefore act on the soul, giving it a certain disposition, but they are not the soul itself: the most proper essence of the soul resides in the *volere* that is the seal of the creator on its creature. In Spinoza, since mind and body are the same individual, 'the order of the actions and passions of our body is simultaneous in nature with the order of the actions and passions of the mind' (Spinoza 2002, *Ethics* III, pr. 2 schol, p. 280). Moreover, since the mind is not a substance but a plurality of ideas, and since ideas are passions, the mind will be nothing other than a plurality of passions.   — *Platonov*

ıce and once and for all: its power varies with the instability of the rela-
ween outside and inside. The passions are not, therefore, the property
of an already given human nature, a property that would exist prior to any
encounter that would activate or arouse it. The passions are relations constituting the human individual and its interiority: they do not occur *within* the
individual, but in the space *between* individuals. Interiority is therefore itself
a mere effect of these relations. What Spinoza refers to as the three 'primary'
affects (desire, pleasure and pain) are simply the constitution and variation of
an interiority that, insofar as it is *conscius sui* (and *ignarus causarum rerum*) –
in short, insofar as it imagines – transforms *circumstantiae* into an Origin and
objects of desire into Values.[59] If these affects are 'primary' with respect to the
individual, they are not primary from the point of view of immanent causality,
this causality that gives rise to the individual as a *connexio singularis*, a singular interweaving, a singular stitch or knot. A useful comparison can be made
with Althusser's interpretation of Epicurus: 'all the elements are both here
and beyond, to be rained down ... but they do not yet exist and they remain
abstract insofar as the unity of a world has not brought them together in the
Encounter that will bring them into existence'.[60] In other words, the primary
affects are only abstract elements before they enter into concrete relations.
These affects cannot exist in a pure form, as originary elements whose combinations give birth to all the others. These affects 'exist' only in and through the
infinity of metamorphoses that external relations impose upon them: hatred,
love, hope (security/joy), fear (despair/remorse) and so on. Spinoza, however,
allows us to go even further: we cannot even refer to an individual affect as a
transitive relation to an object.[61] Because immanent causality appears in the
sphere of the finite as *nexus causarum*, as a weave of causes, every individual
affect is always-already overdetermined by other affects:

---

59   '... I acknowledge no other primary affect beyond these three: in the pages that follow, I
      will show that all the others are derived from these three' (Spinoza 2002, EIIIP11S, p. 285
      [translation modified]).

60   Althusser 1994, vol. 1, p. 560. It would be interesting to see Paci's critique (using Dewey and
      Whitehead) of the atomism of the sensible in this context. See 'La struttura relazionale
      dell'esperienza' (Paci 1959, pp. 73–84).

61   The same relation that binds a subject and an object has no universality, as Spinoza
      stresses: 'Different men can be affected by one and the same object in different ways, and
      one and the same man can be affected in different ways by one and the same object at
      different times' (Spinoza 2002, *Ethics* III, pr. 51, p. 303).

1)   by the memory of another affect or emotion it has been associated with in the past;[62]

2)   by the similarity of something with another object we have been affected by;[63]

3)   by the emotion felt by someone we ourselves feel for or are affected by;[64]

4)   by our feeling for someone who produces an affection in something or someone we ourselves are affected by;[65]

5)   by the emotion felt by someone similar to us;[66]

6)   by the approval of other men;[67]

7)   by someone else's feeling for an object we ourselves are affected by;[68]

8)   by the emotion felt by someone toward us;[69]

9)   by the emotion of someone toward someone else;[70]

10) by the fact that the one we feel for belongs to a class or nation by which we are affected (based on the experience of previous encounters with individuals belonging to them).[71]

This complicated weave of relations is the mode of existence of all affective life. Let us say – going beyond Spinoza's specific use of the term – that the effect produced by this weave should be called *fluctuatio animi* ['waverings of the mind', fluctuations of the soul]. According to Spinoza, *fluctuatio animi* is 'a condition of the mind arising from two conflicting affects',[72] that is, from the contradiction between two primary affects with respect to the individual taken abstractly. But if we once again assume the perspective of immanent causality, i.e. if we assume the perspective from which the *nexus causarum* is *prius* to the *res singularis*, *fluctuatio animi* becomes the conceptual name of the psyche in an ontology of relation. Once we have abandoned the idea of substantiality, the singular thing can metaphorically assume the figure of the ripple or wave [*flutto*], the brief, momentary form that gives individuality to the otherwise undifferentiated sea. 'Substance' is no longer what stands under

---

62   Spinoza 2002, *Ethics* III, pr. 14, p. 286.
63   Spinoza 2002, *Ethics* III, pr. 16, p. 287.
64   Spinoza 2002, *Ethics* III, pr. 21 and 23, pp. 289–90.
65   Spinoza 2002, *Ethics* III, pr. 22 and pr. 24, pp. 290–1.
66   Spinoza 2002, *Ethics* III, pr. 27, p. 292.
67   Spinoza 2002, *Ethics* III, pr. 29, p. 293; Spinoza 2002, *Ethics* III, pr. 53, pr. 55, pp. 305–7.
68   Spinoza 2002, *Ethics* III, pr. 31 and pr. 35, pp. 294–6.
69   Spinoza 2002, *Ethics* III, pr. 33, p. 295.
70   Spinoza 2002, *Ethics* III, pr. 34, p. 296.
71   Spinoza 2002, *Ethics* III, pr. 46, p. 302.
72   Spinoza 2002, *Ethics* III, pr. 17, p. 287.

or beneath, *sub-stantia*; it is now simply a restless surface with no definitive form. As Spinoza puts it in a wonderful passage, 'we are in many respects at the mercy of external causes and are tossed about like the waves of the sea when driven by contrary winds, we waver and fluctuate, unsure of the outcome and of our fate'.[73]

If we now come back to the sole passage in which Spinoza uses the term 'relation' in a technical sense, we can see how inadequate it is:

> The definitions of jealousy and of other waverings of the mind I pass over in silence, both because they arise from the combination of the emotions which I have already defined, and also because most of them have no names, which shows that it is enough for practical purposes just to know them in general. For the rest it is clear, from the definitions of the emotions I have explained, that all the emotions spring from desire, pleasure, or pain; or rather, that there are no emotions apart from these three, which are customarily called by various names on account of their relations and extrinsic denominations.

Here Spinoza appears to suggest that the three primary affects exist as *proprietates* of an *essentia intima* that can assume different forms in its varied relations with reality. But it seems more in line with the philosophy of *essentia=potentia* to affirm that it is the composed ('secondary') affects, which are only constituted in relation with an outside, that are the only true affects; in turn, this philosophy compels us to see the three primary affects less as substrates than as a set of determined abstractions (common notions, in Spinoza's terms) necessary to conceptualise the composed affects.[74]

6   Relation: Constitutive or *ens rationis*?

On the physical plane, individuals are constituted by relative movements between parts. In the same way, the social individual is constituted by those

---

73   Spinoza 2002, *Ethics* III, pr. 59, p. 310 (translation modified).

74   Spinoza says this explicitly in *Ethics* III, pr. 56 schol: '[I]t is sufficient for our purpose – namely, the determination of the strength of the emotions, and the power of the mind over them – to have the general definition of each emotion. It is sufficient, I say, for us to understand the common properties of the emotions and of the mind, so that we can determine what and how great is the power of the mind in controlling and restraining the emotions' (Spinoza 2002, p. 308).

relations Spinoza calls passions. Spinoza will finally find a name for this social individual in the *Tractatus politicus*: the *multitude*. These passions are not understood the way they are in Descartes, namely as the inner echo of some external occurrence; instead, Spinoza grasps them as events that affect the mind and body at the same time – in short, he understands them as *practices*.[75] Passions can be identified with practices only if the actions of an individual are not treated (as they are by Descartes) as voluntary responses to the urgings of a soul stirred by the passions. For Spinoza, not only are intellect and will one and the same, but intellections and volitions can only ever exist in the singular: these singular events are passions. These idea-passions, these passionate ideas, cannot therefore be inward states of mind, and they are 'in' the mind only insofar as the mind is entirely one with the body. Passions, then, are the body and its actions. Spinoza writes:

> [T]he decisions of the mind are simply the appetites themselves, which therefore vary in accordance with the varied disposition of the body. For each person regulates everything in accordance with his emotion, and those who are harassed by contrary emotions do not know what they want, but those who are harassed by no emotion are easily driven this way and that way. All this clearly shows that both the decision of the mind, and the appetite and the determination of the body, are simultaneous in nature, or rather are one and the same thing which, when it is considered under the attribute of thought and is explained through it, we call a decision, and when it is considered under the attribute of extension and is deduced from the laws of motion and rest, we call a determination.[76]

For Spinoza, the passions are therefore relations constituting the individual, its imaginary and its social practices. Spinoza's analysis of the function of ritual in the Hebrew state is a perfect historical example of the way these idea-passions crossing through the social body both pervade and sculpt the practices of each individual. Spinoza often insists that these passions mould a politico-social formation out of an uncivilised people, and they can even be said to constitute the Hebraic individual as a social being.

---

75   This results in an extremely clear way from the definition of the affect: 'By affect I understand the affections of the body by which the body's power of acting is increased or diminished, helped or hindered, and at the same time the ideas of these affections' (Spinoza 2002, *Ethics* III, def. 3, p. 278).

76   Spinoza 2002, *Ethics* III, pr. 2 schol, p. 281. What stands out in this proposition is the importance of Hobbes's analyses for these positions of Spinoza.

What then are we to make of Spinoza's contention that relations are nothing more than rational entities, than *entia rationis*? We need to make a distinction between different types of relations. We might say that all relations belonging to the causal order, to the system of relations instituting the causal efficacy of divine power, are constitutive relations. When Spinoza refers to relations as 'rational entities', he is not referring to these relations; he is instead referring only to those relations that emerge from the comparison between the individual 'clots' (so to speak) in the causal order. Relations like identity, difference, opposition and so on are nothing more than *entia rationis* with a precise function: they help us classify the veritable *connexiones singulares* that individuals in fact are. These classifications have their foundation in the imagination and memory, not reason. Once again, Leibniz provides a helpful distinction:

> Relations are either relations of comparison or of coordination [*concours*]. The first concern accord [*convenance*] or discord [*desconvenance*] and include relations of resemblance, equality, inequality, etc. Relations of coordination include some form of connection [*liaison*], such as, for example, cause-effect, part-whole, situation and order.[77]

We can say, then, Leibniz's relations of comparison, of accord and discord, are what Spinoza calls *entia rationis*, whereas what he calls relations of coordination are constitutive on the ontological plane.

From this perspective, we can see that Spinoza clearly separates himself from the Platonic tradition as it is paradigmatically expressed in Plotinus. Plotinus considers all those relations he defines as 'inactive' – i.e. that are based on a comparison – to participate in a form and a reason [*eideos e logos*]:

> If reality implied embodiment, we should indeed be forced to deny reality to these conditions called relative; if, however, we accord the preeminent place to the unembodied and to reasons and at the same time maintain that relations are reasons and participate in ideal forms, we are bound to seek their causes in that higher sphere. Doubleness, it is clear, is the cause of the thing being double, and from it is derived halfness.[78]

Spinoza's refutation of the hypostatisation of terms like identity, difference, opposition, etc. (and his general refutation of all mathematical relations) only assumes its real importance, however, when he is compared to Hegel.

---

77   Leibniz 1960, vol. 5, p. 129.
78   Plotinus 1962, VI, 1, 9, p. 450.

The chapter on 'absolute relation' in the *Science of Logic* moves from substance to cause, action and reaction, and then to reciprocal action;[79] the chapter called 'The Essentialities or Determinations of Reflection' moves from identity to difference, then from opposition to contradiction.[80] To speak like Plotinus, the relations produced by Hegel's immanent causality therefore participate in forms and reasons – in other words, they are intrinsically logical. By reducing these relations to intrinsically logical forms, Hegel reproduces in modern terms the great cosmogonic myth found in Plato's *Timaeus*. This myth presents the soul of the world, created by the demiurge from the categories of the identical, the diverse and being, as preceding that great living sensible being that is the body of the word and as constituting its vital and cognitive principle.[81] But for Spinoza, the relations generated by immanent causality are a-logical (as is confirmed by the theory of the infinite intellect as *natura naturata*). This is precisely what Spinoza is reproached for in Hegel's *Lectures on the History of Philosophy*. Spinoza's substance never becomes subject and his *causa sui* is never raised to the level of the concept, because its structure is *ab origine* a-conceptual. Even the initial division between *esse in se* and *esse in alio* that orients the opening definitions in the *Ethics* cannot be taken literally. They are not to be understood according to a teleological model in which *in se* and *in alio* assume the form of a dialectic of alienation and reappropriation. This initial distinction is posited only in order to be negated: the mode as *esse in alio* does not exist in substance as *esse in se* in the same way, for example, that for Locke an idea is in the mind, in a self that is conscious of what is present within it. If the mode is structurally referred to the other, then substance is only the relational system of these references. Substance can be 'in itself' only in the form of this necessary structure of referral, and it in this sense that Althusser called Spinoza's totality a totality without closure.[82]

7   Contingency of Relation

Because passions are relations that constitute both the individual – its self-image and its image of the world – and society, these relations can be said to *precede* both society and the individual. These relations are, therefore, the

---

79   Hegel 1989, p. 554 ff.
80   Hegel 1989, p. 408 ff.
81   Plato, *Timaeus*, 34c–37c.
82   See Althusser 1976.

between Jean-Luc Nancy speaks of in *Being Singular Plural*.[83] Spinoza's position is as removed from the Hobbesian theory of man's natural unsociability
(*homo homini lupus*) as it is from the Aristoteleo-Scholastic theory of man as
zoon politikon. Neither mechanism nor finalism: the social is *always-already-
there* to the extent that the individual does not exist prior to or outside of the
passions-relations – these passionate relations – crossing through it. Man is,
for Spinoza, always-already socialised, and Part Three of the *Ethics* is nothing
other than the registering of this fact, just as Part One recognises the existence
of reality (through the exclusion of the Leibnizian *Grundfrage*) and Part Two
acknowledges the facticity of human thought (through the exclusion of questions concerning the *de jure* conditions of knowledge).

We should not, however, think of these passions-relations that constitute
human nature (a human nature which exists only in and through these relations between individuals) as a kind of invariant, some irreducible fact that can
only be as it is and not otherwise. These relations are not an invariant behind
which we would find God's plan lurking, as if this God, after being deposed
from the throne of Origin, managed to survive in his theoretical effects, either
in the form of eternal laws that still present the image of his immutability,
or through the transcendentalisation of these relations (such that the passions would be conceived as the transcendental form of concrete encounters
between individuals). Spinoza clearly states in Propositions 56 and 57 of Part
Three of the *Ethics* that each passion is a relation that is both complex and
singular, a relation we might even call 'historical':

> There are as many species of pleasure, pain, and desire, and consequently
> of each emotion which is composed of these (such as waving of the mind)
> or which is derived from these (namely love, hatred, hope, fear, etc.) as

83 Nancy 1996. Nancy writes: 'From now on, this is the minimal and absolutely irrecusable
ontological premise. Being is played out between us and can have no sense other than
the dis-position of this "between"' (Nancy 1996, p. 47). He adds: 'In this way, being is
simultaneous. Just as, in order to say being we must repeat it in saying "being is", so too
being is only simultaneous with itself. The time of being (the time it is) is this simultaneity,
this co-incidence that supposes a more general "incidence", movement, displacement or
deployment, the originary temporal drift and derivation of being: its spacing' (Nancy
1996, p. 58). Contending that the time of *being-between* and *being-with* is simultaneous
prevents us from thinking these concepts in all their radicality. As we mentioned above,
simultaneity is the temporal metaphor of spirit. We should instead, it seems to me,
suggest that the articulations and schema of succession and simultaneity are constituted
by the 'between' and the 'with', in such a way that no space of absolute simultaneity is
possible.

there are species of objects by which we are affected'; and, 'Any emotion of each individual differs from the emotion of another only in so far as the essence of one differs from the essence of the other'.[84]

What we are calling an 'ontology of relation' can therefore only be called an 'ontology' on condition that we undertake a radical modification of the traditional sense of this word. This ontology can in no way be considered a first philosophy, like the substantialist ontologies of the past (Wolff's title says it all: *Philosophia prima sive ontologia*).[85] An ontology of relation should instead be considered a 'second' philosophy, a philosophy that must always be thought in the contingency of the *connexio singularis* of historically given relations. Far from being a first philosophy, such an ontology would be nothing less – or more – than the methodological banishment and methodical abandonment of such a pretension.

Translated by Jason E. Smith

---

84   Spinoza 2002, *Ethics* III, pr. 56 and 57, pp. 307–9.

85   In the 'Preface' to *Être singulier pluriel*, Nancy writes: 'This text does not hide its ambition to redo the entirety of "first philosophy" by giving it a foundation in the "singular plural". But this is not my ambition: it is necessitated both by the thing itself and by our history' (Nancy 1996, p. 13). Later, he writes: 'By its very definition and essence, this "first philosophy" should, like Maldoror's poetry, be "made by all, not by one"' (Nancy 1996, p. 45). To assert that this philosophy, its collective writing and the history giving rise to it are necessary can only be a powerful and persuasive rhetorical expedient. In fact, no philosophy is necessary, and history never calls for any philosophy, nor does it determine either its form or its substance. Philosophy is, to recall Althusser's beautiful image, simply the 'void of a distance taken', and can do no more than intervene in a conjuncture delimited by certain material conditions; it can in no way be the sense or expression of this conjuncture.

CHAPTER 3

'The World by Chance': On Lucretius and Spinoza

1   The Subterranean Current of the Materialism of the Encounter

In a 1982 text, 'The Underground Current of the Materialism of the Encounter,' Louis Althusser outlines the features of a tradition that seems to have crossed the centuries yet remained invisible on the surface, invisible because hard-fought, misunderstood, removed.[1] This tradition he calls *materialism of the rain, of the deviation, of the encounter, and of the taking-hold.* Epicurus, Lucretius, Machiavelli, Spinoza, Hobbes, Rousseau, Marx, the Heideggerian *es gibt*, the Wittgensteinian *fallen*. What do these authors have in common? The resistance, the irreducibility to a history of Western thought understood as the history of reason or metaphysics, resistance to the great Hegelian-Heideggerian periodisation. The core of this materialism of the aleatory is characterised by Althusser in three theses:

1)   the affirmation of the primacy of the encounter over form, of absence over presence, of the encounter over the form that springs forth from it;
2)   the negation of every teleology;
3)   the affirmation of reality as a process without a subject.

The rejection of the Subject and of the End is a theme dear to the Althusserian production of the 1960s and 70s. What instead is new (or at least what is empha-sised in this text) is the theme of the primacy of the encounter over form, of the primacy of the nothing of the encounter over form, meaning by this 'that nothing except the factual circumstances of the encounter has prepared the encounter itself'.[2] Encounters to be evaded, avoided, scarcely touched on, encounters that are brief, enduring yet always temporary. The primacy of the nothing over form and, Althusser adds, of aleatory materialism over every for-malism, that is, over every form of structuralist combinatory among given ele-ments, means precisely that every form is the result of a triple abyss:

---

1   Althusser 2006.
2   Morfino and Pinzolo 2000, p. 11.

1)   of being able not to have been;
2)   of being able to be brief;
3)   of being able to no longer be.

This, according to Althusser, allows one to avoid another figure of metaphysics, the hypostatisation of the laws that result from the encounter, considering as eternal the form of order and the form of beings to which the encounter gives rise: *the fact of a given order*.

2   Lucretius's Way

When Althusser presents the subterranean current of the materialism of the encounter, he does so, in this text as in other analogous texts ('The Only Materialist Tradition'), in an autobiographical context. Nothing prevents one from considering these writings as the traces of a theoretical autobiography: the Althusserian road to Marx. And yet from a historiographical point of view the pages of Althusser can perhaps be read if not as the observation of the existence of a current, whose metaphor already concedes too much to a historicist and idealistic tradition, then perhaps as a challenge, as a heuristic device that allows one to read in a different way (not necessarily following Althusser in the details of his interpretation) some of these authors and the relationships between their discourses. I have done this kind of work on the Spinoza-Machiavelli relationship, and I propose now to do something analogous, although on a reduced scale, regarding Spinoza and Lucretius.[3]

Naturally when the relationship of Spinoza with Atomism is evoked, the famous correspondence with Hugo Boxel cannot be avoided, in which Democritus, Epicurus and Lucretius are cited as positive philosophical *auctoritates*, the only case in all of Spinoza's work, if the two long passages of the *Political Treatise* on Machiavelli are excluded. The context, as is well known, is a discussion about the existence and the nature of ghosts. Spinoza concludes the exchange of letters with Boxel, which included a series of testimonies of historians and philosophers regarding the existence of ghosts, with this abrupt taking of a position:

> The authority of Plato, Aristotle and Socrates carries little weight with me. I should have been surprised if you had produced Epicurus, Democritus, Lucretius or one of the Atomists or defenders of the atoms. It is not

---

3   Morfino 2002a.

surprising that those who have thought up occult qualities, intentional species, substantial forms and a thousand more bits of nonsense should have devised spectres and ghosts, and given credence to old wives' tales with a view to disparaging the authority of Democritus, whose high reputation they so envied that they burned all the books which he had written amidst so much acclaim.[4]

What is the meaning of this return to Democritus, Epicurus, and Lucretius? Surely not taking a position in favour of the Atomistic ontology that Spinoza, we know, did not share. In order to understand the basic reasons for this last passage one must run through the correspondence with Boxel backwards.

After a first interlocutory letter in which Boxel poses the question of ghosts in an apparently neutral way, to which Spinoza responds by defining ghosts as *nugas et imaginationes*, in the second letter Boxel clearly exposes what is at stake:

I say I believe that there are ghosts. My reasons are, first, that it contributes to the beauty and perfection of the universe that they should exist. Second, it is probable that the Creator has created them because they resemble him more closely than do corporeal creatures. Third, just as there is a body without soul, so there is a soul without body. Fourth and last, I believe that there is no dark body in the upper air, region or space that is without its inhabitants, and therefore the immeasurable space extending between us and the stars is not empty but filled with inhabitants that are spirits.[5]

The existence of ghosts is demanded from an anthropocentric, finalist, and hierarchical conception of the universe; and therefore testimonies about their existence are proofs of the existence of such a universe. Hereafter from the single reply that Spinoza proposes through four points, the meaning of the summons to Greek Atomism and to Lucretius becomes clear in this context; it is a question, as Laurent Bove has written, of a summons 'to the rational study of the world without any foreign addition, which expels every hidden world, every asylum of ignorance, every mystery, for the benefit of the pure immanent joy of understanding'.[6] Spinoza seems here to appeal to what Monod calls 'the cornerstone of the scientific method', the postulate of the objectivity of nature,

---

4   Spinoza 2002, *Letter* LVI, pp. 905–6.

5   Spinoza 2002, *Letter* LIII, p. 895.

6   Bove 1994, p. 471.

that is, 'the *systematic* refusal to consider the possibility of reaching a "true" knowledge by means of any interpretation of the phenomena given in terms of final causes, that is, of a "plan"'.[7]

In what sense, then, would Lucretius's testimony be significant? Because Lucretius could not be suspected, he on whose text the young Machiavelli learned to follow the *actual truth of things*, of 'narrat[ing] things, not as they are, but as they would like them to be'.[8] In fact, Spinoza writes, he [the witness of apparitions] 'makes things up to justify the fear that has seized him regarding his dreams and fancied apparitions, or also to confirm his courage, his credibility and his esteem'.[9]

Fear and superstition are the common enemies of Lucretius and Spinoza. Against them both pleaded the cause of the knowledge of nature based on two fundamental points: the rejection of every finalist model of explanation of natural phenomena and the affirmation of the existence of natural laws that regulate becoming. On these two points it is possible to establish a true and proper genealogy between Lucretius-Spinoza. We see them in brief in *De Rerum Natura*.

3   Against Finalism

Without wanting to overestimate the analogy, there is the same connection between the ignorance of the nature of things (what Althusser calls the opacity of the immediate), finalism as an anthropo-theo-centric prejudice, and inversion in the finalist explanation of causes and effects. And regarding this last it is difficult to think that Spinoza in the Appendix to Part I of the *Ethics* did not have before him the famous passage of the Lucretian Book IV in which it is openly denounced:

> One error here you must with might and main
> Avoid – in fear and trembling flee this fault:
> do not imagine the eyes' bright gleam created
> in order that we might see, or that we might
> step the long stride for this, thigh ends in calf,
> and calf in foot, firm-based yet flexible;
> or that our arms were strung with brawn and muscle

---

7 Monod 1970, p. 37.

8 Spinoza 2002, Letter LII, p. 894.

9 Spinoza 2002, Letter LII, pp. 894–5.

and hands bestowed, our servants, left and right,
that we might do what life required of us.
These and all other like interpretations
are falsely reasoned and preposterous;
no part of us grew there that we might use it,
but what grew there created its own use.
There was no seeing before the eye took form,
no words, no pleas, until the tongue was made;
tongues, rather, came into being far ahead
of speech, and ears took form long, long before
a sound was heard. In short, each of our parts
existed, I think, before its use arose;
they can't have grown, then, to fulfil a function.[10]

And to the limited finalist vision of the world is counterposed, on the one hand, the infinite space furrowed from infinite seeds and, on the other hand, the *substantia infinita infinitis modis*: this infinite abyss into which every finalist prejudice sinks is perfectly represented in the parallel of the tiny worm 'living in the blood as we are living in our part of the universe'.[11]

4   The *foedera naturae*

It is said that finalist superstition is generated in ignorance. But in the ignorance of what? It is ignorance of 'what can be / and what cannot; yes, and what law defines / the power of things, what firm-set boundary stone'.[12] It is ignorance of the pacts of nature, the *foedera naturai*, the laws that regulate becoming – becoming that is always certain insofar as it is regulated by a *ratio* that is not, however, either transcendent or transcendental, but is none other than the name of the conformation of bodies, of their being as they are and not otherwise. And it is characteristic for this determination that everything arises from nature, that, according to Lucretius, mythological creatures, i.e., creatures constituted with a double nature, cannot exist:

But there were no Centaurs, nor at any time
could creatures of double nature and two bodies

---

10   Lucretius, *De rerum natura*, IV, vv. 823–42.
11   Spinoza 2002, *Letter* XXXII, p. 849.
12   Lucretius, *De rerum natura*, V, vv. 87–90.

be built out of unrelated parts, yet equal
enough in powers and substance on both sides.
And here is proof for even the dull of mind.
First: at about three years, the horse has reached
his prime; not so, the child: for often still
in sleep he'll seek his mother's milky breasts.
Later, when horses are aging, and their strength
and muscle are failing, as life runs toward its close,
then, for the boy the bloom of youth is just
beginning, just starting to clothe his cheeks with down.[13]

Mythological creatures cannot exist, nor have they existed, because every
being has its own temporality, its own determinate rhythm that cannot be harmonised, except in the poetic imagination, with that of another. Regarding this
proposition Moreau, in one of the few articles devoted to the Epicurus-Spinoza
relationship, notes that just as in Epicureanism and in particular in Lucretius
'the rigorous world of laws is opposed to the world of mutations without principle,' there is in Spinoza an opposition 'between the world of metamorphosis
and the world of the regularity of forms'.[14]

5   The Soul and the Body

Therefore, when Spinoza evokes Lucretius against Boxel it is obviously a reference to an anti-finalist and deterministic philosophical model. In what way
can this model be used in the question of the existence of ghosts? In letter 54
Spinoza compares ghosts to Harpies, Griffins, and Hydras – fantastic beings
produced from the imagination – and a little further on adds that it is not possible for there to be a mind without body, just as it is not possible for there to be
'memory, hearing, sight, etc... without bodies'.[15] There are determinate laws
that preside over the appearing of forms in nature. Lucretius writes:

It can't be that just anything you like
be thought possessed of wisdom and soul-substance.
In air there are no trees; in the salt sea
clouds can't exist, nor fish live on dry land;

---

13   Lucretius, *De rerum natura*, V, vv. 878–89.
14   Moreau 1994, pp. 464–5. See also Moreau 1989, pp. 9–18.
15   Spinoza 2002, *Letter* LIV, p. 899.

there can't be blood in wood, or sap in stone.
It's fixed and ordained where things may grow and live.
Soul, then, can't come to being with the body,
all by itself, far, far from flesh and blood.[16]

This *certa ratio*, this determinate norm that ensures that everything has 'its special spot [*certa loca*] assigned / for growth, where, once created, it persists', also ensures that thought cannot be given without the body. The determination and order of nature exclude it.[17]

6   The World by Chance

The summons to Atomism, then, seems to be in Spinoza an appeal to the scientific study of the laws of nature against every form of religious superstition. However, if the exchange of letters is read with attention, after Boxel's second letter (Letter 53), it can be observed that the epicentre of the discussion moves decidedly from the question of the existence of ghosts to that of chance. Of course the discussion regarding ghosts maintains a space, but, if you listen carefully, Spinoza's tone in dealing with the two questions is quite different: whereas regarding ghosts the tone is ironic nearly to the point of provocation (for example, regarding the genitals of ghosts), regarding the question of chance the tone is extremely serious and technical.

In the second letter, Boxel raises the question of chance. As said before, Boxel brings to light here what are the *enjeux* of the question of the existence of ghosts. Let us read it again:

I say I believe that there are ghosts. My reasons are, first, that it contributes to the beauty and perfection of the universe that they should exist. Second, it is probable that the Creator has created them because they resemble him more closely than do corporeal creatures. Third, just as there is a body without soul, so there is a soul without body. Fourth and last, I believe that there is no dark body in the upper air, region or space that is without its inhabitants, and therefore the immeasurable space extending between us and the stars is not empty but filled with inhabitants that are spirits.[18]

---

16   Lucretius, *De rerum natura*, V, vv. 126–33.

17   Lucretius, *De rerum natura*, III, vv. 618–21.

18   Spinoza 2002, *Letter* LIII, p. 895.

The finalist order of the universe demands the existence of ghosts. There is, however, someone who can remain immune from such reasoning, according to Boxel: 'This reasoning will not convince those who perversely believe that the world was made by chance [*qui mundum fortuito creatum esse / dat de wereld by geval gemaakt is*]'.[19] Boxel's sentence, scribbled down here almost carelessly, is a threatening warning: watch out, for one who denies the existence of ghosts denies the existence of God and therefore falls into atheism. The warning is so perfectly picked up by Spinoza that, after some verbal skirmishing and before taking apart one by one the four points through which Boxel has demonstrated the existence of ghosts, he devotes a lot of space to the refutation of Boxel's equation: deniers of ghosts = atheists.

Regarding the question of whether the world is created by chance, Spinoza expounds in these terms his own conception:

> My answer is that, as it is certain that chance and necessity [*fortuitus et necessarius*] are two contrary terms, so it is also clear that he who affirms that the world is the necessary effect of the divine nature is also denying absolutely that the world was made by chance [*casu*].[20]

Divine causality excludes happenstance, and necessity excludes chance. The accusation of atheism is rejected and, with a rhetorical expedient well known to readers of Spinoza, is returned to the sender: one who supposes the world by chance does not assert a necessary relationship between God and the world but presupposes at the origin of the world a free choice of the divine will.

To these arguments, Boxel, frightened not in the least, responds by specifying what he meant:

> A thing is said to happen fortuitously when it comes about regardless of the doer's intention. When we dig the ground to plant a vine or to make a pit or grave, and find a treasure of which we have never had a thought, this is said to happen by chance. He who acts of his own free will in such a way that he can either act or not act can never be said to act by chance if he chooses to act; for in that case all human actions would be by chance, which would be absurd. 'Necessary' and 'free', not 'necessary' and 'fortuitous' are contrary terms.[21]

---

19 Spinoza 2002, *Letter* LIII, p. 895.
20 Spinoza 2002, *Letter* LIV, p. 898.
21 Spinoza 2002, *Letter* LV, pp. 900–1.

Boxel refutes Spinoza's arguments with precision: the issue is not whether the world is a necessary effect of God, the question is God's intention. If the finalist order of the universe is denied, so, in fact, is God denied. Boxel renews the veiled accusation of atheism.

Spinoza feigns nothing, speaks of the radical difference in principles, and in a slightly pedantic way redefines the pair of opposites: the true pair is fortuitous/necessary and free/constrained. However, he turns a deaf ear to the essential question, takes Boxel's example literally and, in fact, ridicules it:

> Tell me, pray, whether you have seen or read any philosophers who have maintained that the world was made by chance, taking chance in the sense you give it, that God had a set aim in creating the world and yet departed from his resolve. I am unaware that any such idea has ever entered the thoughts of any man.[22]

However, perhaps tired with these verbal skirmishes that have no other aim than bouncing accusations back at Boxel, he seems at the end of the letter to lose patience. Boxel thinks that Spinoza denies God as an intelligent creator, and it is difficult to refute him. Thus, having abandoned all prudence, in the last part of the letter we find, first, a famous passage of Feuerbachian flavour *avant le lettre*, and then a summoning of the Atomists, with a particular insistence on Democritus, as the only reliable witnesses on the question of ghosts.[23] Having started with the 'world created by chance', the letter ends with Democritus. That this is not 'accidental' will become clear after reading this passage of Thomas Aquinas made famous by Dante in the *Inferno*:

> Therefore those only can assert that many worlds exist who do not acknowledge any ordaining wisdom, but rather believe in chance, as Democritus, who said that this world, besides an infinite number of other

---

22   Spinoza 2002, *Letter* LVI, p. 903.

23   'When you say that you do not see what sort of God I have if I deny in him the actions of seeing, hearing, attending, willing, etc., and that he possesses those faculties in an eminent degree, I suspect that you believe there is no greater perfection than can be explicated by the afore-mentioned attributes. I am not surprised, for I believe that a triangle, if it could speak, would likewise say that God is eminently triangular, and a circle that God's nature is eminently circular. In this way each would ascribe to God its own attributes, assuming itself to be like God and regarding all else as ill-formed' (Spinoza 2002, *Letter* LVI, p. 904). Here Spinoza seems to repeat a famous saying of Epicurus according to whom 'impious is not the one who denies the gods of the common people but the one who applies the opinions of the common people to the gods'.

worlds, was made from a casual concourse of atoms [*Et ideo illi potuerunt ponere plures mundos, qui causam mundi non posuerunt aliquam sapientiam ordinantem, sed casum, ut Democritus, qui dixit ex concursu atomorum factum esse hunc mundum, et alios infinitos*].[24]

It is a question of a true and proper admission. Boxel, satisfied, does not write to him any more.

7   Chance and Fortune

However, the question of chance deserves to be deepened, because it is subject to easy simplifications or misunderstandings. In order to disentangle the skein one must make a detour through Aristotle and his conceptions of chance [*automaton*] and fortune [*tuche*]. Aristotle takes up these concepts in Book II of the *Physics*, paragraphs 4–6. In paragraph 4 in particular, before proposing his theory of chance he analyses as is customary the different previous positions, taking into consideration Democritus's theory according to which chance would be the cause of 'this heavenly sphere and all the worlds':[25] 'by chance', Aristotle writes, 'the vortex arose ... i.e., the motion that separated and arranged the universe in its present order'.[26] According to Aristotle, this position is indefensible because 1) it asserts chance in the generation of the heavens and of the worlds 2) it denies chance in the generation of plants and animals: 'For it is not any chance thing that comes from a given seed but an olive from one kind and a man from another'.[27] According to the Stagirite, it is not only a question of a mistaken position; it is also diametrically opposed to the true position. In fact, 1) in the heavens nothing happens fortuitously, whereas 2) in the sublunary world many things happen by chance.

But note well that we find in the description that Aristotle makes of the Democritean position some interesting cues: as in Lucretius and Spinoza, there is asserted a necessity that regulates the becoming of forms, and yet the world is posited by chance as Boxel secretly reproaches Spinoza. In order to deepen the discourse we must return to Aristotle and to his conception of chance. This he defines as concern for events that do not take place either always or mostly, but happen for the sake of an end in an accidental way (fortuitous events are

---

24   Aquinas 1912, I, 47, 3, p. 260.
25   Aristotle 1984, vol. 1, p. 26 (translation modified).
26   Ibid.
27   Ibid.

those that at origin have a choice, whereas random events are those that do not). Let us read Aristotle's example:

> A man is engaged in collecting subscriptions for a feast. He would have gone to such and such a place for the purpose of getting the money, if he had known. He actually went there for another purpose, and it was only accidentally that he got his money by going there; and this was not due to the fact that he went there as a rule or necessarily, nor is the end effected (getting the money) a cause present in himself.[28]

Chance commonly understood as whatever does not have a cause does not exist for Aristotle; it only makes sense for Aristotle regarding a causal order and, indeed, it presupposes it. Everything that happens has a cause: a stone falls by virtue of its nature; a man goes to the market in order to make a purchase. It is a question of natural processes. However, these do not happen in solitude but in the middle of other natural processes. It happens that some processes are intertwined with others: the stone falls and hits a man who is passing by, the man gone to the market meets a debtor and collects his loan. In both cases it is a question of the encounter between two causal processes: in fact, the man who is hit passed by there for determinate reasons, the debtor found himself in the market for determinate reasons. Now, what in this intertwining of causal processes makes us speak about chance and fortune? An apparent teleology, an 'as if': it would seem that this intertwining is prepared by a meaning, by an intention. It could seem that the stone had fallen with the intention of killing, as if at the origin had been the aim to kill; it could seem that the man had gone to the market in order to collect, as if at the origin had been the aim to collect, but in reality none of this is so: the stone's aim was to fall downwards, its cause *per se*, and by accident it has hit the man; the man's aim was to go to the market to make a purchase, his cause *per se*, and by accident he has encountered the creditor.

On the basis of this theory of chance (of which fortune is obviously a subset), Aristotle is in a position to refute Democritus's position:

> Chance and fortune are causes of effects which, though they might result from intelligence or nature, have in fact been caused by something accidentally. Now since nothing which is accidental is prior to what is *per se*, it is clear that no accidental cause can be prior to a cause *per se*. Chance and fortune, therefore, are posterior to intelligence and nature. Hence,

---

28   Aristotle 1984, vol. 1, p. 27.

however true it may be that the heavens are due to chance, it will still be true that intelligence and nature will be prior causes of this universe and of many things in it besides.[29]

When Spinoza responds to Boxel, he in fact uses an argument much like Aristotle's. Boxel tells him that by accidental or fortuitous he means an event like the discovery of a treasure following the digging for a well, and Spinoza asks him if he has ever felt like someone who supports a God who had planned something and then changed his idea at the last moment. If he had wanted to be more precise – but perhaps caution and respect for his own interlocutor did not allow it – he could have spoken about a God intending to make a minestrone that by chance, combining the ingredients, gave rise to a world.

8   The Primacy of the Encounter Over the Form

We have seen that in tracing the essential points that would characterise the authors of the subterranean current of aleatory materialism Althusser had established three points:

1)   the primacy of the encounter over form;
2)   the negation of every form of finality;
3)   the affirmation of reality as a process without a subject.

The second and the third points we have found at the centre of the Spinozist return to the work of Lucretius. But what about the first one? Is the affirmation of a regularity of nature, of necessity as the persistence of determinate forms, not in direct antithesis with the primacy of the encounter over form?

When Spinoza cites Democritus, Epicurus and Lucretius, he cites them against Socrates, Plato and Aristotle; he cites them above all against occult quality, intentional species, and substantial form. The most obvious reading of this passage sees an opposition between a qualitative world and a world that is quantitatively understood. But perhaps one could read this passage according to a nuance certainly not alternative but different: an opposition between a philosophy of the encounter and a philosophy of form. In what sense would this be the case, however? Have we not identified in the affirmation of the laws that regulate the becoming of forms one of the fundamental elements of the established theoretical alliance of Spinoza with Lucretius?

---

29   Aristotle 1984, vol. 1, p. 30 (translation modified).

In order to grasp all the importance of the question one must return to Book II of the *Physics*, precisely to paragraph 8 in which we find one of the Stagirite's philosophically most beautiful and most powerful pages. Here Aristotle analyses a possible fault in his theoretical construction, at whose centre is the concept of form; this gap is strictly inherent in the definition of chance as an apparent teleology. Aristotle wonders if every teleology is not in reality apparent, an appearance of finality, in other words, if every form is not in reality an effect of chance. Here is the extraordinary Aristotelian passage:

> A difficulty presents itself: why should not nature work, not for the sake of something, nor because it is better so, but just as the sky rains, not in order to make the corn grow, but of necessity? (What is drawn up must cool, and what has been cooled must become water and descend, the result of this being that the corn grows.) Similarly if a man's crop is spoiled on the threshing-floor, the rain did not fall for the sake of this – in order that the crop might be spoiled – but that result just followed. Why then should it not be the same with the parts in nature, e.g. that our teeth should come up of necessity – the front teeth sharp, fitted for tearing, the molars broad and useful for grinding down the food – since they did not arise for this end, but it was merely a coincident result; and so with all other parts in which we suppose that there is purpose? Wherever then all the parts came about just what they would have been if they had come to be for an end, such things survived, being organized spontaneously in a fitting way; whereas those which grew otherwise perished and continue to perish, as Empedocles says his 'man-faced oxprogeny' did.[30]

Everything could have happened by necessity and not for the sake of an end. It rains, this is a fact. And rain can have positive effects, to make crops grow, or negative effects, to spoil crops on the threshing floor. In the two cases it does not rain for an end, but necessarily [*ex anagkes*]. Aristotle wonders if every form could not be thought on the model of rain and its possible effects on grain. Forms would be none other than the result of a successful combination of necessity, a good organisation that for this reason persists; by contrast, bad organisations perish and have perished like calves with human faces. Forms, then, do not exist because they are produced with an end to existing, but because they are casually adapted to existence. This primacy of the encounter over form is a hypothesis that Aristotle discards, relying on the use of the language that structures it, which is identified with the very ontological structure

---

of reality: as Wieland puts it perfectly, 'wherever we speak of chance we have always-already positively stated first of all teleological structures'.[31]

When Spinoza counterposes Lucretian concepts to those of the medieval Aristotle, substantial forms, etc., does he not perchance have in mind the affirmation of the primacy of the encounter over form?

At the end of Book I, Lucretius himself seems to designate such a horizon:

> For surely not by planning did atoms
> find rank and place, nor by intelligence,
> nor did they regulate movement by sworn pact
> [...]
> till, trying all kinds of movements and arrangements,
> they came at last into such patterned shapes
> as have created this Sum of Things.[32]

Neither nature nor intelligence are at the origin of form, but rather the innumerable motions and attempts at union. From this follow three theoretical consequences of fundamental importance:

1) the infinity of the worlds that will be revived by Bruno himself using Lucretius against Aristotle;
2) the fact that the world has a birth and a death;
3) perhaps the most important from the theoretical point of view, what Althusser calls the primacy of the encounter over form and which is perfectly exemplified in this passage of Lucretius:

> For time changes the nature of all the world;
> all things must pass from one state to another.
> No thing stays like itself: all things change place;
> nature makes everything turn into something else.
> For one thing rots, grows weary and weak with time,
> then out of its rubbish another thing grows up.
> So, then, time changes the nature of all the world,
> and earth takes one condition, then another,
> can't bear what it could, and can, what it could not bear.
>   Then, too, earth tried creating hosts of strange
> creatures, fantastic things in face and form,

---

31   Wieland 1962, p. 328.
32   Lucretius, *De rerum natura*, I, vv. 1021–8. See also V, vv. 185–94, vv. 420–30.

androgynes – twixt and tween, not one, not t'other –
some without feet, and again some lacking hands,
some mute and mouthless; eyeless, some, and blind,
some with body and limbs all in adhesion,
unable to act, unable even to move
to avoid danger and take what life requires.
Still more such marvels and miracles she created,
all to no end, since nature deterred their growth;
they longed for the flower of life but could not reach it,
or even find food or join in the act of love.
For many things, we see, must work together
that creatures may procreate and forge their kind.[33]

The regularity of forms and their becoming that we had grasped at the basis of Lucretian naturalism is in reality founded on the abyss. Form does not persist by virtue of its own teleology: every form is the effect of a conjunction that only in the presence of the *concurrere multa rebus* can become a conjuncture, a conjunction that endures. Like Aristotle's rain that falls on the field of grain and makes it grow.

It was said that Lucretius had denied the existence of mythological creatures on the basis of the *foedera naturae* that regulate the becoming of forms. However, this negation does not imply the affirmation of the immutability and limitation of forms, but rather the necessity of thinking, and not imagining, their real multiplicity and instability: paraphrasing Shakespeare, it could be said that Lucretius asserts that there are more things on earth and in the heavens than literature can dream of.

And is it not perhaps this primacy of the encounter over form that Spinoza counterposes through Lucretius to the philosophy of substantial form, to the universe hierarchically ordered through those forms that these ghosts are only a metaphor for? And that in Spinoza there would be present an analogous conception of the primacy of the encounter over form demonstrates as much the theory of the individual in Part Two of the *Ethics* as does the axiom of Part Four of the *Ethics*: on the one hand, form as the *certa ratio* of a composition, of an agreement, of a concurrence (and the form of the political individual is also defined in the same terms), on the other hand, the radical contingency of every form, whether it be a little flower or a world, meaning the term contingency in the sense that Spinoza confers on it in the corollary to Proposition 31 of Part II

---

33   Lucretius, *De rerum natura*, V, vv. 828–50.

of the *Ethics*, that is, *possibilitas corruptionis*. And perhaps a symptom of this primacy of the encounter over form is the example that Spinoza proposes in order to show the opposition between scientific and religious explanation in the appendix of Part One: a stone that falls and kills a man. Necessity against finalism, to be sure! But it cannot escape anyone aware of Spinoza's philosophical strategy that we are dealing with one of the very examples Aristotle himself uses in order to illustrate the concept of chance: 'The stone that struck the man did not fall for the sake of hitting him; therefore it fell as if by chance, because it might have fallen by the action of an agent and for the sake of striking'.[34]

We are dealing with chance even though a teleology seems to be at work, which is in reality not the case. Through the same example Spinoza thinks about necessity against finalist prejudice. But using this very example, does he not himself perhaps want to assert what Althusser calls the primacy of the encounter over form? This concurrence of circumstances that produced the man's death (*'saepe enim multa simul concurrunt'*, exclaims Spinoza) is not the space of the intersection of teleological processes dominated by the regularity of forms but is the same mode in which divine immanent causality acts: it concurs, it agrees (that is the literal translation of the Greek *sumbebekos*), this is at the basis of the generating, enduring, and perishing of forms, as is shown perfectly by the sketch of the ontology of history in Chapter III of the *TTP* that concludes with the oxymoron *directio dei sive fortuna*. Of course Spinoza says that God is cause *per se* and not by accident, and to Boxel's insinuations responds that he means that the God-World relationship is necessary and not fortuitous. This *a parte Dei*. But when Spinoza, reprising Boxel's terminology, talks about *mundus*, what exactly is he talking about, since in the *Ethics* the term occurs only once and without any technical sense? When Spinoza talks about necessity he certainly refers to the relationship that connects *natura naturans* and *natura naturata*. For Spinoza every form is the product of concurrence, every essence is in reality a *connexio*, in Lucretian terms a *textura*: the world is by chance. Natural laws are not, then, the guarantee of the invariance of forms but the necessity immanent to conjunctions, the necessity of the rain that makes the grain in the field grow and spoils it on the threshing floor. And perhaps a second indication of this is the passage in the appendix that follows the example of the stone about the structure of the human body, constituted in such a way 'that no one part shall injure another'. Is it not perhaps an implicit reference to that passage in Aristotle, in which the possibility that every form is the product of chance, of concurrence, is harboured?

---

34   Aristotle 1984, vol. 1, p. 29 (translation modified).

Primacy of the encounter over form, primacy of chance over the necessity to which it gives rise: in some cases, a concurrence of circumstances is given that has allowed some forms to endure, 'whereas those which grew otherwise perished and continue to perish, as Empedocles says his "man-faced oxprogeny" did'.

Translated by Ted Stolze

CHAPTER 4

The Primacy of the Encounter over Form

From the theoretical point of view, the most important work Louis Althusser produced in the 1980s is most likely the manuscript that the editors of Althusser's *Écrits* presented as the 'The Underground Current of the Materialism of the Encounter'. This is an extremely fascinating text in which the clandestine history of a materialism that refuses the classical opposition between idealism and materialism is outlined. Against this opposition that is internal to the history of Western metaphysics, we are presented with a materialism of contingency and of the aleatory that is not dominated by the great principle *'nihil est sine ratione'* that has resonated, as Heidegger tells us, throughout the history of Western metaphysics before being formulated by Leibniz. The biggest risk posed by this text is in the very fascination it inspires: this text dazzles more than it enlightens; it is full of flashes of brilliance that break with philosophical commonplaces, full of intuitions that open up passages that, for the most part, are not followed up on with the patient work of the concept. The biggest risk, then, is to see in this text an abandonment of the powerful rationalism of the writings of the 1960s in favour of a philosophy of the event, of chance, or, worse, of freedom. The challenge is not so much to deny the ambiguities this text gives rise to but to recognise them and underline them, in order to cut through them with a theoretical *coup de force*, placing an unwritten thesis at the theoretical centre of the text: the thesis of the primacy of the encounter over form. The fundamental issue that immediately crops up is, what is the relation between this thesis and the thesis, repeated constantly in the 60s and 70s, of the primacy of the relation over the elements? Is there any contradiction between them? Does the first thesis allude to a pre-existence of the elements that the second thesis denies? At stake here is nothing less than the possibility of thinking a materialism of the aleatory without jumping the rails of rationalism.

1   The Primacy of Class Struggle

As mentioned above, the primacy of relations over elements characterises the works of the first Althusser. In this sense, Althusser's position as it is articulated in his 'Response to John Lewis' is well known. In opposition to the humanist concept that man makes history while transcending it, Althusser affirms that a) it is the masses that make history and b) that class struggle is the motor of history. The two theses are not, however, on the same plane, since the first must be subordinated to the second: 'That means that the revolutionary power of the masses comes precisely from the *class struggle*'.[1] In other words, it is not possible to think the existence of classes outside the struggle between them: 'You must therefore begin with the class struggle if you want to understand class division, the existence and nature of classes. *The class struggle must be put in the front rank*'. Then, just a few lines later, he concludes: 'Absolute primacy of the class struggle'.[2]

As Stanislas Breton has underlined, the thesis of the primacy of class struggle over the existence of classes can be translated, in abstract terms, into the thesis of the primacy of relations over the elements.[3] But here it is a matter of determining what, exactly, primacy means. It seems to me that the term can be read, in a first approximation, from the point of view of the Aristotelian tradition, as what is primary by nature: *proto physei* signifies a priority that is not temporal but ontological. But without going back to Aristotle, we can also understand the term in light of the first proposition of the first part of Spinoza's *Ethics*: 'A substance is by nature prior to its affection [*Substantia prior est natura suis affectionibus*]'.[4] This is an ontological primacy that must be asserted on an epistemological level against a naive empiricism that considers the things appearing before a subject to be a subsistent reality. In this sense, the scholium to proposition 10 of the second part of the *Ethics* dedicated to the correct *ordo philosophandi* is decisive:

> All must surely admit that nothing can be or be conceived without God. For all are agreed that God is the sole cause of all things, both of their essence and of their existence; that is, God is the cause of things not only in respect of their coming into being [*secundum fieri*], as they say, but also in respect of their being. But at the same time many assert that that without which a thing can neither be nor be conceived pertains to the essence of the thing, and so they believe that either the nature of God pertains to the essence of created things or that created things can either be or be conceived without God; or else, more probably, they hold no consistent opinion. I think that the reason for this is their failure to observe the proper order of philosophical inquiry. For the divine nature,

---

1   Althusser 1976, p. 50.
2   Ibid.
3   Breton 1993, p. 418.
4   Spinoza 2002, *Ethics* I, pr. 1, p. 218.

which they should have considered before all else – it being prior both in cognition and in Nature – they have taken to be last in the order of cognition, and the things that are called objects of sense they have taken as prior to everything.[5]

This important methodological note on the primacy of totality follows an assertion of great philosophical importance: 'the essence of man is constituted by definite modifications of the attributes of God'.[6] This means that it makes no sense to pose the problem of man in terms of an atemporal essence, because the essence of man is constituted by modifications and can be correctly thought only if posited in relation to the totality.

Introducing the *Positivismusstreit* into German sociology, Adorno takes a similar position from a methodological point of view, asserting that facts are not an ultimate, impenetrable given, as the sociology of the time affirmed, but let appear what posits and constitutes them as such:

> The interpretation of facts leads to totality ... There is not any social fact that does not have its place and meaning in that totality. This is preordinate to every single subject that represents the totality in his own monadological constitution.[7]

Of course, such a position cannot be taken in a naïve manner; it must be understood in relation to the tradition of expressive causality found in Leibniz and Hegel.

2   The Primacy of Relations: Telos, or Alea?

Althusser dedicated the final paragraph of 'The Object of *Capital*' to the difference between the Marxist and Leibnizian/Hegelian conception of causality. It was significantly titled 'Marx's Immense Theoretical Revolution'. Althusser holds that in the theory of history and political economy developed in *Capital* we find a concept of causality that, though Marx never theorised it on a strictly

---

5   Spinoza 2002, *Ethics* II, pr. 10 schol, pp. 249–50.
6   Spinoza 2002, *Ethics* II, pr. 10 cor, p. 249.
7   Adorno 1969, p. 21. About this Macherey writes: ' ... the totality Adorno speaks of is not totally unrelated to substance such as Spinoza defines it, substance that conditions all modal determination to the extent that it itself can only be apprehended modally' (Macherey 1992b, pp. 222–36).

philosophical level, addresses the questions of the determination of the elements of a structure and the structural relations between these elements through the efficacy of this structure itself. In this sense, we have a model of causality that is neither mechanistic nor holistic:

> Very schematically, we can say that classical philosophy (the existing Theoretical) had two and only two systems of concepts with which to think effectivity. The mechanistic system, Cartesian in origin, which reduced causality to a *transitive* and analytical effectivity: it could not be made to think the effectivity of a whole on its elements, except at the cost of extra-ordinary distortions (such as those in Descartes' 'psychology' and biology). But a second system was available, one conceived precisely in order to deal with the effectivity of a whole on its elements: the Leibnizian concept of *expression.* This is the model that dominates all Hegel's thought. But it presupposes in principle that the whole in question be reducible to an *inner essence,* of which the elements of the whole are then no more than the phenomenal forms of expression, the inner principle of the essence being present at each point in the whole, such that at each moment it is possible to write the immediately adequate equation: *such and such an element* (economic, political, legal, literary, religious, etc., in Hegel) = *the inner essence of the whole.* Here was a model which made it possible to think the effectivity of the whole on each of its elements, but if this category – inner essence/outer phenomenon – was to be applicable everywhere and at every moment to each of the phenomena arising in the totality in question, *it presupposed that the whole had a certain nature, precisely the nature of a 'spiritual' whole in which each element was expressive of the entire totality as a* 'pars totalis'. In other words, Leibniz and Hegel did have a category for the effectivity of the whole on its elements or parts, but on the absolute condition that the whole was not a structure.[8]

Marx therefore has recourse to a model of causality that is neither mechanical nor organic, a model that, without Marx knowing it,[9] was also that of Spinoza's immanent causality. The theoretical problem, however, consists in differentiating in detail the Spinozan model from the Hegelian one which is widely

---

8 Althusser 1970, pp. 186–7.

9 'The only theoretician who had had the unprecedented daring to pose this problem and outline a first solution to it was Spinoza. But, as we know, history had buried him in impenetrable darkness. Only through Marx, who, however, had little knowledge of him, do we even begin to guess at the features of that trampled face' (Althusser 1970, p. 187).

deployed in the Marxist tradition. At the end of this paragraph, Althusser multiplies the formulations that underline this difference: 'structural causality', 'overdetermination' (categories introduced in *For Marx*), *Darstellung*, metonymical causality, immanent cause, theatre without an author. Some years later, without adding anything of substance to his argumentation, Althusser will also oppose 'whole' to 'totality'[10] ('Is it Simple to be a Marxist in Philosophy?') and a 'whole without closure'[11] to the closed totality of the idealist tradition.

In order to shed light on this point, we need to consider the thesis of the primacy of relations in the tradition of expressive causality. Leibniz holds that relations constitute reality insofar as they order the spatio-temporal structure of phenomena. But if these relations structure the world such as it appears, they nevertheless require two foundations in their turn: a spiritual substance not constituted by relations (and therefore beyond all relation), on the one hand, and a divine intellect, without which, according to Leibniz, 'nothing would be true',[12] on the other. For his part, Hegel dissolves all substantiality into the most radical relationality. But this relationality is not the pure, unqualified play of action and reaction. It is conceived of instead as the presence of an all-pervading time that *orders* relations rather than being *constituted* by them. This presence is understood to be the contemporaneity of a principle that is immanent to the play of relations (the beautiful soul, the abstract juridical person, and so on), a power that decides in advance what developments the play of relation can give rise to. The obscurity at the heart of reciprocal action [*Wechselwirkung*] necessarily tends toward the light of the concept: this tension and tendency is lodged *ab initio* in the schema of simultaneity, the great temporal metaphor of the Spirit [*Geist*].

It seems, then, that both Leibniz and Hegel were able to pose the question of relations in the most radical way, and yet they both seem to have fled in the face of the extreme consequences these positions imply. Leibniz's theory of pre-established harmony, for example, permits substance to enter into the play

---

10   'Marx did not have the same idea of the nature of a social formation as Hegel, and I believed that I could demonstrate this difference by saying that Hegel thought of society as a *totality*, while Marx thought of it as a complex whole, structured in dominance. If I may be allowed to be a little provocative, it seems to me that we can leave to Hegel the category of *totality*, and claim for Marx the category of the *whole*' (Althusser 1976, p. 181).

11   'Spinoza served us as a (sometimes direct, sometimes very indirect) reference: in his effort to grasp a "non-eminent" (that is, non-transcendent) not simply transitive (à la Descartes) nor expressive (à la Leibniz) causality, which would account for the action of the Whole on its parts, and of the parts on the Whole – a Whole without closure, which is only the active relation between its parts' (Althusser 1976, pp. 140–1 [translation modified]).

12   Leibniz 1960, vol. 5, p. 210.

of relations only when it has the form of a possible essence in the divine intellect. Leibniz therefore reduces relation to the combinatory game of a God presented as both architect and sovereign, a game always-already decided in advance by the divine will's tendency toward the good. In the same way, Hegel's theory of the ruse of reason is said to weave the great tapestry of universal history, a tapestry whose warp and woof is the Idea and whose passions are the individual woven threads. Both pre-established harmony and the ruse of reason make relationality serve the ends of teleology: the primacy of teleology over relationality, we could say, to echo the Althusserian formulation we started from. In both cases, the conception of time is the secret of this primacy, the theological eternity of Leibniz and its Hegelian secularisation into the contemporaneity of an epoch or age.

In his 'An Outline for a Concept of Historical Time', Althusser tried to construct a concept of time freed from this double hypothesis: the time of totality is neither eternal, nor contemporaneous, nor synchronic (in an explicitly polemical argument with 'structuralism'), but is the complex articulation of differential times not harmonised in a simple essence.[13] So if the thesis of the primacy of relations, as Althusser himself admits, can be read in the terms of idealist theory, it is necessary to find a formula able to express this conception with a force equal, and opposed, to the tradition of expressive causality. Primacy of the aleatory over relationality? In my opinion, the clearest formula is: the primacy of the encounter over form. However, as mentioned beforehand, the thesis is nowhere to be found in 'The Underground Current'.

3   The Seven Theses of 'The Underground Current' and the
        Materialism of the Encounter

First, let us consider Althusser's outline of this materialism. Althusser sketches the features of a tradition that seems to have crossed the centuries while remaining invisible on the surface. This tradition he calls the *materialism of rain, of the deviation, of the encounter, and of taking hold*. Epicurus, Lucretius, Machiavelli, Spinoza, Hobbes, Rousseau, Marx, the Heideggerian *es gibt*, the Wittgensteinian *fallen*. What do these authors have in common? Their resistance, their irreducibility to a history of Western thought understood as the history of reason or metaphysics, a resistance to the great Hegelian-Heideggerian periodisation.

When he defines this materialism, Althusser says that it is included in these theses:

---

13   Althusser 1970, pp. 91–118.

1. 'thesis of the primacy of positivity over negativity (Deleuze)';[14]
2. 'the thesis of the primacy of the swerve over the rectilinearity of the straight trajectory (in which the Origin is deviation, swerve, and not reason)';[15]
3. 'thesis of the primacy of disorder over order';[16]
4. 'the thesis of the primacy of "dissemination" over the postulate that every signifier has a meaning (Derrida)';[17]
5. 'thesis of the primacy of absence over presence (Derrida)';[18]
6. 'thesis of the primacy of "nothing" over every "form" ';[19]
7. 'thesis of the primacy of aleatory materialism over every formalism'[20]

We can now summarise in a single schema the symmetrical use of the key terms:

positivity	negativity
swerve	straight line
disorder	order
dissemination	position
absence	presence
nothing	form
aleatory materialism	formalism

The fundamental philosophical references in these theses are Deleuze (thesis 1), Epicureanism (thesis 2 and 6), and Derrida (thesis 4 and 5). Between the fourth and fifth theses Althusser makes reference to Wittgenstein's *Fall* and Heidegger's *es gibt*. But the multiplication of theoretical references is unhelpful: without discussing in detail the pertinence of each one of these references (it could be done, and we could show that these references are no more than vague suggestions), I will simply say that they might be misleading when

---

14   Althusser 2006, p. 189.
15   Ibid.
16   Ibid.
17   Ibid.
18   Althusser 2006, p. 191.
19   Althusser 2006, p. 192.
20   Ibid. Matheron reports that 'this phrase was added to the manuscript' (Althusser 1994, p. 579).

brought together with the conceptuality used in the definition of the materialism of the encounter. In my opinion, the risk posed by this series of theses is
perfectly summarised by an expression that Althusser uses in referring to
Heidegger: the 'transcendental contingency of the world'. This expression is
almost meaningless but, to the extent that it is intelligible, it seems to me to
institute an hypostatisation or opposition between the subject and the world
whose encounter would necessarily take the form of contingency.

   These theses should therefore be provisionally left aside with all their ambiguity in order to take into consideration what I consider to be the fundamental
thesis: the primacy of the encounter over form. Let us see how Althusser characterises the philosophy of encounter as he addresses a brief interlude of its
underground history:

1.   For *a being* (a body, an animal, a man, state, or Prince) *to be*, an
     encounter has *to have taken* place (past infinitive). To limit our-
     selves to Machiavelli, an encounter has to have taken place between
     beings with affinities [*des affinissables*]; between such-and-such
     an individual and such-and-such a conjuncture, or Fortune, for
     example – the conjuncture itself being junction, con-junction con-
     gealed (albeit shifting) encounter, since it has already taken place,
     and refers in its turn to the infinite number of its prior causes, just
     as (let us add) a determinate [*défini*] individual (for instance,
     Borgia) refers to the infinite sequence [*suite*] of prior causes of
     which it is the result.

2.   There are encounters only between series [*séries*] of beings that are
     the results of several series of causes – at least two, but these two
     soon proliferate, by virtue of the effect of parallelism or general
     contagion (as Breton put it, profoundly, 'elephants are contagious').
     One also thinks here of Cournot, a great but neglected thinker.

3.   Every encounter is aleatory, not only in its origins (nothing ever
     guarantees an encounter), but also in its effects. In other words,
     every encounter might have not taken place, although it did take
     place; but its possible non-existence sheds light on the meaning of
     its aleatory being. And every encounter is aleatory in its effects, in
     that nothing in the elements of the encounter prefigures, before the
     actual encounter, the contours and determinations of the being
     that will emerge from it.[21]

---

21   Althusser 2006, pp. 192–3.

To summarise:

1. Every being is the product of an encounter;
2. Every encounter is the effect of other encounters *ad infinitum*;
3. Every encounter might not have taken place;
4. The elements that have given rise to the encounter do not already contain the being that will emerge from the encounter.

4   The Function of the Void

What role does the void play in such a philosophy? I would like to maintain that the emphasis on the concepts of 'nothing,' the 'null' and the 'void' has a purely rhetorical function; that contingency and the aleatory are the effect of an encounter and not of the nothing or the void. If this rhetorical function is transformed into a theoretical proposition, it risks transforming the theory of the encounter into a theory of the event or of freedom.

We can see the form in which these terms appear in the outline of the authors of the 'underground current':

–   in Epicurus and Lucretius, the void is what allows the parallel fall of atoms while the null or nothing is the clinamen, 'the "nothing" of the swerve' that initiates the piling up of atoms;[22]
–   in Machiavelli, the nothing lurks in the conditions for Italian unity: 'a nameless man [*homme sans nom*]', who comes from 'a *nameless corner* of Italy [*dans un coin d'Italie sans nom*]'. Althusser further affirms that among the conditions for regeneration are 'a man of nothing [*homme de rien*] who has started out from nothing [*parti de rien*]'.[23]
–   in Spinoza, the void is 'the object [itself] of philosophy' in the paradoxical sense that his philosophy voids the concepts of teleology, epistemology, morality and politics through a labour of 'deconstruction' that, following the lessons of Machiavelli, 'who evacuated [*fit la vide*] all of Plato's and Aristotle's philosophical concepts in order to think the possibility of making Italy a national state'.[24]

---

22   Althusser 2006, p. 191.
23   Althusser 2006, p. 172.
24   Althusser 2006, pp. 176, 178, 175.

- in Hobbes, the void appears as the foundation of freedom, as the absence of any obstacle to movement;[25]
- in Rousseau, the void comes on stage in the figure of the forest of the state of nature, that represents '*a radical absence* [néant] *of society*'[26] and in the figure of the cataclysm that puts an end to this state, and in the 'abyss...represented by the relapse into the state of nature' that determines the true meaning of *The Social Contract.*[27]

If we pay attention to the theoretical strategy that commands the appearing of these terms, we can see clearly that the emphasis placed on them is purely rhetorical: the nothing of the Epicurean *clinamen* as well as Rousseau's nothing of society are the effect of a philosophical strategy deployed in order to undo the conceptual horizon within which these authors found themselves, namely that of Aristotle and *jusnaturalism*. The nothing of Machiavelli that Althusser insists on when he speaks of Valentino is, in turn, a pure and simple mistake. Far from being an '*homme de rien*' who came from nothing, Cesare is the son of Alessandro VI, protected and advised by his father and nominated to the post of Gonfaloniere of the Papal states. The philosophical voids of Spinoza and Machiavelli are the description of a precise philosophical strategy. It is true that Althusser flirts with Derrida's 'deconstruction', but far from being assimilable to a hermeneutic tradition that annuls all differences, we are confronted in fact with a limit case of philosophical activity, which consists in occupying, in a conflictual mode, a position in 'the thick of an already occupied world'.[28] Hobbes's void, finally, is nothing other than the absence of determinations external to action, certainly not an absolute absence of determinations.

That the concepts 'void', 'nothing' and 'null' are not necessary for thinking the encounter is demonstrated, it seems to me, by the fact that these concepts disappear when Althusser comes around to dealing with Marx (and we should not lose sight of the fact that the reconstruction of the underground current is at bottom nothing more than a methodological premise for this rereading of Marx) and opposes, in Marx's thought, an aleatory conception of the mode of

---

25   Althusser 2006, p. 181.

26   Althusser 2006, p. 184.

27   Althusser 2006, p. 186.

28   Althusser 1976, p. 165. In a later text, this theoretical strategy is likened to the 'theory of the urban guerilla and the encirclement of cities by the countryside dear to Mao' (Althusser 1998, p. 11).

production to a teleological one.[29] The only two occurrences of the term 'void' have the task of showing the difference between the aleatory and teleological conceptions of the mode of production: 'Here the specific histories no longer float in history, like so many atoms in the void, at the mercy of an "encounter" that might not take place. Everything is accomplished in advance; *the structure precedes its elements and reproduces them in order to reproduce the structure*.'[30] And:

> We are at the opposite pole of the conception of the '*encounter between the bourgeoisie*', an element that floats as much as the others, and *other floating elements*, an encounter that brings an original mode of production into existence, the capitalist mode of production. Here there is no encounter, for the unity precedes the elements, *for the void essential to any encounter is lacking* [ce vide nécessaire à toute rencontre aléatoire]. Whereas it is in fact a question of thinking *the fact to be accomplished*, Marx deliberately positions himself within the *accomplished fact*, and invites us to follow him in the laws of its necessity.[31]

The void is now nothing more than the condition of possibility of floating, of fluctuation. It is the concept necessary for thinking fluctuation; it is the absence of any plan before the encounter among elements. The void has no meaning in itself.[32]

Starting from this point, the inadequacy of all those theses that do not underline the element of encounter seems to be clearly outlined: terms such as 'positivity', 'deviation', 'disorder', 'dissemination', 'absence' and 'nothing' risk being ambiguous or misleading if not understood by means of the category of encounter. They have the merit, to be sure, of making links to other thoughts, emphasising certain affinities, and building alliances on the philosophical

---

29   This is said *apertis verbis* on pp. 15–16 of the typescript: the aim of the text is to 'to call Marx's philosophical phantasms by their name, idealism, and…to call the authentic materialist tradition he belongs to by its name…. This is why I would take up again here the task at the point where my first clumsy essays and later rectifications left things. To see more clearly, and if possibly finally clearly into Marx's theory, and into his theoretical thought' (Archives IMEC).

30   Althusser 2006, p. 200.

31   Althusser 2006, p. 202.

32   On this point, see Morfino and Pinzolo 2005, pp. 151–2; see also Morfino 2005. Further proof of the theoretical inessentiality of these concepts is their absence in a typescript dated September 22, 1966, with the title 'On Genesis', in which Althusser proposes to show how a 'theory of the encounter' or 'theory of conjunction' should replace 'the ideological (religious) category of genesis' (see Althusser 2011).

Kampfplatz, but they also tend to conceal what is truly unprecedented in Althusser's materialism.

5 Althusser's Two Rains

Let us now go back to the first page of Althusser's text. It is, from a literary point of view, very beautiful:

> It is raining.
> Let this book therefore be, before all else, a book about ordinary rain.
> Malebranche wondered 'why it rains upon sands, upon highways and seas,' since this water from the sky which, elsewhere, waters crops (and that is very good), adds nothing to the water of the sea, or goes to waste on the roads and beaches.
> Our concern will not be with that kind of rain, providential or anti-providential.
> Quite the contrary: this book is about another kind of rain, about a profound theme which runs through the whole history of philosophy and was contested and repressed there as soon as it was stated: the 'rain' (Lucretius) of Epicurus' atoms that fall parallel to each other in the void; the 'rain' of the parallelism of the infinite attributes in Spinoza and many others: Machiavelli, Hobbes, Rousseau, Marx, Heidegger too, and Derrida.[33]

In the following lines, Althusser arrives at a definition of the underground current, namely a 'materialism of rain'.[34] Yet Althusser's text does not keep the promise of its splendid opening. This will not be a book about rain. The metaphor of rain will rarely return, and not always with pertinence to the passages in which it appears: the rain of Epicurus's atoms, Machiavelli's Italian states, Spinoza's parallel attributes, the men in Rousseau's forest, the parallel marches of workers and students in the French May. These rains are modelled on Epicurus's rain of atoms, the vertical and parallel fall of primal bodies that, with the *clinamen*, pile up and give birth to worlds. But this rain, it should be emphasised, is not a metaphor for the thesis of the primacy of the encounter over form, but rather of another thesis that is perhaps complementary to it, the thesis of the primacy of the *non*-encounter over the encounter: before the

---

33   Althusser 2006, p. 167.
34   Ibid.

encounter that originates a world, atoms fall like raindrops without encountering one another, and their existence as elements that will make up a world is entirely abstract.

The rain that opens the writing, the rain that falls on the harvest fields, on the road, on the desert or the sea, is left aside as if it were a beautiful image with no relevance. But in my opinion, this is actually the theoretical core of the text: this is actually the rain Aristotle spoke of, long before Malebranche, in a fundamental paragraph of *Physics* (§ 8, book II). It is a paragraph that closes a book, the second book, where some of the concepts that constitute the veritable cardinal points of the Western tradition emerge: substance [*ousia*], chance [*automaton*], and fortune [*tuche*]. Now, within the weave of this conceptual fabric Aristotle inserts the fundamental thesis of his philosophy: the primacy of form over matter. Form as structure, as the internal organisation of living beings, is the nature (and therefore substance) of matter and it can be traced back to three of the four senses in which we speak of cause (efficient, formal, and final).[35] And it also appears at the moment when Aristotle traces a line of demarcation with respect to the tradition for which 'fortune and chance are among the causes', taking his distance from an atomism that posits chance at the origin of the world and also from the popular religion of *Tuche*, for which fortune would be a cause hidden to human thought, something divine or demonic. It is once again the concept of form that allows him to draw out this line of demarcation through the construction of the theory of chance and fortune. It is well worth the effort to dwell on this a bit longer.

6   Rain Falling on Fields of Grain

Aristotle distinguishes among 1) things that always happen in the same way, 2) those that happen normally and for the most part in the same way, and 3) those that occur neither always nor normally, which he calls fortuitous. Fortune and chance are not involved in the first two types of events, but only those events in the third group which happen in view of an end, whether or not there is some choice at their origin. Chance therefore involves those events that take place neither always nor normally and for the most part, but occur both in view of an end in an accidental way and if there is no choice at their origin, while fortune is involved in those events that do not take place always or normally, but accidentally, and have a choice at their origin. Let us read Aristotle's example:

---

35   See Repellini's commentary in Aristotle 1995, p. 95.

Example: A man is engaged in collecting subscriptions for a feast. He would have gone to such and such a place for the purpose of getting the money, if he had known. He actually went there for another purpose and it was only incidentally that he got his money by going there; and this was not due to the fact that he went there as a rule or necessarily, nor is the end effected (getting the money) a cause present in himself – it belongs to the class of things that are intentional and the result of intelligent deliberation. It is when these conditions are satisfied that the man is said to have gone 'by chance'. If he had gone of deliberate purpose and for the sake of this – if he always or normally went there when he was collecting payments – he would not be said to have gone 'by chance'.[36]

The chance that is commonly understood as what has no cause does not, for Aristotle, exist; it only has a sense with respect to a causal order that, therefore, it presupposes. Everything that happens has a cause: a rock falls by virtue of its nature; a man goes to the market to buy things. These are natural processes. However, these events do not happen all by themselves, but in the midst of other natural processes. It happens that some processes are intertwined with others: a rock falls and hits a man who is passing by, a man goes to the market to meet his debtor and collect his debt. In both cases there are encounters between two causal processes: in fact, the man who is hit is going that way for a determined reason, just as the debtor goes to the market for a determined reason. Now, what in this weaving together of causal processes makes us speak of chance and fortune is an apparent teleology, an 'as if': it seems as if this weave of processes has a sense, is traversed by an intention. It can seem as if the rock fell with the intention of killing, it can seem that the man went to the market in order to collect his debt as if at the origin there was the goal of collecting. But in reality there is no such thing: the goal of the rock is to fall to the ground, its cause *per se*, and by accident it kills the man; the man's goal was to go to the market to spend money, his cause *per se*, and by accident he encountered his creditor.[37]

On the basis of this theory of chance Aristotle is able to refute Democritus's position, for whom chance is the cause of 'this heavenly sphere and all the worlds':[38]

---

36   Aristotle 1984, vol. 1, p. 27.

37   For this interpretation of Aristotelian theory of chance and fortune, I make reference to the fine commentary by Repellini (Aristotle 1995, pp. 102–4).

38   Aristotle 1984, vol. 1, p. 26.

Chance and Fortune are causes of effects which though they might result from intelligence or nature, have in fact been caused by something incidentally. Now since nothing which is incidental is prior to what is *per se*, it is clear that no incidental cause can be prior to a cause *per se*. Chance and fortune, therefore, are posterior to intelligence and nature. Hence, however true it may be that the heavens are due to spontaneity, it will still be true that intelligence and nature will be prior causes of this All and of many things in it besides.[39]

In these lines, Aristotle affirms the primacy of the intellect and of nature over chance and fortune, i.e., to translate Aristotle's language into Althusser's terminology, the primacy of form over the encounter. However, in paragraph 8 Aristotle hesitates, sensing that a radical objection might be made to his theoretical construction, an objection that is completely integral to the definition of chance as apparent teleology. Aristotle wonders if *every* teleology is not in reality only apparent; in other words, if every form is not in reality an effect of chance. Here is the extraordinary Aristotelian passage:

A difficulty presents itself: why should not nature work, not for the sake of something, nor because it is better so, but just as the sky rains, not in order to make the corn grow, but of necessity? (What is drawn up must cool, and what has been cooled must become water and descend, the result of this being that the corn grows.) Similarly if a man's crop is spoiled on the threshing-floor, the rain did not fall for the sake of this – in order that the crop might be spoiled – but that result just followed. Why then should it not be the same with the parts in nature, e.g. that our teeth should come up of necessity – the front teeth sharp, fitted for tearing, the molars broad and useful for grinding down the food – since they did not arise for this end, but it was merely a coincident result; and so with all other parts in which we suppose that there is purpose? Wherever then all the parts came about just what they would have been if they had come to be for an end, such things survived, being organized spontaneously in a fitting way; whereas those which grew otherwise perished and continue to perish, as Empedocles says his 'man-faced oxprogeny' did.[40]

Everything could have happened by necessity and not for the sake of an end. It rains; this is a fact. Rain can have positive effects, making crops grow, or negative effects, spoiling crops on the threshing floor. In both cases it does not

---

39 Aristotle 1984, vol. 1, p. 30 (translation modified).
40 Aristotle 1984, vol. 1, p. 31.

rain for the sake of an end, but out of necessity [*ex anagkes*]. Aristotle wonders if every form might be thought on this model of rain and its possible effects on grain. Forms would be none other than the result of a successful combination of necessity, a good organisation that for this reason persists; by contrast, bad organisations perish and have perished like those calves with human faces. Forms, then, do not exist because they are produced with a view toward existing, but because they are causally adapted to existence.

Aristotle discards this hypotheses, on the basis of the use of the language whose structures, he thinks, are identical with the very ontological structures of reality: and in language, as Wieland perfectly summarises, 'where we speak of chance, teleological structures are already presupposed'.[41]

7   The Primacy of the Encounter over Form: Rereading Darwin

What I would like to argue is that Althusser's position is diametrically opposed to Aristotle's, and that the thesis that is never written *apertis verbis* in 'The Underground Current' is in fact its fundamental theoretical centre: the primacy of the encounter over form.

Beginning with a survey of Althusser's text (however relevant such a survey might be when we are dealing with an editorial 'montage'), we find that the word 'form' occurs twenty-five times in the singular or plural (the term 'formation' occurs four times), the term 'encounter' appears one hundred and twenty-two times in the singular and four times in the plural, and that the term *'prise'* ['take'] occurs as a substantive or a past participle thirty-four times. The high frequency of these terms in various combinations (the form taken by the encounter, the encounter that does or does not take hold, etc.) is the first textual evidence for the centrality of this thesis.

A second argument seems to me, however, more relevant. The thesis of the primacy of the encounter over form can be read in a totally new light when we juxtapose it with an author that Althusser refers to only once: Charles Darwin. Let us consider the context in which Althusser cites Darwin:

> If we must therefore say that there can be no result without its becoming (Hegel), we must also affirm that there is nothing which has become except as determined by the result of this becoming: this is retroaction itself (Canguilhem). That is, instead of thinking contingency as a

---

41   Wieland 1962, p. 146.

modality of necessity, or an exception to it, we must think necessity as the becoming-necessary of the encounter of contingencies.

Thus we see that not only the world of life (the biologists, who should have known their Darwin, have recently become aware of this), but the world of history, too, *gels* at certain felicitous moments, with the taking-hold of elements combined in an encounter that is apt to trace such-and-such a figure: such-and-such a species, individual, or people.[42]

The role Althusser lets Darwin play here is extremely clear: Darwin is played off against Hegel, with Marx in turn at stake. What is at stake is the possibility of distinguishing between an aleatory and a teleological theory of the mode of production. Darwin's role is fundamental because it provides Althusser a model for applying the thesis of the primacy of the encounter over form in its treatment of the natural world. No 'transcendental contingency of the world', just the emergence of every natural form from a complex encounter among an extremely large number of elements.

As stated above, in paragraph 8 of his *Physics* Aristotle contemplated the possibility of such a theory before refusing it. In the first pages of his *Historical Sketch of the Progress of Opinion on the Origin of Species*, Darwin actually quotes this same passage from Aristotle, adding: 'We here see the principle of Natural Selection shadowed forth, but how little Aristotle fully comprehended the principle, is shown by his remarks on the formation of the teeth'.[43] Now, that Darwin's theory is opposed to Aristotle's is in a certain sense admitted even in common sense. What is much less obvious is that the theory of Darwin is opposed to Hegel's philosophy. The theory of natural selection, and Althusser is clearly referring to this, has for a long time been interpreted as a theory of progress, of the evolution of forms, in a way that is completely compatible with the syntax of Hegel's logic (as is demonstrated, moreover, in Engel's *Dialectics of Nature*).[44]

Let us now try to read the *Origins of Species* from this perspective. *A first theoretical element* of fundamental importance is the erosion of the concept of form itself, produced by the observation of species' variations in their natural state. Darwin remarks that 'no one definition [of the term species] has satisfied all naturalists',[45] and that 'the term "variety" is almost equally difficult to

---

42   Althusser 2006, pp. 193–4.
43   Darwin 1988, vol. 16, p. xiii.
44   See above, pp. 19–45.
45   Darwin 1988, vol. 16, p. 34.

define';[46] the monstrosities shade into variety and are either a 'deviation of structure, generally injurious, or not useful to the species'.[47] Species, varieties, and monstrosities are therefore grades of individual differentiation that are not separated by strong ontological coordinates. This introduces uncertainty and arbitrariness into naturalist classifications. According to Darwin, we can construct a sort of progressive ladder which goes from individual differences (small differences that occur in the descendants of a same parent, the first step toward variety) to larger and more persistent differences in variety (stages of variety that are more stable and characteristic), up to subspecies and finally to species:

> The passage from one stage of difference to another may, in many cases, be the simple result of the nature of the organism and of the different physical conditions to which it has long been exposed; but with respect to the more important and adaptive characters, the passage from one stage of difference to another, may be safely attributed to the cumulative action of Natural Selection ... A well-marked variety may therefore be called an incipient species.[48]

A second fundamental theoretical element lies in focusing on the struggle for existence as the selective mechanism of forms. Darwin asks himself 'how have all those exquisite adaptations of one part of the organization to another part, and to the condition of life, and of one organic being to another being, been perfected'.[49] And he asks, 'how is it that varieties, which I have called incipient species, become ultimately converted into good and distinct species, which in most cases obviously differ from each other far more than do the varieties of the same species'?[50] The well-known answer is that useful variations are conserved in the struggle for existence. But the expression 'struggle for existence' must be understood in a broad and metaphorical sense: in an analogy with the concept of domestic selection, which is the subject of the first chapter of *The Origin of Species*, Darwin calls this complex weave of relations 'natural selection'. This concept is not however presented as an instance of transcendent (and therefore finalist) selection; useful variations are in fact conserved as an effect of the organism's 'infinitely complex relations to other organic beings

---

46   Ibid.
47   Ibid.
48   Darwin 1988, vol. 16, p. 43.
49   Darwin 1988, vol. 16, p. 50.
50   Darwin 1988, vol. 16, pp. 50–1.

and to external nature'. The expression 'struggle for existence' should therefore be understood in a metaphorical sense: the concept that underpins it is the reciprocal dependence of all individuals, and it is a struggle for existence between individuals of the same species, between different species, and finally, of all individuals against the conditions of life. In other words, the struggle for existence never acts as a single and simple instance, but as a network of infinitely complex relations between plants, animals and climatic conditions of a determined geographical location (as Canguilhem correctly notes, Darwin's environment is 'bio-geographical').[51] Let us look at Darwin's example:

> In Staffordshire, on the estate of a relation, where I had ample means of investigation, there was a large and extremely barren heath, which had never been touched by the hand of man; but several hundred acres of exactly the same nature had been enclosed twenty-five years previously and planted with Scotch fir. The change in the native vegetation of the planted part of the heath was most remarkable, more than is generally seen in passing from one quite different soil to another; not only the proportional numbers of the heath-plants were wholly changed, but twelve species of plants (not counting grasses and carices) flourished in the plantations, which could not be found on the heath. The effect on the insects must have been still greater, for six insectivorous birds were very common in the plantations, which were not to be seen on the heath; and the heath was frequented by two or three distinct insectivorous birds. Here we see how potent has been the effect of the introduction of a single tree, nothing whatever else having been done, with the exception of the land having been enclosed, so that cattle could not enter. But how important an element enclosure is, I plainly saw near Farnham, in Surrey. Here there are extensive heaths, with a few clumps of old Scotch firs on the distant hilltops: within the last ten years large spaces have been enclosed, and self-sown firs are now springing up in multitudes, so close together that all cannot live. When I ascertained that these young trees had not been sown or planted, I was so much surprised at their numbers that I went to several points of view, whence I could examine hundreds of acres of the unenclosed heath, and literally I could not see a single Scotch fir, except the old planted clumps. But on looking closely between the stems of the heath, I found a multitude of seedlings and little trees which had been perpetually browsed down by the cattle. In one square yard, at a point some hundred yards distant from one of the old clumps, I counted

---

51   Canguilhem 2008, p. 106.

thirty-two little trees; and one of them, with twenty-six rings of growth, had, during many years tried to raise its head above the stems of the heath, and had failed. No wonder that, as soon as the land was enclosed, it became thickly clothed with vigorously growing young firs. Yet the heath was so extremely barren and so extensive that no one would ever have imagined that cattle would have so closely and effectually searched it for food. Here we see that cattle absolutely determine the existence of the Scotch fir; but in several parts of the world insects determine the existence of cattle. Perhaps Paraguay offers the most curious instance of this; for here neither cattle nor horses nor dogs have ever run wild, though they swarm southward and northward in a feral state; and Azara and Rengger have shown that this is caused by the greater number in Paraguay of a certain fly, which lays its eggs in the navels of these animals when first born. The increase of these flies, numerous as they are, must be habitually checked by some means, probably by other parasitic insects. Hence, if certain insectivorous bird were to decrease in Paraguay, the parasitic insects would probably increase; and this would lessen the number of the navel-frequenting flies – then cattle and horses would became feral, and this would certainly greatly alter (as indeed I have observed in parts of South America) the vegetation: this again would largely affect the insects; and this, as we have just seen in Staffordshire, the insectivorous birds, and so onwards in ever-increasing circles of complexity.[52]

Darwin adds that relations are not, however, always as simple as this: 'battle within battle must be continually recurring with varying success'.[53] Natural beings are 'bound together by a web of complex relations'[54] and the average number of individuals of a species is produced by 'many different checks, acting at different periods of life, and [which] during different seasons or years, probably come into play'. Selection is therefore in no way a kind of conscious choice of nature (in fact nature does not really appear as a whole, but only as a 'web of complex relations') nor does it itself produce the variations. It acts only insofar as it weaves the complex relations on individual variations:

It may metaphorically be said that Natural Selection is daily and hourly scrutinizing, through the world, the slightest variations: rejecting those that are bad, preserving and adding up all that are good; silently and

52   Darwin 1988, vol. 16, pp. 58–9.
53   Darwin 1988, vol. 16, p. 59.
54   Ibid.

insensibly working, whenever and wherever opportunity offers, at the improvement of each organic being in relation to its organic and inorganic conditions of life.[55]

A *third fundamental theoretical element* is the Darwinian concepts of order and time. *Order* is nothing other than the temporary balancing of forces in this web of complex relations. It is not some type of transcendent or immanent nature that guides the action of individuals, but a complex web whose balance can be lost with the variation of any of the factors that enter into its complex structure:

> [...] in the long-run the forces are so nicely balanced, that the face of nature remains for long periods of time uniform, though assuredly the merest trifle would give the victory to one organic being over another. Nevertheless, so profound is our ignorance, and so high our presumption, that we marvel when we hear of the extinction of an organic being; and as we do not see the cause, we invoke cataclysm to desolate the world, or invent laws on the duration of the forms of life![56]

Time then has no influence over natural selection and it should not be thought that 'all life forms were necessarily undergoing change through some innate law':[57]

> Lapse of time is only so far important, and this importance in this respect is great, that it gives a better chance of beneficial variations arising, and of their being selected, accumulated, and fixed. It likewise tends to increase the direct action of the physical condition of life, in relation to the constitution of each organism.[58]

Order and time cannot be, therefore, articulated in a theoretical syntax which transforms the theory of natural selection, i.e., the theory of the complex relations of natural beings, into a philosophy of nature and of history under the banner of the teleological evolution of forms, a sort of 'poor man's Hegelianism', as Althusser nicely put it in 'Is it Simple to be a Marxist in Philosophy?'[59]

---

55   Darwin 1988, vol. 16, pp. 68–9.
56   Darwin 1988, vol. 16, p. 59.
57   Darwin 1988, vol. 16, p. 86.
58   Ibid.
59   Althusser 1976, p. 186.

8   Darwin and Aleatory Materialism

Far from being a marginal reference in 'The Underground Current', Darwin's theory seems to me to be its invisible centre. The fundamental core of Darwin's thesis is not the thesis concerning the evolution of forms (against fixism). It is instead the thesis concerning the primacy of the encounter over form, i.e., the contingency not so much of the world (a term which has no sense in Darwin's thought) but of each and every form, insofar as each is the result of a complex weave of encounters, each of which is necessary, but according to a necessity that, if I may deploy an oxymoron, is completely aleatory, that is, deprived of both project and *telos*. In this sense, the elements that have come together are not there for the sake of the form, with each having its own history, each an effect in its turn of a weave of encounters that have taken place or, to the contrary, of encounters that have been missed.[60] In this sense, that is, if we agree that both *telos* and project are rejected (as well as the correlative concept of nature as order), Darwin seems to provide a model that is perfectly compatible with the thesis of the primacy of the encounter over form and of the relation over the elements. The complex weave of relations that constitutes the stable face of nature in a given period is not an order and guarantee of stability, but a complex weave of encounters, where the very fact that one of them takes place or does not can reconfigure the entire ensemble of encounters, as Darwin writes, 'in circles of increasing complexity'.

---

60   Aristotle writes: 'For the generation is for the sake of the substance and not this for the sake of the generation' (Aristotle 1984, I, p. 996). And: 'In order of time, then, the material and the generative process must necessarily be anterior; but in logical order the substance and form of each being precedes the material. This is evident if one only tries to define the process of formation. For the definition of house-building includes that of the house; but the definition of the house does not include that of house-building; and the same is true of all other productions. So that it must necessarily be that the elementary material exists for the sake of the homogeneous parts, seeing that these are genetically posterior to it, just as the heterogeneous parts are posterior genetically to them. For these heterogeneous parts have reached the end and goal, having the third degree of composition, in which development often attains its final term. Animals, then, are composed of homogeneous parts, and are also composed of heterogeneous parts. The former, however, exist for the sake of the latter. For the active functions and operations of the body are carried on by these; that is, by the heterogeneous parts, such as the eye, the nostril, the whole face, the fingers, the hand, and the whole arm. But inasmuch as there is a great variety in the functions and motions not only of the whole animal but also of the individual organs, it is necessary that the substances out of which these are composed shall present a diversity of powers' (Aristotle 1984, I, p. 1006).

THE PRIMACY OF THE ENCOUNTER OVER FORM

It seems to me that it is precisely this model that allows Althusser to distinguish between a teleological and an aleatory conception of the mode of
production: the Darwinian example of the effect of an enclosure on the flora
and fauna of Staffordshire allows for a suggestive resonance (and no more than
a resonance, clearly) with the effect of the enclosures on the birth of the capitalist mode of production in England.

As is well known, upon reading *The Origin of Species*, Marx wrote this to
Engels: '[a] book which, in the field of natural history, provides the basis for our
view'.[61] This judgment of Marx's was canonised with the famous phrases
uttered by Engels over Marx's tomb: 'Just as Darwin discovered the law of
development of organic nature, so Marx discovered the law of development of
human history'. In order to understand this judgment it is, however, necessary
to understand the way in which Marx and Engels read Darwin. The aleatory
that holds sway in Darwin's theory, the complete absence of any idea of progress or of the gradual perfecting of living forms, is completely denied both by
Marx and by Engels. In an 1861 letter to Lassalle, it is true, Marx does affirm that
in Darwin a 'death-blow [is] dealt here for the first time to "teleology" in the
natural sciences', but immediately afterward he adds that '[the] rational meaning [of "teleology"] is empirically explained'. *The Origin of Species* was nothing
more than the empirical confirmation of the teleological syntax of Hegel, just
as the laws of evolution of the modes of production was nothing more than the
empirical confirmation of the Hegelian philosophy of history (or its being
turned right side up, if you prefer). Rediscovering Darwin while getting rid of
Darwinism allows Althusser to read Marx in a completely different way, finding in some chapters of *Capital* an aleatory conception of the mode of production. Of course, Darwin here is not used as a biological foundation or basis for
the conception of history. He is instead a methodological model and safeguard
against any and all linear conceptions of the development of forms at whatever level of complexity might be involved. As Althusser writes in a passage we
have already read, 'For *a being* (a body, an animal, a man, state, or Prince) *to be*,
an encounter has *to have taken* place (past infinitive)'.

That all of this is not simply a conjecture, a nice exercise in philosophical
construction with no historical support, is demonstrated by a note (one of the
very few in the text) that Althusser adds to the single occurrence of the name
Darwin in his text: 'See the fine and very successful Darwin conference recently
organized in Chantilly by Dominique Lecourt and Yvette Conry'.[62] In the acts

---

61   Marx to Engels, 19 December 1860, Marx Engels 1975–2005, vol. 41, p. 232.
62   Althusser 2006, p. 194.

of this colloquium,[63] held in Paris from September 13–16, 1982, there is a beautiful article by Dominique Lecourt, one of Althusser's closest students, with the title 'Marx through the lens of Darwin', in which we find meticulously reconstructed the Hegelian conceptual framework Marx and Engels used to read Darwin, showing how these, 'contrary to what the Marxist tradition, notably, would have us believe, have passed Darwin by', and that 'this contempt resulted in the strange bedfellows of Marxism and evolutionism'.[64]

In conclusion, Lecourt writes that 'the order of exposition in *Capital*... allows us to see ... a countermovement of Marx's thought ... in the chapter on "primitive accumulation", as well as in the chapter on the "working day"'.[65] And at the centre of this countermovement there is the category of the 'encounter' (and not the 'void or the nothing'): but Marx, instead of developing this theme, one for which he could have found illustrious predecessors in Machiavelli and Epicurus, instead takes cover in the Hegelian concept of becoming.

But what does Darwin have to do with this countermovement? Lecourt devotes his conclusion to Darwin. What would have happened if Marx had read Darwin other than as a theory of necessary progress, that is, if the encounter had not taken the form of a misunderstanding?

> He would have found in Darwin not some occasion for transposing Darwin's contingency into a theory of history, since this theory would by itself have denounced in advance the reasons for such a transposition. I repeat, he would have instead had the occasion to change his philosophical position, and to open up, against the conservative tendency of his inverted Hegelianism, a perspective for his thought in the direction of a countermovement by which it was mutely animated. He would have, perhaps, come to the idea that history is neither 'more nor less easy' to know than nature; that the metaphysical couple history/nature should be itself put into question; and that thinking history outside of this couple is to expose oneself to the recognition that nowhere is the guarantee of its sense, or its 'progress' hidden away.[66]

Translated by Jason E. Smith

---

63   Conry 1983.
64   Lecourt 1983, p. 241.
65   Lecourt 1983, p. 247.
66   Lecourt 1983, pp. 247–8.

CHAPTER 5

The Syntax of Violence between Hegel and Marx

1   The Midwife of History

There is a well-known sentence in Marx on the matter of violence that is a good starting point for drawing a diagram of the syntax of violence in Marx and Hegel. At the end of Chapter 24 of *Capital*, Marx exclaims: 'Violence [*Gewalt*] is the midwife [*Geburtshelfer*] of every old society pregnant with a new one. It is itself an economic power [*Potenz*]'.[1]

This passage seems to provide us with a key to the meaning of the plurality of histories described within this chapter, especially because it can be found in the conclusion to this chapter on primitive accumulation. Is this truly the case? We will come back to this matter further on. For now let us limit ourselves to a closer analysis of Marx's proposition. What does the metaphor used here refer to? First, that violence is indeed an economic power, but also that it is a marginal element within the historic process, and second, that a new society already exists at the heart of the older one and is simply waiting to rise up from within it. If we interrogate the use of the metaphor of pregnancy within the philosophical tradition more generally, we find that it is at the centre of Leibniz's monadology and of the idea of temporality that it implies: 'the present is pregnant with what is to come',[2] exclaims Leibniz in paragraph 22 of the *Monadology*. 'The present is pregnant with the future, the future can be read in the past',[3] he adds in paragraph 13 of the *Principles of Nature and of Grace*. The metaphor indicated the way in which the different states of every monad follow one another according to a *lex seriei* that is, by virtue of a pre-established harmony, the very law of History and of its Progress. Marx's proposition therefore seems to establish a linear development of historical time in which a *lex seriei* governs the transition from one society to another, marked by moments in which violence appears.

As is also well known, Engels dedicated some chapters of the *Anti-Dühring* to defining the role of violence in history, a role he finds perfectly synthesised

---

1   Marx Engels 1975–2005, vol. 35, p. 739.
2   Leibniz 1970, p. 645.
3   Leibniz 1970, p. 640.

in Marx's proposition. With the aim of better understanding the theoretical stakes at play here, I intend to demonstrate that the conception of violence found in Marx's famous sentence is commanded by a Hegelian conceptual syntax whose logical structure can be detailed in two fundamental chapters of Hegel's *Science of Logic* as well as in the historical dialectic found in some decisive passages from Hegel's philosophy of right and his philosophy of history.

2   Violence in 'Actuality' [*Wirklichkeit*]

The first of the two theoretical sites where Hegel deals with the question of violence, of *Gewalt*, is in the third section of the *Doctrine of Essence*, concerned with *Wirklichkeit* or 'Actuality'. In this section, the binary logic produced by the dialecticisation of the categories of the metaphysical tradition tends, finally, to arrive at the unity of the concept. Here, right on the threshold of the concept, in the *Zwischen* between the realm of necessity and the realm of freedom, the first significant occurrence of the term *Gewalt* appears in the dialectic of causality: namely, a *wirken* that presupposes an alterity, something external. The cause acts on itself as if it were an other, which therefore appears as a passive substance. First, it takes away its being other and returns into itself, and, second, it posits this return into itself as a determination, i.e., it determines it. The passive substance therefore has a double nature, because on the one hand it is presupposed as independent, as an alterity, and on the other hand, it is identical with the agent of causality.

It is at this level of the deduction that Hegel inserts the concept of *Gewalt*. Violence emerges with the action of active substance on passive substance, which is said to suffer or undergo – *leiden* – violence. Let us examine the long passage that Hegel dedicates to the formulation of this concept:

> Violence is the *manifestation of power* [*Erscheinung der Macht*], or power *as external* [*die Macht als Äußerliches*]. But power is external only in so far as causal substance in its action, that is, in the positing of itself, is at the same time presupposing, that is, it posits itself as sublated [*aufgehobenes*]. Conversely, the act of violence is equally an act of power. It is only on an other presupposed by itself on which the violent cause [*gewaltige Ursache*] acts, its effect thereon is a negative relation *to itself*. The passive is the self subsistent that is only something *posited*, something that is broken within itself; an actuality which is condition, and condition, too, which is now in its truth, that is, an actuality that is only a possibility, or, conversely, an in-itself that is only the *determinateness of the in-itself*, is only passive. Therefore not only is it possible to do violence

to that which suffers it, but also violence *must* be done to it; that which acts violently on the other can do so only because it is the power [*Gewalt*] over it, the power in which it *manifests* both itself and the other. Through violence, passive substance is only *posited* as what it is in truth, namely, to be only something *posited*, just because it is the simple positive, or immediate substance; what it is *before-hand* [*das Voraus*] as condition, is the illusory [*Schein*] immediacy which active causality [*wirkende Causalität*] strips off from.[4]

The action of power [*Macht*], the power of acting substance on passive substance, is a violent [*gewaltige*] action; but it is an action that it performs on itself, i.e., on substance that is at once both the presupposition of this act and that is in itself identical to this action. This substance is what makes possible the manifestation of action itself. What *appears* as a violence exercised by an agent on something passive is an optical illusion; in reality, the agent does nothing but strip or take away the immediacy of the passive element (or better, the passive substance that is posited as a presupposition of its action) and reveals the presupposed exteriority and immediacy as something posited by this power. Violence is, in conclusion, the *Erscheinung*, the phenomenal appearing of power through which passive substance becomes what it always-already is, what it was always destined to be.

Hegel concludes in this manner:

Passive substance therefore only receives its due through the action on it of another power [*Der passiven Substanz wird daher durch die Einwirkung einer andern Gewalt nur ihr Recht angethan*]. What it *loses* is that *immediacy*, the substantiality which is *alien to it*. What it, as something alien, *receives*, namely, to be determined as a *positedness*, is its own determination. But now in being posited in its positedness, or in *its own* determination, the outcome is not that it is sublated, but rather that it only *unites with its own self* and therefore *in being determined* is, in fact, *originative*. On the one hand, therefore, the passive substance is *preserved* or *posited* by the active substance, namely, in so far as the latter makes itself into a sublated [*aufgehobene*] substance; but, on the other hand, it is the *act of the passive substance itself* to unite with itself and thus to make itself into the originative and into *cause*. Its *being posited* by an other, and its own *becoming* are one and the same thing [*ein und daßelbe*].[5]

---

4 Hegel 1989, pp. 567–8.
5 Hegel 1989, p. 568.

Passive substance gets from violence what it deserves (its 'due'). It loses its immediacy and is given its determination as a positedness. Passive substance is therefore posited by active substance as being posited in itself, and so 'receive[s] the *effect* of the latter within it'; but it also produces a 'reaction ... *against the first active cause*'.[6] And yet where in determined causality the cause that an individual *is* and the cause that an individual *has* were still distinct, in action and reaction each individual is both cause and effect. Action and reaction do not therefore produce the bad infinity of indeterminate regression and the indeterminate progress of transitive causality, but an 'infinite reciprocal action' that is nothing other than a causality folded back onto itself that abandons the imperfect geometric metaphor of the straight line in order to assume the perfect metaphor of the circle. And thus the path to reciprocal action or 'reciprocity' [*Wechselwirkung*] is opened up, as a mutual causality of substances that reciprocally presuppose and condition each other. Every residue of immediacy is then sublated (as posited), and we are confronted in this way no longer with substrates but with substances. Reciprocal action is causality itself, the concept of causality itself, causality that has risen to the level of the concept: *causa sui*.

Let us now move away from the Hegelian discourse to observe the strategy from afar. In order to make possible the leap from the realm of necessity to the realm of freedom, from substance to subject, from darkness to transparency and to light, an instance of violence must necessarily intervene. This instance has the function of lifting this darkness. Nevertheless this violence appears as violence only to a superficial glance, because in fact it only *appears* to act on an immediate presupposition, on some obscure contingency or accident [*Zufälligkeit*]. In reality this contingency, this darkness that has been posited by the light of the concept has been transformed into freedom by the power of necessity. The light uses darkness, gives it dignity; liberates it from the sombre night of the senseless in order to set it off within the drawn-out *chiaroscuro* of a world that gradually allows a scale of determinations to appear. Violence is a black line on a white sheet, violence that is only apparently so, since by means of it the sheet is made noble and dignified, and through violence it becomes what it was destined to be: a well-drawn-out design, sense. If now the implicit effects of the Hegelian discourse on causality taken in its global strategy are considered, it is clear that the emergence of sense is possible only with violence, a violence that is nevertheless only apparent. In short: 1) violence is necessary; and yet 2) violence is not real, it is not *wirklich*, not only because violence does not act, *wirken*, or produce an effect, *Wirkung*, i.e., violence is not

---

6   Ibid.

the motor of the process, but also because its occurrence is the effect of an optical illusion produced by the last level of binary logic of the metaphysical categories (*'Wirkung und Gegenwirkung'*), illusion of a duality that will be resolved in the unity of the Idea.

3   Violence in 'Teleology'

Let us now look at the second theoretical site in the Greater Logic. Just as in the objective logic, in the subjective logic the term 'violence' appears in the diachrony of the system at a crucial point in terms of strategy: it is the signpost pointing the way that leads from teleology to the Idea. As with *Wirklichkeit*, here in the subjective logic violence again appears at a threshold, in a *Zwischen* between objectivity and subjectivity, or even better, on the border or at the limit of this duality, just before it is sublated into a superior unity, the adequate concept, i.e., the Idea. Therefore violence appears – in the scenario laid out by Hegel's conceptual syntax – once again in the transition between object and subject, at the point where objectivity rises to its highest level, teleology, and just before it becomes subjectivity, the Idea.

Teleology emerges in Hegel from the well-known dialectic between mechanism and finalism. The positivity of finalism lies in the essential unity, while its negativity arises from the imposition of this essential unity in such an extrinsic and accidental way that it makes the mere accidentality of a mechanical tautology preferable. The way to overcome the negative side of finalism was demonstrated by Kant, who distinguished between internal and external finality or 'purposiveness':

> One of Kant's great services to philosophy consists in the distinction he has made between relative or *external*, and *internal* purposiveness [*Zweckmäßigkeit*]; in the latter he has opened up the Notion of life [*Begriff des Lebens*], the Idea, and by so doing has done positively for philosophy what the *Critique of Reason* did but imperfectly, equivocally, and only negatively, namely, raised it above the determinations of reflection and the relative world of metaphysics.[7]

According to Hegel the task is to take this Kantian intuition up once again in order to push it to its extreme consequences, i.e., betraying and in this way rendering true Kant's undertaking, thinking once again metaphysics as a

---

7   Hegel 1989, p. 737.

science, but avoiding the dogmatic naïveté of a Wolff or of a Mendelssohn through the severe discipline of the transcendental.

Once the primacy of internal teleology has been established, Hegel goes on to analyse the individual moments through which the speculative concept of teleology is deduced:

The subjective end. The end is the subjective concept understood as the 'effort' or '*élan*' to become an exterior, to posit itself as an exteriority. It has an analogy with the concept of force, but it is a force whose move towards exteriorisation is solicited entirely by itself; it is also analogous with the concept of cause, but in this case a cause that is the cause of itself or an effect that is immediately cause. The end is subjective and its activity is directed against an exterior objectivity. Indeed, it has before itself an objective (mechanical and chemical) world which its activity relates to as something already existent. In this way, Hegel determines the dialectic of the end:

> the movement of the end can now be expressed as having for its aim to sublate its *presupposition* [*Voraussetzung*], that is the immediacy of the object [*Unmittelbarkeit des Objects*], and to *posit* the object as determined by the Notion.[8]

The means. An interior is posited within the end and, at the same time, an external world that is completely indifferent to the determinations of the end is presupposed. Hegel shows how, given this conceptual framework, the end requires a means through which it can fulfil itself. This means, which has an external existence, functions as a medium term:

> The finitude of the end consists accordingly in this, that its determining is altogether external to itself, and so its first determining, as we have seen, divides itself into a positing and presupposing [*in ein Setzen und in ein Voraussetzen*].[9]

In other words, Hegel underlines how in this relationship the notion or concept and objectivity are related in an extrinsic way, because the means is a mechanical object. Nevertheless, the means can be pervaded by the end and is susceptible to this communication of sense only because in itself it is identical with the end.

---

8   Hegel 1989, p. 742.
9   Hegel 1989, p. 743.

THE SYNTAX OF VIOLENCE BETWEEN HEGEL AND MARX

The realised end. The end that is active in its means must not therefore determine the immediate object as an extrinsic object; the latter should melt, of itself, into the unity of the concept. In other words, the exterior activity of the end, by means of the means, should overcome or surpass itself: 'the negative attitude [*Verhalten*] of purposive activity towards the object is thus not an *external* attitude, but the alteration and transition [*Veränderung und Übergang*] in its own self into the end'.[10]

Within this theoretical framework, Hegel determines violence as an effect of the action of the end on the object through the means:

> That the end relates itself immediately to an object and makes it a means, as also that through this means it determines another object, may be regarded as *violence* [*kann als Gewalt betrachtet werden*] in so far as the end appears to be of quite another nature than the object, and the two objects similarly are mutually independent totalities. But that the end posits itself in a *mediate* relation with the object and *interposes* another object *between* itself and it may be regarded as the *cunning of reason* [*List der Vernunft*]. The finitude of rationality has, as remarked, this side, that the end enters into relationship with the presupposition, that is, with the exteriority of the object.[11]

Activity is therefore the act of subtracting itself from the appearance of exteriority, a self-overcoming that can appear as violence only if the end, the means and the external object on which the end acts are considered as alterities whose exteriority cannot be mediated. In reality, the realised end reveals itself to be the point that determines the dialectic of these three moments which belong to the unfolding of the concept or notion: 'the teleological process is the translation [*Übersetzung*] of the Notion that has a distinct concrete existence as Notion into objectivity; this translation into a presupposed other is seen to be the meeting of the Notion *with itself through itself*'.[12]

Therefore, Hegel concludes, 'it can be said of the teleological activity that in it the end is the beginning, the consequent the ground, the effect the cause, that it is a becoming of what has become, that in it only what already exists comes into existence, and so forth', and that violence, as in the dialectic of *Wechselwirkung*, is nothing other than the illusion of an opacity that has been

---

10   Hegel 1989, p. 746.
11   Ibid.
12   Hegel 1989, pp. 747–8.

posited as such in order to be rendered transparent.[13] The realised end com-mands the moves of the subjective end, of the means and of the object from the final point of the process, using them as pieces on a chessboard to carry out its own strategy to the end: violence is nothing but the optical effect seen by whoever observes this process from a limited point of view (and in this sense the Hegelian expression '...kann als Gewalt betrachtet werden' is symptom-atic), of someone who looks at the finite without understanding that the unity of the process is completely impregnated by the concept. If we want to name the subject of the view from without, which sees violence in the finite without penetrating the global rationality within which it is inserted, we can single out one faculty, the intellect, which holds the finite firmly in place without grasp-ing its vital relationship with the infinite.

Nevertheless one point must be underlined in the Hegelian argumentation: the appearance on the theoretical scene, right in the middle of the Hegelian redefinition of the concept of teleology, of the expression List der Vernunft, which is part of a completely different context of the system, namely objective spirit, the philosophy of history. The cunning of reason is the name that Hegel gives to the strategy of reason in history, to its way of using the instincts, pas-sions, desires and deeds of individuals to realise its own universal plan, leaving these individuals behind as 'empty shells'. What Hegel constructs within his theory of teleology is the logico-ontological structure of historicity, in which violence, as we will soon see in a more analytic way, is always exercised upon what no longer has any reality, any life, and is therefore eliminated as an ines-sential element of the process.

4   Violence in the Philosophy of Right

The atemporal structure of the Greater Logic determines the historical dialec-tic of violence. In Elements of the Philosophy of Right, violence occupies the theoretical space of a threshold, the border between the state and the history of the world. It appears as Krieg or war in the part dedicated to 'Right between States', where Hegel defines the nature of the relations between independent states. States are arrayed against each other in the same situation as men in the state of nature posited by Hobbes, with the difference being that here there is no lex naturalis that can be made effective by a coercive super partes power. In other words, according to Hegel, the Kantian project of a perpetual peace that is obtainable through a confederation of states that are able to manage

---

13   Hegel 1989, p. 748.

and regulate all conflict is mere wishful thinking: 'There is no praetor to judge between states' – concludes Hegel – 'at best there may be arbitrators or mediators, and even these exercise their functions only contingently, i.e. in accordance with particulars wills'.[14]

Therefore, when the particular wills of individual states cannot come to an understanding, the matter 'can only be settled by *war* [*Krieg*]'.[15] However, the violence that breaks out in this specific form of *Wechselwirkung* is not contingent – it allows the glimmers of the concept to shine through the course of world history:

> It is as *particular* entities that states enter into relations with one another. Hence their relations are on the largest scale a highly animated play of external contingency and the inner particularity of passions, interests and purposes, talents and virtues, vices, force, and wrong – a play wherein the ethical whole itself, the independence of the state, is exposed to contingency. The principles of the spirits of peoples are in general restricted on account of their particularity, for it is in this particularity that, as *existent* individuals, they have their objective actuality and their self-consciousness. Their deeds and destinies in their relations to one another are the manifest dialectic of the finitude of these spirits, and out of it arises the *universal spirit, the spirit of the world*, free from all restriction, producing itself as that which exercises its right – and its right is the highest right of all – over these finite spirits in world history as the *world's court of judgement.*[16]

Through the dark sea of the *Wechselwirkung* of subjective passions, interests, vices, virtues and acts of violence the light of the concept shines through: the history of the world is not in fact the judgement of the mere '*power* [*Macht*]' of spirit that passes judgement, i.e., the abstract and non-rational necessity of a blind destiny [*blinde Schicksal*]',[17] but the development of the self-consciousness and the freedom of spirit: 'The history of spirit is its own act [*seine Tat*]. Spirit is only what it does, and its act [*Tat*] is to make itself the object of its own consciousness'.[18]

States, peoples, and individuals are conscious of the level of evolution of the spirit that they carry within while at the same time being the unconscious

---

14   Hegel 2008, p. 262.
15   Ibid.
16   Hegel 2008, p. 315.
17   Hegel 2008, p. 316.
18   Ibid.

instruments of the work of spirit that elaborates through them its own transition to a higher level:

> Justice and virtue, injustice, force and vice, talents and their deeds, pas-
> sions strong and weak, guilt and innocence, grandeur in individual and
> National life, in dependence, fortune and misfortune of states and indi-
> viduals, all these have their specific significance and worth in the field of
> conscious actuality; therein they are judged and justice – thus only
> imperfect justice – is meted out to them. World-history, however, falls
> outside the point of view from which these things matter. Each of its
> stages is the presence of a necessary moment in the Idea of the world
> spirit, and that moment attains its *absolute right* in that stage. The people
> whose life embodies this moment secures its good fortune and fame, and
> its deeds are brought to fruition.[19]

History is spirit giving itself the form of events, of immediate natural actuality.
Now, the people, which corresponds to an immediate natural principle,
'is entrusted with giving complete effect to it in the advance [*Fortgang*] of
the self-developing self-consciousness of the world spirit'.[20] In the history
of the world, this people is for this particular age the dominant people, and it
can play this epoch-making role only once, although in a total way:

> In contrast with this its absolute right of being the bearer of this present
> stage [*gegenwärtigen Entwicklungstufe*] in the world spirit's develop-
> ment, the spirits of the other peoples are without rights, and they, along
> with those whose epoch [*Epoche*] has passed, no longer count in world
> history.[21]

The *Gewalt* of the *Logic* manifests itself in the historical form of the *Krieg*. It
breaks out against those peoples that obscure the transparency of the spirit of
an age. Whoever suffers violence gets their due within the development of the
process. As Hegel has written in the objective logic, '*Der passiven Substanz
wird daher durch die Einwirkung einer andern Gewalt nur ihr Recht angethan*'.
He who suffers sees inscribed on his body, as in the famous story by Kafka,
the judgment of the *Weltgericht*. But, more profoundly, the point of view
that sees violence is still limited, illusory, just as Hegel writes in the subjective

---

19   Hegel 2008, p. 317.
20   Ibid.
21   Ibid.

Logic, '[...] *kann als Gewalt betrachet werden*'. It is seen from the point of view of a faculty such as the intellect that would like to give substance to the particular moment without inserting it into the frame of totality: the peoples who suffer violence are in effect deprived of spirit, not-contemporary, furnished with a form of phantasmatic existence, without life, survivors of an already passed *Zeitgeist* in the history of the world. These peoples, therefore, in suffering violence, carry out the judgment of the tribunal of world history, similarly to the way in which Hegel describes punishment as the reaffirmation of the negated law in the criminal. Hegel writes in the *Philosophy of Right*:

> § 100. The injury which falls on the criminal is not merely just in *itself* – as just, it is *eo ipso* his will as it is in itself, an existence [*Dasein*] of his freedom, *his* right [*Recht*] – but it is also a right *posited in the criminal himself*, i.e. in his objectively existent will, in his action. For his action is the action of a rational being and this implies that it is something universal and that by doing it the criminal has set up a law which he has explicitly recognized in his action and under which in consequence he should be subsumed as under his right.[22]

5   Violence in the *Anti-Dühring*

A reading of these texts has clarified the way in which violence in Hegel's conceptual syntax constitutes a necessary moment in the becoming-subject of substance. The Engelsian repetition of the Hegelian dialectic, although inverted (i.e., no longer based on the Idea but on the economic) keeps the conceptual syntax which governs the passage from necessity to freedom, from the *Wechselwirkung* of nature and of history up to the transparency finally realised in communism, almost completely intact.[23] This emerges in a paradigmatic way in a text of great historical importance within the Marxist tradition, the *Anti-Dühring*. In the second section ('Political Economy') of this work, a veritable encyclopaedia of socialism, we find a 'Theory of Violence' which was re-elaborated in an autonomous text that was published posthumously with the title *The Role of Violence in History*.

The Engelsian theses on violence are constructed in a polemic with Eugen Dühring, an exponent of German Social Democracy, according to whom 'the

---

22   Hegel 2008, pp. 102–3.
23   For a demonstration of this thesis, see '*Causa sui* or *Wechselwirkung*: Engels between Spinoza and Hegel', included in this volume.

formation of *political* relationships is *historically the fundamental thing*, and instances of *economic* dependence are only *effects* or special cases, and are consequently *facts* of a second order'.[24] The primordial element is, according to Dühring, 'direct political violence [*politische Gewalt*] and not any indirect economic power',[25] and, consequently, 'all economic phenomena must be explained by political causes, that is by violence'.[26]

Dühring uses the relationship between Robinson Crusoe and Friday as a symbol of the primacy of political violence over economic factors. Against this example, Engels demonstrates that no violence can be considered as a first cause, because in reality it presupposes certain conditions to be exercised. In the case of Crusoe and Friday, it is not sufficient that the former has 'a sword in hand' to make Friday his slave. In order to be able to make use of a slave, a man must posses the instruments and materials for his slave's labour and the means of bare subsistence for him: violence is therefore only the means, while the end is economic advantage.

Political violence cannot be considered as an original fact, it must be historicised. Engels shows how violence is not a 'mere act of the will'. It instead presupposes certain conditions, the production of weapons, whose technical level is decisive in the resolution of conflicts: 'the triumph of violence is based on the production of arms, and this in turn on production in general – therefore, on "economic power [*Macht*]", on the "economic situation", on the material means which violence has at his disposal'.[27]

The *first movement* of Engels's discourse therefore consists of an historical relativisation of violence: from a primal metaphysical cause to an instrument determined by socio-economic factors. Engels takes the example of the revolution in the art of war provoked by the introduction of gunpowder in the fourteenth century. This was not an 'act of violence [*Gewalttat*], but a step forward in industry, that is, an economic advance'.[28] Engels concludes that '...nowadays any zealous N.C.O. could explain to Herr Dühring how greatly, besides, the conduct of a war depends on the productivity and means of communication of the army's own hinterland as well as on the theatre of war'.[29]

The *second movement* consists of a precise definition of the 'role played in history by violence as contrasted with economic power':[30]

---

24   Marx and Engels 1975–2005, vol. 25, p. 146.
25   Ibid. (translation modified).
26   Marx and Engels 1975–2005, vol. 25, p. 147 (translation modified).
27   Marx and Engels 1975–2005, vol. 25, p. 154.
28   Marx and Engels 1975–2005, vol. 25, p. 155.
29   Marx and Engels 1975–2005, vol. 25, p. 164.
30   Marx and Engels 1975–2005, vol. 25, p. 170.

In the first place, all political power is originally based on an economic, social function, and increases in proportion as the members of society, through the dissolution of the primitive community, become transformed into private producers, and thus become more and more divorced from the administrators of the common functions of society. Secondly, after the political force has made itself independent in relation to society, and has transformed itself from its servant into his master, it can work in two different directions. Either it works in the sense and in the direction of the natural economic development, in which case no conflict arises between them, the economic development being accelerated. Or it works against economic development, in which case, as a rule, with but few exceptions, violence succumbs to it.[31]

Through the *Wechselwirkung* of the factors constituting the history of human society, the *telos* of the economic development ceaselessly emerges (just as, in Hegel, the development of the Idea emerges). Violence can therefore accelerate or decelerate the flow of historical development, but it can never change it. However, in the Engelsian discourse still another nuance emerges that brings it even closer to the Hegelian theory of violence:

To Herr Dühring violence is the absolute evil; the first act of violence [*Gewaltsakt*] is to him the original sin; his whole exposition is a jeremiad on the contamination of all subsequent history consummated by this original sin; a jeremiad on the shameful perversion of all natural and social laws by this diabolical power [*Teufelsmacht*], violence. That violence, however, plays yet another role in history, a revolutionary role [*eine revolutionäre Rolle*]; that, in the word of Marx, it is the midwife of every old society pregnant with a new one, that it is the instrument with the aid of which social movement forces its way through and shatters the dead, fossilised political forms – of this there is not a word in Herr Dühring.[32]

As in Hegel, violence is the phenomenal appearing of power, of the action exercised by what is vital on what is stiff and dead, on what has a positive existence [*Realität*] but no longer has any actuality [*Wirklichkeit*], being the remnant of an age that is over (a fossil). Violence in Engels is the economic cunning that destroys political power when it is opposed to the development of the productive forces, a form of destruction whose paradigm is given by the French

31   Ibid.
32   Marx and Engels 1975–2005, vol. 25, p. 171.

Revolution. The communist revolution, repeating and radicalising the French
Revolution, will produce 'humanity's leap from the kingdom of necessity to the
kingdom of freedom'.[33]

6   The Role of Violence in the Order of the Discourse of Hegel
       and Engels

It has been shown how the passage from substance to subject, from the realm
of necessity to the realm of freedom is possible only on the condition of the
intervention of the moment of violence. What is, then, this violence? Let us
briefly repeat the results of our Hegelian itinerary: violence is, in 'Wirklichkeit',
the phenomenon of the action of power on something presupposed or on an
alterity; in the 'Teleology', it is the effect of the action of the subjective end on
an objective world through a means. Such a conceptual grammar allows us to
observe that the historical appearance of violence in the form of *Krieg* in the
Weltgeschichte as an action of the dominant state on the dominated states is
both:

  –   the effect of the action of the notion, of the *logos*, on an alterity that
       itself has been posited as a necessary presupposition of its action;
  –   the illusion of the finite produced by the incapacity of the intellect
       to grasp the totality of the process.

The necessity of violent action on a presupposed passivity dematerialises the
effects of violence. The first appearance of the term 'violence' in the 'Logic of
Essence' specifically posits the being-always-already of violence, its atemporal-
ity, which will render every form of historical violence a repetition of an action
that has always-already occurred. As Ernst Bloch has written, violence in the
Hegelian system is exactly the violence that is studied at school desks, a violence that always occurs and yet never does, exactly because the contingency
which characterises it is traversed by a higher necessity: things that suffer violence get their due in the development of the process. Hegel never focuses his
attention on what violence destroys, on what its actions erase forever, because
the order of his discourse forbids despair before the abyss of pain, forbids a
definitive loss – provoked by violence – that cannot be restored to and by the
dialectic of the process. Violence is the illusion of the finite, as clearly indicated by its occurrence in the 'Teleology'; it is at bottom nothing more than a

---

33   Marx and Engels 1975–2005, vol. 25, p. 270.

symptom of the concept's reappropriation of exteriority. What is destroyed was posited in order to be destroyed and its destruction is the experience that will be conserved as spirit makes it way along its historical path.

If we substitute the economic for the logos, if we put back on its feet the dialectic that was initially on its head, we find an identical syntax in Engels, a syntax that produces a series of meaningful effects:

1) the univocity of violence, its being merely the indicator of the direction of the historical process and not its motor;
2) the punctual occurrence of violence, its being an epiphenomenon of a leap in level;
3) its dematerialisation, being exercised on what is stiff and dead.

Now, in the famous Marxist conclusions in Chapter 24 of *Capital* on the 'expropriation of the expropriators', it is possible to discover a syntax of this same kind:

> The capitalist mode of appropriation, the result of the capitalist mode of production, produces capitalist private property. This is the first negation of individual private property, as founded on the labour of the proprietor. But capitalist production begets, with the inexorability of a law of Nature, its own negation. It is the negation of the negation. This does not re-establish private property for the producer, but gives him individual property based on the acquisitions of the capitalist era: i.e., on cooperation and the possession in common of the land and of the means of production.[34]

Violence here is unidirectional. It indicates precisely the direction of the historical process; it is punctual, and appears at leaps in level; it is dematerialised by the view that grasps the totality of the process, in its double movement of negation which leads from feudalism to communism and from necessity to freedom.

7   Dialectic or Archaeology of Violence?

The question now is whether this dialectic of violence, which clearly appears in the concept of double negation as well as in the metaphor of childbirth, is

---

34   Marx and Engels 1975–2005, vol. 35, p. 751.

truly the philosophical backbone of Chapter 24, or if it is a kind of distortion. In a work published posthumously in 1992, Althusser opposes, in the economic works of Marx, a teleological conception of the mode of production to an aleatory one. A concept of violence commanded by the Hegelian syntax is undoubtedly linked to the former: the feudal mode of production is pregnant with the capitalist mode of production. The latter is contained as a seed in the former (again Leibniz and preformism), and violence appears at the moment of birth. It assists in the birth of the inevitable. But what concept of violence is linked to the second? In the first paragraph Marx writes: 'The economic structure of capitalistic society has grown out of the economic structure of feudal society. The dissolution of the latter set free the elements of the former'.[35] The first proposition seems to be ascribable to a teleological and preformistic logic; but the second escapes such a model. The dissolution has liberated the elements, but they are not already combined according to a logic of necessity: their combination is aleatory. As Althusser writes in a typescript entitled 'Sur la genèse [On Genesis]' (1966):

1. . . . the elements defined by Marx 'combine' – I prefer to say (in order to translate the term *Verbindung*) 'conjoin' by 'taking hold' [*prenant*] in a new structure. This structure cannot be thought, in its appearance, as the effect of a filiation, but as the effect of a *conjunction*. This new Logic has nothing to do with the linear causality of filiation, nor with Hegelian 'dialectical' logic, which only says out loud what is implicitly contained in the logic of linear causality.

2. And yet, *each* of the elements that come to be combined in the conjunction of the new structure (in this case, of accumulated money-capital, 'free' labour-power, that is, labour-power stripped of the instruments of labour, technological inventions) is itself, as such, a *product*, an *effect*.

What is important in Marx's demonstration is that the three elements are not *contemporary* products of one and the same situation. It is not, in other words, the feudal mode of production that, by itself, and through a providential finality, engenders *at the same time the three elements* necessary for the new structure to 'take hold'. Each of these elements has its own history', or its own *genealogy* (to take up a concept from Nietzsche that Balibar has used very well for this purpose): the three genealogies are relatively *independent*. We even see Marx show that a single and same element ('free' labour-power) can be produced as the result of *completely different genealogies*.

---

35   Marx and Engels 1975–2005, vol. 35, p. 706.

Therefore the genealogies of the three elements are independent of one another, and independent (in their co-existence, in the co-existence of their respective results) of the existing structure (the feudal mode of production). Which excludes any possibility of a resurgence of the myth of genesis: the feudal mode of production is not the 'father' of the capitalist mode of production in the sense that the latter would be contained '*as a seed*' in the first.[36]

If we read chapter 24 from this perspective, violence loses its unidirectionality, its punctuality and its immateriality, all conferred upon it by the Hegelian philosophical syntax, understood as a necessary good Friday on the road to spirit (or to communism). We find violence in its plurality of forms, its pervasiveness and its materiality in a historicity ordered not by the rhythm of an essence but by a fundamental polychronism, by a multiplicity of times.

Plurality of Forms. The term *violence* is the abbreviated and generic form of a plurality of real processes: conquests, enslavements, robberies, murders.[37] It is not the unique directional indicator of a transitional process from one society to another which occurs everywhere at the same moment. It dissolves *some* of the forms of existence of the feudal society, liberating *some* elements that will come together to form a capitalist society, but never through a model of simple and transitive causality: the English proletariat (the localisation of the process is an important methodological caution against totalising philosophies of violence) is the effect of a plurality of causes which in no way could have been anticipated in advance (the dissolution of the feudal castes, the fencing of common lands for sheepwalks, the spoliation of church properties by the Reformation, the clearing of the estates, i.e., the ejection of tenants from large properties). Each of these processes should be analysed in its own specific temporality (for example, the difference between the relative quickness of the theft of the Church's wealth and the clearing of the estates of the Scottish Highlands and in Ireland and the lengthy process of the expropriation of common lands that occurred between the fifteenth and eighteenth centuries, although mutating in nature from 'individual acts of violence' to the use of the 'law [as] the instrument of theft').[38] Violence, in this way, acquires a sense only in a history conceived in the time of the future perfect, *ex post*, in which the fluctuation that preceded the conjunction is imprisoned in a linear and teleological time.

---

36   Althusser 2011.
37   Marx and Engels 1975–2005, vol. 35, p. 705.
38   Marx and Engels 1975–2005, vol. 35, p. 715.

Pervasiveness. Violence is not punctual at all, it does not appear as a sign of a leap of level, but acts in a pervasive way on all levels, in the violent separation of the producers from the means of production (according to different modalities and temporalities, as has been mentioned), in the 'grotesquely terrible' legislation against vagabondage which induced the 'discipline necessary to the wage system'[39] produced by this separation, and finally in the legislation 'to "regulate" wages, i.e. to force them within the limits suitable for surplus-value making, to lengthen the working day and to keep the labourer himself in the normal degree of dependence'.[40] But this plurality of levels does not make up a *Stufenfolge*, a series of successive steps chiselled out by violence, but instead an intricate intertweaving in which sometimes violence produces expected effects and sometimes unexpected ones, while at others times it produces a pure and simple loss with no effect at all.

Materiality. In this perspective, violence acquires once again all of its weighty materiality. Pain again becomes visible in bodies, the pain of hunger, of poverty, of imprisonment, of discipline, of exhaustion. Not an illusory epiphenomenon of an historical process that sweeps away all that is dead, but a plural and omni-pervasive weave of the genesis and structure of the capitalist mode of production (obviously without thinking that the logic of the violence of the structure could be thought as the *telos* of the violence of genesis). It is not a *dialectic* of violence but instead an *archaeology* of violence, capable of identifying, within the complex stratifications and differentiations of historically determined violences the pain inflicted on every single body. And in this way, the pages of Chapter 24 once again evoke 'the dwelling of the peasants and the cottages of the labourers . . . razed to the ground or doomed to decay' in the process of the transformation of land into sheepwalks,[41] 'the suppression of the monasteries [that] hurled their inmates into the proletariat',[42] the 'theft [on a colossal scale] of state lands',[43] the *Acts of Enclosure*, i.e., the 'parliamentary form of the robbery',[44] the *clearing of estates*, i.e., the 'process of wholesale expropriation of the agriculture population from the soil';[45] and also the bloody legislation on vagabondage against a vast mass of men transformed into 'beggars, brigants and vagabonds', the whip, the chains, the prisons, the scorching iron on the flesh, the cutting of the ears, the exceptional penal laws

---

39   Marx and Engels 1975–2005, vol. 35, p. 726.
40   Marx and Engels 1975–2005, vol. 35, p. 727.
41   Marx and Engels 1975–2005, vol. 35, p. 709.
42   Marx and Engels 1975–2005, vol. 35, p. 785.
43   Marx and Engels 1975–2005, vol. 35, p. 715.
44   Ibid.
45   Marx and Engels 1975–2005, vol. 35, p. 792.

against workers' coalitions, the barbarism and atrocity of the colonial system, the kidnapping of men, the famines produced by speculation, the assassinations, the thefts, the price on the heads of men, women and children. And these pages refer back to other extraordinary pages, those of Chapter 8 on the working day, where violence manifests itself in the infinite lengthening of the time of the work day, the cutting of the time for lunch and rest, the imposition of night work and the relay system in its extreme and almost incredible form (children obliged to work for several shifts consecutively). Marx renders almost tangible the inhuman fatigue imposed upon the bodies of men and even children, an inhuman fatigue which provokes great physical and psychic suffering, illness and death.

We have called this analysis an archaeology of violence, an archaeology capable of showing how violence can produce historical effects (or *not* produce them), without ever rewarding itself with the title of the Meaning of History. As Benjamin has written in one of his most beautiful theses, 'there is never a testimony of culture that is not at the same time a testimony of barbarisms [*Es ist niemals ein Dokument der Kultur, ohne zugleich ein solches der Barbarei zu sein*]'.[46] But what can we deduce from this archaeology on the level of the political discourse on violence? Politics cannot be grafted onto a philosophy of history as its necessary outcome, without being thought as the messianic eruption into a time otherwise without qualities. The secularisation of both of the great models of Christian temporality must be refused; the secularisation of Paul, according to whom God came as a 'thief in the night', and that of Joachim of Fiore, who divides time into three successive epochs of humanity. Politics is an intervention in a conjuncture. It is an intervention within a horizon dominated by a plural temporality whose intricacies sometimes offer to virtue the 'miraculous occasion' and sometimes renders virtue ineffective. This intervention must be thought according to the Machiavellian model of the Centaur, half man and half beast: this means that political intervention cannot avoid the question of violence precisely because the existing socio-political order is always-already violent. And yet we can never relieve violence of the weight of the pain it provokes, nor ensure that violence will ever have a sense.

Translated by Jason E. Smith

---

46   Benjamin 1997, p. 30.

CHAPTER 6

The Many Times of the Multitude

The question of the temporality of the multitude is not so much about conceiving the multitude, in a time that has already been qualitatively established,
as the subject of a politics or philosophy of history, a utopia or dystopia, as
it is about reflecting on what specific concept of time is implicit in the extraordinary category Spinoza formulated in his most mature work – the *Political
Treatise* – as the cornerstone of his political theory. If, as several commentators
have noted,[1] the concept of the multitude is radically different from that of the
people, it is primarily because they are based on different temporalities, an
issue that in my opinion has not yet received adequate thought.[2]

---

1 I am thinking here of Antonio Negri, of course, who writes that: 'The multitude is the name
   of an *immanence*. The multitude is a whole of singularities. On these premises we can immediately begin to trace an ontological definition of *what is left of reality* once the concept of the
   people is freed from transcendence. The way in which the concept of the people took shape
   within the hegemonic tradition of modernity is well known. Hobbes, Rousseau and Hegel
   have, each for his own part and in different ways, produced a concept of the people starting
   from sovereign transcendence: in those authors' minds the multitude was regarded as chaos
   and war. The thought of Modernity operates in a twofold manner on these grounds: on the
   one hand, it abstracts the multiplicity of singularities and, in a transcendental manner, uni-
   fies it in the concept of the people; on the other hand, it dissolves the whole of singularities
   (that constitute the multitude) into a mass of individuals. The modern theory of natural
   right, whether of empirical or idealist origin, is a theory of transcendence and of dissolution
   of the plane of immanence all the same. On the contrary, the theory of the multitude requires
   that the subjects speak for themselves, and that what is dealt with are *unrepresentable singularities* rather than *individual proprietors*' (Negri 2008, p. 114; see also Virno 2004).
2 There are a series of remarks in Negri's *The Savage Anomaly* (Negri 1991) and *Insurgencies*
   (Negri 1999) that are deserving of closer analysis. However, because they imply a complete
   disjunction between ontology and history, I do not consider them relevant to the theoretical
   account put forward in this essay. Regarding an interpretation of this sort, we might para-
   phrase the famous question Lactantius poses in *De ira Dei*: '*Si Multitudo, unde malum?*' Or,
   rephrasing the question in terms of temporality, if the time of the multitude is the *present* of
   its deployed constituent power, why does this present not coincide with the historical
   present?

1   Transcendental Intersubjectivity and Simultaneity

As a first approach to the question, let us consider the concept of the multitude through Husserl's concept of intersubjectivity, which he presents in his
Cartesian Meditations. It is here that he asks the fundamental question of his
work: how do we get beyond our 'sphere of consciousness [*Bewusstseins-
bereich*]',[3] off the 'island of consciousness [*Bewusstseinsinsel*]'?[4] This is where
the problem of intersubjectivity arises: it makes little sense to posit the universe of being as external to the universe of knowing, as Descartes did, establishing a fixed law of correspondence between the two (a correspondence
requiring a divine guarantee); all that is needed is that other *egos* and an objective world be transcendentally constituted within me. This offers a way out of
transcendental solipsism, out of the immanence of consciousness, allowing us
to move toward the transcendence of the Other.

Husserl approaches the problem by analysing how the sense of an *alter ego*
arises in me. The first step is a methodological reduction of the sphere of
belonging, namely, to exclude 'from the thematic field everything now in question', or to '*disregard all constitutional effects of intentionality relating immediately or mediately to other subjectivity* [fremde Subjektivität]';[5] Husserl
maintains however that:

> [S]uch an abstraction is not radical; such aloneness in no respects alters
> the natural world-sense, 'experienceable by everyone' [*Für-Jedermann-
> Erfahrbahr*], which attaches to the naturally understood Ego and would
> not be lost, even if a universal plague had left only me.[6]

Therefore, within what is proper to me as a monad, 'purely in myself and for
myself with an exclusive ownness [*in abgeschlossener Eigenheit*]',[7] the intentionality of the Other is to be found: 'there becomes constituted for me the new
existence-sense that goes beyond my monadic very-ownness; there becomes
constituted an ego, not as "I myself", but as mirrored in my own Ego, in my
monad [*sondern als sich in meinem eigenen Ich, meiner Monade spiegelndes*]'.[8]
This second ego is not 'present', it is not given to us 'authentically', but is

---

3 Husserl 1950, p. 82.
4 Husserl 1950, p. 83.
5 Husserl 1950, p. 93.
6 Ibid.
7 Husserl 1950, p. 94.
8 Ibid.

constituted as an *alter ego*. The question of the intentionality of the other remains a difficult one to resolve: 'A certain mediacy of intentionality must be present here, going out from the substratum, "primary world [*primordiale Welt*]' (which in any case is the incessantly underlying basis)".[9] This mediacy should render the *Mit-da* representable without it ever being able to be presented as a *Selbst-da*. It is a matter of making-co-present, a kind of appresentation that is different from what takes place in external experience where, for example, the front of a viewed object appresents its hidden side to me. The appresentation of the Other is of a different sort: 'the ego and alter ego are always and necessarily given in an original "pairing" [*ursprüngliche Paarung*]',[10] a pairing that is a presentation in the form of a couple, group, or multitude. It is a passive synthesis of association such that, based on the fact that I have an animate body, if another body similar to mine appears in my primordial sphere, 'it must enter into a phenomenal pairing [*phänomenale Paarung*] with mine',[11] such that body acquires sense as an animate body through a transfer of sense.

The question now becomes how this sense can have a value of being. According to Husserl,

> The appresentation [*Appräsentation*] which gives that component of the Other which is not accessible originaliter is combined with an original presentation (of 'his' body as part of the Nature given as included in my ownness [*seines Körpers als Stück meiner eigenheitlich gegebenen Natur*]). But in this combination [*Verflechtung*], moreover, the Other's animate body and his governing Ego are given in the manner that characterizes a unitary transcending experience.[12]

This experience of the Other can only be verified 'by means of new appresentations that proceed in a synthetically harmonious fashion'.[13] Husserl continues: 'It is clear that, with the other Ego, there is appresented, in an analogising modification, everything that belongs to his concretion: first, his primordial world, and then his fully concrete ego'.[14] Thus, through appresentation another monad is constituted in my monad, a monad I will never be able to grasp *originaliter* but which has a transcendental character nonetheless.

---

9   Husserl 1950, p. 109.

10   Husserl 1950, p. 112.

11   Husserl 1950, p. 113. The resemblance of the body that has entered into my primordial domain to my own is precisely what makes it 'another body' (Husserl 1950, p. 110).

12   Husserl 1950, p. 114.

13   Ibid.

14   Ibid.

This experience of the Other is what founds the objectivity of the world and the community of the monads, that is, their common temporality:

> with its complicated structure, it effects a similar *connexion mediated by presentation*: namely a connexion between, on the one hand, the uninterruptedly living self-experience (as purely passive original self-appearance) of the concrete ego accordingly, his primordial sphere and, on the other hand, the *alien sphere* presentiated therein. It effects this, first, by its identifying synthesis of the *primordially given* animate body of someone else and the same animate body, but *appresented* in other modes of appearance, and secondly, spreading out from there, by its identifying synthesis of the same Nature, given and verified primordially (with pure sensuous originality) and at the same time appresentation-ally. In that way *the coexistence of my <polar> Ego and the other Ego*, of my whole concrete ego and his, my intentional life and his, my 'realities' and his, in short, a *common time-form* [*eine gemeinsame Zeitform*], is primally instituted; and thus every primordial temporality [*primordiale Zeitlichkeit*] automatically acquires the significance of being merely an original mode of appearance of Objective temporality to a particular subject. In this connexion we see that the temporal community [*zeitliche Gemeinschaft*] of the constitutively interrelated monads is indissoluble, because it is tied up essentially with the constitution of *a world and a world time* [*Weltzeit*].[15]

The contemporaneity of the monads, their *temporal co-existence*, founds the uniqueness of the monadic community, the uniqueness and objectivity of the world, the uniqueness of the space, and the uniqueness of the real temporality.

This community has two orders of formation: in the lower order, the other monad is constituted in me as alien, the other monads are *realiter* separate from mine, there is no real connection between their moments of conscious-ness and mine. In the higher order, if I direct my understanding toward the other person, I discover that his or her animate body is within my perceptual field: his field is within mine. This reciprocity is what founds the monadic com-munity, a transcendental intersubjectivity which 'necessarily bear[s] within itself the same Objective world'.[16] To put it simply, we might say that the first order is Cartesian while the second is Leibnizian. As Husserl himself writes:

---

15   Husserl 1950, pp. 127–8.
16   Husserl 1950, p. 130.

> [T]*he constitution of the world essentially involves a 'harmony' of the*
> *monads*: precisely this harmony among particular constitutions in the
> particular monads; and accordingly it involves also a harmonious genera-
> tion that goes on in each particular monad.[17]

The constitution of transcendental intersubjectivity thus requires the concept
of the monad as a unifying mirror of a world-environment and the concept of
a monadic community as a reciprocity of their mirrorings, a synchrony of the
worlds. This harmony does not have a metaphysical structure, however; nor are
the monads metaphysical inventions or hypotheses. The way out of solipsism
cannot be found, as Husserl himself stresses, in 'an unacknowledged metaphysics, a concealed adoption of Leibnizian traditions'.[18]

2   Metaphysical Intersubjectivity

By rejecting an unacknowledged metaphysics, Husserl rejects both the
Cartesian solution – by which God creates the primary temporality of the *cogitatio* at each instant – as well as the pre-established Leibnizian harmony which
synchronises the time of all the monads by making their internal time a mirror
of world history situated from a different viewpoint (but synchronous with it).
What is specific to Husserl's response resides in the idea of monadic community as temporal co-existence:

> It is essentially necessary that the *togetherness* of monads [*ihr bloßes
> Zugleichsein*], their mere co-existence, be a *temporal* co-existence
> [*wesensnotwendig zeitlich Zugleichsein*] and then also an existence tem-
> poralized in the form: *'real'* temporality [*Verzeitlicht-sein in der Form
> realer Zeitlichkeit*].[19]

The problem is that this temporal co-existence can never be perceived in
reality, because a monad is never able to have access *originaliter* to the vital
flow of another monad. The temporality of the *alter ego* is always only appresented; it is never presented directly. What lies hidden in this temporal co-
existence of monads, in this non-metaphysical harmony, is nothing less than a
God, whether it be Berkeley's transcendent God or Hegel's objective Spirit:

---

17   Husserl 1950, p. 109.
18   Husserl 1950, p. 148.
19   Husserl 1950, p. 139.

temporal co-existence is Husserl's name for God. Intersubjectivity can only be metaphysical: as soon as the Augustinian move to seek the truth *in interiore homine* is repeated, a move that Husserl makes in the conclusion to his *Meditations*,[20] only a God makes it possible for us to escape from our interiority and find our way back to the world.

3 Intersubjectivity and Transindividuality

But does Spinoza's immanent God guarantee the temporal co-existence of the egos? If so, the time of the multitude could very well be that of temporal co-existence. Still, a reading of this sort would imply an interpretation of immanent causality that is in the same tradition as what Althusser calls the model of 'expressive' causality. In this sense, the egos would be contemporaneous with the absolute substance or Spirit. Also in this sense, the model would have to be the famous passage from the *Phenomenology of Spirit* in which the *absolute Substanz*[21] is revealed as mutual interpenetration of the singular and the universal:

The 'I' which is the object of its Notion is in fact not 'object'; the object of Desire [*Begierde*], however, is only independent, for it is the universal indestructible substance, the fluid self-identical essence. A self-consciousness, in being an object, is just as much 'I' as 'object'. With this, we already have before us [*vorhanden*] the Notion of *Spirit*. What still lies ahead for consciousness is the experience of what Spirit is – this absolute substance [*diese absolute Substanz*] which is the unity of the different independent self-consciousnesses which, in their opposition, enjoy perfect freedom and independence: 'I' that is 'We' and 'We' that is 'I'. It is in self-consciousness, in the Notion of Spirit, that consciousness first finds its turning-point, where it leaves behind the colourful show of the sensuous here-and-now and the nightlike void of the supersensible beyond, and steps out into the spiritual daylight of the present [*in den geistigen Tag der Gegenwart*].[22]

---

20   Husserl 1950, p. 157, n. 1.
21   Vergani 2004, pp. 535–52.
22   Hegel 1977, p. 110.

138   CHAPTER 6

The absolute substance constituted by the interpenetration of the 'I' and the
'We' is given in the temporal dimension of presence: Spirit = absolute substance = (I = We) = present. Now, for Kant, 'presence' is one of the predicable
concepts falling under the category of interaction or *Gemeinschaft* whose
transcendental schema is Simultaneity.[23] If, therefore, the multitude is understood as a Hegelian or Husserlian absolute substance, it would be correct
to translate this key term as 'the people', since *Zeitgeist* and *Volksgeist* coincide
in it.[24]

Still, this might very well offer another way to conceive of the temporality of
the multitude, through the attempt to read a sort of Spinoza/Leibniz alternative in the history of thought, exemplified by the two theoretical models of
intersubjectivity and transindividuality. Of course, we might perform an indi-
vidualistic, monadological reading of the modes, so to speak, something that
has been done a number of times in the history of interpretations (and which
Paolo Cristofolini has recently proposed). Once we reject an acosmic interpretation *à la* Hegel, we might be tempted to understand Spinoza's mode as an
individual that pre-exists and founds relations. The essence of man in particular would be defined by the mind-body dyad whose essential properties would
be joy, sadness, and desire. The mode, like the monad, would therefore have an
essence that precedes existence, an essence which would constitute the foundation for the play of relations. Naturally, as in Husserl, there would be no pre-
established harmony in Spinoza: the play of relation would be open, but only
between individuals who would logically precede all relations. Within this
theoretical horizon, the passions would simply be possible variations of an
essence. The emphasis placed by some critics on Spinoza's theory of affective
imitation is only apparently in opposition to an interpretation of this sort;
in reality this argument is favourable to it. Indeed, Montag has rightly pointed
out that:

...this theory in no way excludes the notion of originally dissociated
individuals who remain dissociated even in their imitation of the affects
of others. In fact, Spinoza's text contains the basis of a reading according
to which affective imitation would become nothing more than an act of

---

23   'Presence [*Gegenwart*]' is one of the concepts derived from the primary concept of
      'Community' or 'Interaction' (see Kant 1996, B pp. 257ff, pp. 276 ff).
24   The question of multitemporality is not explicitly addressed in the *Social Contract*.
      Augusto Illuminati claims nevertheless that an implicit contrast can be discerned
      between the will of all and the general will: the former would give rise to a multitemporal-
      ity, while the latter would result in a simultaneity, a temporal co-existence.

THE MANY TIMES OF THE MULTITUDE

projection, which requires only that I imagine that the other feels pleasure or pain in order to imitate what I imagine that other to feel. This is
precisely Adam Smith's definition of sympathy in chapter 1, part 1, of the
Theory of Moral Sentiments. For Smith, there is no crossing the boundary
between me and the other; I can never know what or even if another
person feels. The operation of sympathy remains internal to what Smith
calls 'spectators', who imagine what they themselves would feel or have
felt in a circumstance similar to the other. Sympathy, for Smith, does not
(strictly speaking) require even the existence of the other. It is possible
for me to sympathize with the dead, given that there is no communication or transfer of feeling or affect across the infinite distance that separates me from all others, all of whom can be no more than projections of
myself.[25]

In other words, the imitation of affects would occupy the same place on the
ontological plane as Husserl's analogical appresentation of the *alter ego* does
on the methodological one: the bridge between individuals is erected starting
from an analogical projection of an interiority (it is not by chance that Husserl
uses, albeit with great caution, the term empathy [*Einfühlung*] in this regard).

Nevertheless, any interpretation of the modes in light of the concept of
monad, even if used provisionally, is extremely problematic. To begin with, let
us examine the scholium that concludes the treatise on physics in Part Two
of the *Ethics*, one which frees the concept of the corporeal individual from
any form of substantiality. It does so by positing a *principium individuationis* in
which a certain ratio [*certa ratio*] of motion and rest of the parts enter into the
process of its composition and its regeneration in relation to the environment:

> [A] composite individual can be affected in many ways, though its nature
> is none the less preserved. Now, so far we have conceived an individual
> which is composed solely of bodies which are distinguished from each
> other only by motion and rest, speed and slowness; that is, which is com-
> posed of most simple bodies. But if we now conceive another individual,
> which is composed of several individuals of a diverse nature, we shall
> find that it can be affected in several other ways, though its nature is
> nonetheless preserved. For since each part of it is composed of several
> bodies, each part ... will therefore be able, without any change of its
> nature, to move now more quickly and now more slowly, and conse-
> quently to communicate its motions to the rest more quickly or more

---

25   Montag 2005, pp. 667–8.

slowly. But if we conceive further a third genus of individuals, composed of the members of this second genus, we shall find it able to be affected in many other ways, without any change of its form. And if in this way we proceed to infinity, we shall easily conceive the whole of Nature to be one individual, whose parts – that is, all bodies – vary in infinite ways without any change of the whole individual.[26]

This scholium has attracted the attention of critics because of Spinoza's reference to *corpora simplicissma* and to nature viewed as a whole individual. To my mind, these are *Holzwege*, paths that lead nowhere: in other words, they are limit terms or, to use Spinozist terminology, *auxilia imaginationis*, which in actuality do not correspond to any ontological reality. It seems clear that Spinoza is not saying that there exist infinite levels of existence of individuals between the simple bodies and nature understood as a complex individual. Rather, there exist infinite levels of existence of individuality of growing complexity *tout court*. What he calls 'Nature' is precisely these infinite levels of complexity that cannot be reduced to the infinitely small or infinitely big (strictly speaking, in fact, neither the *corpora simplicissima* nor Nature as a totality can be understood as individuals in Spinoza's sense).

If we compare Spinoza with the Leibnizian model, we cannot overlook the fact that there is a structural analogy between the different levels of individuality (which precisely express the metaphors of the pond and the garden in paragraph 67 of the *Monadology*). In Spinoza, on the contrary, the complexity of the higher level has no structural analogy with that of the lower one: rather, it constitutes the emergence of an order of individuality that was not contained beforehand in the orders of individuality that entered into its composition. Furthermore: while the body, life, is ordered in Leibniz by a hierarchy of forms whose level – namely, its position in the hierarchical scale of being – is given once and for all (although the perpetual flux of the bodies makes it unthinkable that a soul has real possession of animate beings of a lower order),[27] in Spinoza the mind is in no way the form of the body, it is not the *reductio ad unum* of the plurality of matter. Instead, it is the body itself, but expressed according to a different attribute. This means that minds must be conceived according to the same model of the infinite levels of complexity Spinoza used to describe the structure of bodies; at least this is what Proposition 7 of Part Two of the *Ethics* entails. The individual mind-body cannot be conceived, then, as a closed monad, but must be seen rather, as a composite of individuals

26   Spinoza 2002, pp. 254–5.
27   Leibniz 1970, p. 650.

that enters, in its turn, into the composition of individuals on the higher level: whichever level one chooses to examine, the individual will always be found as a doubly provisional moment between two levels of individuality. What one will find, to use Simondon's terminology, is that the individual is in reality secondary to the process of individuation that constitutes it as such.

To return to the comparison with Leibniz through the theme of relations, it may be noted that the theory of the pre-established harmony entails that each extrinsic determination be founded in reality in an intrinsic determination; or rather, that each exterior relation be founded in a property of the monad, that it be an internal state of the monad (and every state is infinitely complex because it has to express all of the inter-individual at the level of the intra-individual). In Spinoza each intrinsic determination is in reality founded on a complex play of extrinsic determinations (without the extrinsic determinations being able to contain the intrinsic determination beforehand). In other words, each property of an individual is produced by a complex play of relations that has constituted its individuality.

To approach the question from the point of view that interests us here, that of the multitude, the passions are not properties of a given human nature, properties which exist prior to the encounter and which are somehow activated by it; rather, the relations are what constitute the social individual. The *ironic* original locus of the passions is not interiority, but the space *between* individuals whose very interiority is an effect thereof. Certainly, Spinoza defines joy, sadness, and desire as the primary affects.[28] These primary affects could therefore be understood as fundamental properties of the human essence, properties that anticipate the encounters arising from the relation between the individual and its environment, and which receive different nuances based on these encounters. In reality, if these affects are primary to the individual, they are not so if we place ourselves in the point of view of immanent causality, which gives rise to the individual inasmuch as he is a *connexio singularis*, a singular connection. From this perspective, before entering into relations, these primary affects are nothing but abstract elements. Moreover, they cannot even exist in a pure state, as primal elements out of whose combination all the others arise; they only exist in the infinite metamorphoses that relations with the outside impose on them: hate, love, hope (safety/enjoyment), fear (desperation/regret), and so forth. Furthermore, we cannot even speak about a

---

28   'And besides these three I recognize no other primary affect; for I will show in what follows that the other affects arise from them' (Spinoza 2002, p. 285 [translation modified]).

single affect as a transitive relation with an object,[29] because, due to immanent causality which manifests itself as *nexus causarum*, an interweaving of causes in the sphere of the finite, every affect is always overdetermined by others.

The passions cannot be conceived under the category of the property, the inherence of a predicate to a subject, but must be conceived as a complex web of relations. As Montag describes it so well:

> The imagination (which to a certain extent mediates between inner and outer, between self and other, acting as a conduit between my body considered as a singular thing and other equally singular bodies) gives way to an unmediated imitation that is less a reduplication of one person's affect in another than, as we see in part 21, a perpetuation or persistence of affect without the mediation of the person.[30]

The affect is thus not to be found contained in me or in others, but between us: the web of affective life exists between individuals. This means that no inner mirroring of the Other, of the monad of the *alter ego*, is given in my monad, precisely because the *alter ego* is what we are woven out of. While Husserl's attempt to rework monadology in transcendental terms is pulled up short by the insuperable barrier of the unapproachability of the Other through consciousness – surreptitiously introducing a metaphysical concept of harmony without which the ego and the *alter ego* cannot belong to the same time or same world – a barrier of this kind is avoided through the model of transindividuality, precisely because the Other is not beyond the closed circle of the ego, but is always-already in the ego (and certainly from this perspective the contraposition of ego to *alter ego* is nothing more than the substantiation of a grammatical function): it traverses it, it constitutes it as such inside a complex web of bodies, practices, passions, ideas, and words. As Lucretius writes in a brilliant verse which I like to think inspired Spinoza:

Inter se mortales mutua vivunt.[31]

The pivotal philosophical question now becomes: can this complex web still be conceived through the temporal co-existence of a community?

---

29 The same relation that binds a subject and an object has no universality, as Spinoza himself underlines: 'Different men can be affected by one and the same object in different ways, and one and the same man can be affected in different ways by one and the same object at different times' (Spinoza 2002, p. 303).

30 Montag 2005, p. 668.

31 '[M]ortal things trade life for life' (Lucretius, *De rerum natura*, II, v. 76).

4   Multitemporality

To my mind, in order to appreciate the Spinozist concept of multitude in all its radicality, what is required is a concept of temporality that is completely different from temporal co-existence. In fact, the primary temporality of the ego that we sense as present in the moment of the *cogitatio* fades away in Spinoza even before the disappearance of the transcendent God (or immanent God, but conceived according to an expressive model) that constitutes a clock for being.[32]

The temporality of the multitude must be conceived as the locus of the non-contemporaneous, of an impossible contemporaneity, precisely because the individual itself is a multitude: the individual is not contemporaneous with itself, it does not find itself in the primary temporality of the *cogitatio* or in Locke's *self-consciousness*. In opposition to the Cartesian-Lockean tradition, Spinoza subscribes to the tradition of Lucretius and Machiavelli.

4.1   *Lucretius*

There is no theory of time *per se* in Lucretius, although he does allude to it in two places. The first is in the middle of Book I where he asserts that time cannot be said to exist the way void and matter do because time has no existence independently from events; time derives from the occurrence of events:

> Furthermore, there is nothing one could call
> discrete from matter and distinct from void,
> something revealed as a third form of Being...
> Time doesn't exist as such, but from events
> our senses gather what happened in the past,
> what things are with us, and what are going to be.
> No man may assert he senses time as such,
> discrete from things in motion and things at rest...
> Thus you may see: historical events
> do not, like matter, exist in their own right;
> nor may we describe them as we do the void,
> but rather, and properly, call them accidents [*eventa*]
> of matter and of the places where they happen.[33]

---

32 'The existence of the ego is deployed temporally, but according to a temporality that is first and radically determined by the cogitatio. Inversely, if the ego exists only as often and as long as the present moment of the cogitatio endures, this is because the cogitatio itself privileges presence in the present in its own temporality' (Marion 1999, p. 177).

33 Lucretius, *De rerum natura*, I, vv. 430–482.

It would appear that Lucretius is explaining in this passage the theory of temporality that Sextus Empiricus attributes to Epicurus, according to whom 'time is an accident of accidents, that accompanies days and nights and seasons, feelings and absences of feeling and motions and states of rest,' which are 'accidents that occur in different realities'.[34] There are clear traces here of a polemic with the Stoic conception of time, but even more interesting to our query, perhaps, is the polemic with the Platonic theory presented in the *Timeus*, in which the demiurge models time as 'a moving image of eternity ... eternal but moving according to number', creating the 'days and nights and months and years ... when he constructed heaven', and then, in order to distinguish and preserve 'the numbers of time', he created 'the sun and moon and five other stars'.[35] In the order of things created by the demiurge, the parts of time precede – 'logically', we might say, if we were not in the context of a probable discourse – the planets and their motions, which are nothing but instruments to measure the different parts of time, created for this purpose, as signs of an order and divisioning of time that pre-exist them: the revolution completed by the motion of the fixed stars provides the measure of a day, that of the moon provides the measure of a month, and, although nameless, the revolutions of the other five planets signal other clearly defined parts of time.

When Epicurus asserts that time is an accident of things he seems to be refuting precisely this sort of conception of time: time is not a sensory duplicate of an intelligible idea of the eternal, but the effect of the occurrence of events, and therefore it cannot be posited as a theoretical locus of unification for all becoming; rather, time is what results from the plurality of the rhythms of existing things.[36] To use a literal translation of an expression from the *Letter to Herodotus*, time is a 'specific symptom [*symptomon*]' of the occurrence of events.[37]

Returning to Lucretius, we find a clear allusion to a theory of multiple temporalities with regard to the theory of *simulacra*, 'clear-cut tracings of their shapes/that flit fine-textured speedily everywhere/yet separately and singly can't be seen'.[38] Now, these simulacra flow continuously out of the surfaces of

---

34   Sextus Empiricus 2000, p. 180.

35   Plato, *Timaeus*, 94c.

36   Noting the Epicurean distinction between *symptomata* [events], and *sumbebekota* [conjunctions], Michel Serres declares that 'history is the symptom of nature' while 'time is the symptom of symptoms' (see Serres 1977, p. 156).

37   Epicurus 1994, p. 15 (translation modified).

38   Lucretius, *De rerum natura*, IV, vv. 87–99.

bodies, '*texturas rerum tenuis tenuisque figuras*'.[39] It is not a matter of a transitive action of the object on the subject of perception through the simulacrum (an action that would allow the subsequent perceptions to be ranged along a time line), but rather an action of the *textura rerum* through the *textura* of the *simulacra* onto the *textura* of the body:

> Or it is rather true that in the moment
> Of sentience (that is, when one word is uttered)
> Lurk many moments, found there by our reason . . .[40]

In uno tempore, tempora multa latent. In one moment lie hidden a plurality of temporalities.

4.2   Machiavelli

This same weave that forms the theoretical backdrop of the Machiavellian concept of the occasion is spoken of by Jankélévitch:

> The occasion is not the instant of a solitary becoming, but the instant complicated by 'polychronism,' that is, by the sporadic and plural nature of durations. . . . The miraculous occasion depends on polymetry and polyrhythmy, as well as on the momentaneous interference of becomings. More precisely still: it is the point where privileged moments of two distinct chronologies coincide; the occasion is therefore a simultaneity – not an indifferent simultaneity, but a fortunate simultaneity that favors our aims or our knowledge.[41]

Laurent Gerbier has recently written a doctoral thesis exploring the metaphorical weave of Machiavellian texts on time with the specific goal of teasing out the theory that they implicitly contain.

In the venerable tradition of historicism, Gerbier's first move consists in showing that Machiavelli's theory of temporality is an expression in thought of his contemporary world, of his historical horizon. The Italian cities, which had provided themselves with free institutions starting in the eleventh century, liberated themselves from the double tutelage of the Church and the Empire. By doing so, they escaped from the eternity of revelation and the sempiternity

---

39   '[T]hese films of things, fine-textured, finely shaped' (Lucretius, *De rerum natura*, IV, v. 158).

40   Lucretius, *De rerum natura*, IV, vv. 794–8.

41   Jankélévitch 1980, p. 117.

of the empire, thereby exposing themselves to the varying times and to the eruption of novelty.[42] Machiavelli's rejection of metaphysics in favour of an authentic 'physics of politics,' says Gerbier, is a consequence of this. From this perspective, the notion of time in Machiavelli becomes a decisive question. Is it the concept of time of Aristotle's *Physics*, a homogenous succession of empty moments, or a time that, far from being a multiplicity juxtaposed with moments taken *partes extra partes*, simply enumerated, is instead a multiplicity of tensions, overlapping each other in the moment and eviscerated by the reasoning of state [*dal ragionare dello Stato*]? Gerbier believes that, precisely because of Machiavelli's reflection on the historical conjuncture of the Italian cities, he opposed the multiplicity of juxtaposed moments with the multiplicity of strands of time that interweave at each moment. Rather than the unified time of the Church and Empire, with its homogenous succession, for Machiavelli there was an interweaving that constitutes the novelty of the moment.

In Gerbier's view, Machiavelli arrived at this conception of temporality through his counterattack against the famous Augustinian criticism of the reduction of time to motion:

> I once heard a man say that time is simply the movement of the sun and moon and stars. I did not agree. For why should not time rather be the movement of all bodies? Supposing the light of heaven were to cease and the potter's wheel moved on, would there not be time by which we could measures its rotations and say that these were at equal intervals, or some slower, some quicker, some taking longer, some shorter?[43]

The Augustinian argument is clearly useful for asserting the spirituality of time, for establishing the priority of the bond of time with the soul rather than with motion, but Machiavelli, says Gerbier, welcomed the example in all its radicality. 'Every movement', writes Gerbier, 'every operation, every tension actualized in the world effectively engenders its own time; and it is articulation of this multiplicity of times that needs to be understood'.[44] Machiavelli's concept of time is that of strands made out of a multiplicity of interwoven microcontinuities that are irreducible to an abstract, neutral unit of measurement. The course of time cannot be brought back to an ultimate movement, 'it is simply a matter of knowing how each action engenders time or, more

---

42   Gerbier 1999, p. 1.
43   Augustine 2006, pp. 248–9.
44   Gerbier 1999, p. 23.

exactly, gives birth to an order among the chaos of instants, to a proximity, that one can call "my" time'.[45]

It would require another study to uncover this theory from Machiavelli's major historical and political works (*The Prince, The Discourses, The Florentine Histories*) but also from his legations and letters. His theory of time is the theoretical premise for these analyses, the implicit condition of thinkability about the concrete situation in all its real complexity. There is one text, however, in which Machiavelli appears eager to expound his 'philosophy' *apertis verbis*, a sort of epistemological reflection on politics, in the famous letter of September 1506 known as 'Ghiribizzi al Soderini'. Translating the problem into strictly philosophical terminology, Machiavelli seeks in this letter to understand how, in the political sphere, two different causes can produce the same effect and two similar causes can produce a different effect. Here is the 'opinion' of the Florentine Secretary:

> I believe that as Nature has given each man an individual face, so it has given him an individual disposition and individual imagination. From this it results that each man conducts himself according to his disposition and his imagination. On the other hand, because times vary and affairs are of varied types, one man's desires come out as he had prayed they would; he is fortunate who harmonizes his procedure with time, but on the contrary he is not fortunate who in his actions is out of harmony with his time and with the type of its affairs. Hence it can well happen that two men working differently come to the same end, because each of them adapts himself to what he encounters, for affairs are of as many types as there are provinces and states. Thus, because times and affairs in general and individually change often, and men do not change their imaginings and their procedures, it happens that a man at one time has good fortune and at another time bad. And certainly anybody wise enough to understand the times and the types of affairs and to adapt himself to them would have always good fortune, or he would protect himself always from the bad, and it would come to be true that the wise man would rule the stars and the Fates. But because there never are such wise men, since men in the first place cannot command their natures, it follows that Fortune varies and commands men and holds them under her yoke.[46]

45   Ibid.
46   Machiavelli 1965, vol. 2, pp. 896–7.

Nature viewed as varying, which Machiavelli stresses more than once in his letters, is what rules out the application of a linear model of causality to politics. The plurality of dispositions [*ingegni*] and the plurality of types of affairs [*ordini delle cose*] make it unthinkable to model time as a line along which an individual's actions unfold according to an instrumental logic. The changing times that Machiavelli speaks about are placed precisely at the intersection between these two pluralities, in which no room is made for contingency as absence of necessity or, viewed positively, as a manifestation of human freedom. Necessity cannot be postponed or avoided, but it is not linear; and contingency is produced not from an absence of causes but from the complex interweaving of causes which can only be viewed from an internal, partial perspective, never from a panoramic viewpoint. In this sense, Fortune, which Machiavelli refers to at the end of this passage, is none other than the mythological name for multitemporality.

This is the tradition that Althusser calls the underground current of the materialism of the encounter,[47] an indispensable aid in the attempt to understand the specific temporality of the multitude. And it is also, we might note in passing, the only philosophical tradition that Spinoza acknowledged as his own.[48]

5   Eternity and Multitemporality

We now come to Spinoza himself. When we look at his famous letter on the infinite, we discover that the essential terms of Spinozist ontology, substance and modes, can be expressed entirely in temporal terms: the temporality of the substance is eternity, while the temporality of the mode is duration. Time is introduced additionally as a measure of the durations. In order to understand the way Spinoza distinguishes between duration and time, we must refer to the Cartesian theory of space and time, presented in the *Principles of Philosophy*. Through his theory of the *res extensa*, Descartes came to understand each movement as measurable in relation to other movements; he also came to deny the existence of any unmoving bodies that could constitute an absolute unit of measurement. Now, inasmuch as a thing continues to exist, we may say that it endures, that it has a specific duration which, obviously, can only be temporally located by taking other things that endure as a term of

---

47   Althusser 2006.

48   On the relationship between Spinoza and Machiavelli, see Morfino 2002a. On the relationship between Spinoza and Lucretius, see pp. 82–100 of this volume.

measurement. Time is nothing other than the measure of these durations based on a regular duration: that is, the movement of the planets. In general, therefore, the spatial-temporal references of a body cannot be given with respect to an absolute reference, but only with respect to the location and duration of other bodies. Nevertheless, in Descartes, multitemporality remains anchored to a double foundation, both theological and mathematical: on the one hand, the divine creation reconstitutes the time-line of being in the abyss of the *res extensa*; on the other hand, the geometrisation of physics (or the primacy of geometry over physics) guarantees, by virtue of the postulate of the isomorphism of space, that the same moment will elapse in every part of matter.

By making God the immanent rather than the transcendent cause of the world, and by making the will an effect rather than a cause, Spinoza made the temporality of the *res extensa* the only temporality, no longer anchored even to the isomorphism of geometric space, since what we are witness to in Spinoza – far from a mathematisation of being, as one school of criticism would have it – is a historicisation (or politicisation) of physics.[49] Both the temporal continuity of the moments and the discontinuity of a moment with respect to the time-line are based on the transcendence of the divine will: the continuous creation cuts matter into contemporaneous sections, subjugating their plurality to the decision of the divine will (whether it decides in favour of continuity or discontinuity). All this in Spinoza leaves room for a theory of multitemporality, in which the infinite multiplicity of the durations is not liable to totalisation, because eternity cannot be the result of the sum of the durations, hence, an indefinite duration. The concept of *connexio*[50] compels us toward a more radical conception, to conceive of durations as the effects of endless encounters between rhythms. This means that starting from the knowledge of an existing duration, we can access knowledge of the existing durations that exist in relation to it (connected to it), both in the abstract and inadequate form of time – which renders a particular rhythm into an absolute, making it the measure of all the others – as well as in the form of eternity, an adequate conception of the relational nature of time as a complex connection of durations. In so doing, we also stay well away from any attempt to provide time with a metaphysical anchoring to the totality (meaning, modeled on the general scholium of Newton's *Principia*, according to which time is instituted by the omnipresence of God in such a way that every indivisible moment of

---

49   For an analytical proof of this argument see Morfino 2007.

50   On the passage in Spinoza passing from a serial model of causality to one based on connection, see Morfino 1999, pp. 239–54.

the duration endures in all places). So there can be no absolute simultaneities or successions. There are no successions and simultaneities, except in relation to and because of the individual encounters between rhythms and between particular relations of speed and slowness.

One problem does arise, however. When Spinoza excludes the possibility of understanding eternity in terms of the sempiternal in the Explanation to Definition VIII in Part I of the *Ethics*, he seems to be pointing to a conception of eternity understood as eternal present or absolute simultaneity. The most beautiful piece from a literary point of view imbued with a reading of this sort is Ernst Bloch's *The Principle of Hope*:

> The world stands here as *crystal, with the sun in the zenith, so that nothing casts a shadow*...Time is missing, history is missing, development is missing and especially every concrete multiplicity in the one ocean of substance... Spinoza stands there as if there was eternal noon in the necessity of the world, in the determinism of its geometry and of its both carefree and situationless crystal – *sub specie eternitatis*.[51]

Two arguments can be formulated against this kind of interpretation, one philological and the other analogical; neither, however, are conclusive. The philological argument is very simple: the Western theological tradition, from Boethius and Thomas Aquinas and beyond, had forged a certain number of expressions for defining the temporality of God versus worldly temporality. The most celebrated include, among others, *nunc stans* or *tota simul*.[52] Spinoza never uses these kinds of expressions in any of his later works: in no passage does he state that *aeternitas est nunc stans* or *interminabilis vitae tota simul*. These expressions were easily at hand – we might call them the ABCs of theology – yet Spinoza never uses them, not once. What this indicates to me is that, at the very least, he might have believed them to be sources of misunderstanding and error and not up to the demands of his theory on eternity. As far as this point is concerned, it seems to me that the absence of a word in a context where it would normally be expected to occur should be considered just as significant a philological proof as its presence.

The analogical argument can be presented in these terms: the specificity of Spinoza's philosophical strategy consists in evacuating the traditional words of the layers of meaning that had stratified in them over the centuries, so as to give them a new conceptuality through a system of entirely new relations.

---

51   Bloch 1996, vol. 2, pp. 852–3.

52   For more on this, see Morfino 2002a, pp. 160–81.

The clearest example of this is the philosophical work that Spinoza performs around the term 'God': placed at the centre of Part I of the *Ethics*, it is evacuated of any religious or theological meaning to become the name of the blind power of nature. Given that similar examples can be described for terms like 'substance', 'individual', 'mind', 'right', and so forth, it is no wonder that Spinoza introduced an unheard-of concept through a term, *aeternitas*, whose history is as ancient as the West and as inextricably intertwined with the different Western figures of the divine. To those who continue to sustain an interpretation of eternity in the sense of simultaneity or eternal present, we can only respond that it renders Spinoza's entire mature opus unintelligible, with the exception of Parts One and Five of the *Ethics* (but even in these sections we would have to close our eyes to page after page). We would be forced to the conclusion that Spinoza dedicated most of his work to figments – of the imagination, of the passions, of religions, history, and politics – all the while knowing full well that they are simply illusions from the point of view of the 'eternal noon' of substance and absolute simultaneity. Adding insult to injury, we could even hand these critics over to Kojève, who in his *A Note on Eternity, Time, and the Concept* in his *Introduction to the Reading of Hegel* famously objected that:

> Spinoza's system is the perfect incarnation of the absurd. Indeed, if Spinoza says that the Concept is Eternity, whereas Hegel says that it is Time, they have this much in common: the Concept is not a *relationship* ... In both cases, Being *itself* is what reflects on itself in and through, or – better yet – as, Concept. Absolute Knowledge that reflects the totality of Being, therefore, is just as closed in itself, just as 'circular,' as Being itself in its totality: there is nothing outside of the Knowledge, as there is nothing outside of Being. But there is an essential difference ... Spinoza's Concept-Being is *Eternity*, whereas Hegel's Concept-Being is *Time*. Consequently, Spinozist absolute Knowledge, too, must be Eternity. That is to say that it must exclude Time. In other words: there is no need of Time to realize it; the *Ethics* must be thought, written, and read 'in a trice'. And that is the thing's absurdity.[53]

Eternity is salvaged (and with it the *quid* of transcendence that remains with it) and Spinoza is lost!

To come to the point, it seems to me that the relation of the durations is correctly understood in relational terms; eternity must be conceived as immanent to the interweaving of the durations, without violating, however, Spinoza's

---

53   Kojève 1969, pp. 117–18.

interdiction against conceiving of it in temporal terms ('there is no "when", "before", or "after" in eternity').[54] When it is conceived as a contraction of all times, the relational system of the durations is destroyed. When it is conceived in temporal terms, the concept of eternity is destroyed. Perhaps the best approach is to think of it as the principle of objectivity for the relation of the durations (and, as such, not immersed in temporality, in the same way that for Aristotle the soul is the principle of movement for the body but is not itself in motion). This principle consists just as much in its necessity (in its intelligibility) as it does in the interdiction to project the temporality of the modes onto the totality through the ontologisation of the *auxilia imaginationis*, namely, time, measure, and number. Knowledge *sub specie aeternitatis* is not at all locationless, where nothing casts a shadow, as Bloch puts it, but rather, it is knowledge of the shadowy reality. Or better yet, taking a safe distance from the theoretical effects of Plato's metaphor, it is the knowledge of encounters and relationships, a knowledge that derives from the knowledge of the totality, *qua* immanent cause. But it is never knowledge of eternity *per se*, because the substance never falls under the infinite intellect as one object among many, but as a complex relationship between objects (namely, as *connexio*). In other words, the eternity of the substance, which is the immanent structure of the encounters between the modes that endure, never comes to view in presence, as is the case for absolute knowledge in *The Phenomenology of Spirit*, but only in the finite interweaving of temporalities, which is eternal precisely because it is freed from any hypostatisation of time, that is, from any anthropomorphic image of eternity.

6   The Double Order of Multitemporality

In order to conceive the temporality that is specific to the multitude, then, we must give up on the model of temporal co-existence found in Leibniz, Hegel, and Husserl (which not even Jean-Luc Nancy appears to elude in *Being Singular Plural*, when he speaks about simultaneity as the temporality of the *being-with*, of the *being-between/among*),[55] so as to turn to a model of multitemporality

---

54   Spinoza 2002, *Ethics* I, pr. 33 schol. 2, p. 237. For a diametrically opposed interpretation of this passage and of Spinoza's concept of eternity in general, see D'Anna 2002.

55   Nancy writes: '*Being is not without Being*, which is not another miserable tautology as long as one understands it in the co-originary mode of being-with-being-itself. According to this mode, Being is simultaneous [*selon ce mode, l'être est simultané*]. Just as, in order to say Being, one must repeat it and say "Being is", so Being is only simultaneous with itself. The time of being (the time that it is) is this simultaneity [*le temps de l'être (le temps qu'il*

required for the category of the transindividual. If every individual is an unstable composite of rhythms, every individual is a multitude and, therefore, the multitude itself is revealed to be this unstable composite of temporality.

The temporality of the multitude, therefore, is non-contemporaneity: a complex, articulated temporality which is never reducible to the transparency of an essence that can synthesise the plurality of matter into the principle of contemporaneity, the great temporal metaphor of Spirit.

But there is more. Not only is the temporality of the multitude plural, it is plural on two planes: on that of being, which we have analysed thus far; and on that of the imaginary, that is, the various ways of imagining time that emerge out of the multiple ocean of the multitude. We now enter onto the plane of inadequate knowledge (since on the plane of adequate knowledge, multitemporality becomes eternity, understood as knowledge of the necessary articulation of the plurality of times), where qualititative times reside, which hypostatise the colours of the aleatory encounters between bodies.

6.1   The Ontological Level

After having reconstructed/invented the genealogy of multitemporality on the ontological level, let us try to clarify and more precisely determine its sense through some of the great nineteenth-century models without which it would have been impossible to identify the theme in Spinoza.

Let us begin with Ernst Bloch's *Heritage of Our Times* and his attempt to reformulate the Hegelian-Marxist model of survival, in order to understand the rise of Nazism while reflecting on a strategy for the conjuncture. The core of the text, as Bloch himself states in the 1935 preface, comes from his essay on 'Non-Synchronism and the Obligation to its Dialectics'. It begins thus:

> Not all people exist in the same now [*Nicht alles sind im selben Jetzt da*]. They do so only externally, through the fact that they can be seen today. But they are thereby not yet living at the same time with the others [*Damit aber leben sie noch nicht mit den Anderen zugleich*]. They rather carry an earlier element with them; this interferes.[56]

---

est) est cette simultanéité], this coincidence that presupposed "incidence" in general. It assumes movement, displacement, and deployment; it assumes the originary temporal derivative of Being, its spacing' (Nancy 2000, p. 38).

56   Bloch 1990, p. 97. For more on this text, see Bodei 1979, which in addition to offering perceptive commentary on Bloch, also provides a rich storehouse of historical and philosophical background on multitemporality, requiring clear theoretical lines of demarcation to be drawn, however, in order to make use of it.

This anteriority, this non-presentness, is at the heart of Bloch's analysis of German society and Hitler's rise to power.

> The masses also streamed toward it, because at least the intolerable Now [*unerträgliche Jetzt*] seems different with Hitler, because he paints good old things for everyone. There is little more unexpected and nothing more dangerous than this power of being at once fiery and meagre, contradictory and non-contemporaneous. The workers are no longer alone with themselves and the employers. Much earlier powers, from a very different bottom, begin between them.[57]

The time of the young bourgeoisie, deprived of future bourgeois prospects, the time of the farmers and the time of the impoverished middle class are all non-contemporaneous times that innervate Hitler's power: 'With the decline of Hitler the non-contemporaneous will also perhaps seem weaker: yet it remains as the seed and ground of the National Socialist and of every future heterogeneous surprise'.[58]

What Bloch underscores with force in his analysis of German society is that this non-contemporaneity [*Ungleichzeitigkeit*] is not exclusively a subjective non-contemporaneity:

> But even if now, after total proletarianisation and insecurity, after the decline of the higher standard of life and all prospects of a career, the masses of employees do not join the Communists or at least the Social Democrats, quite the contrary, then there is obviously a reaction of forces which conceal the process of becoming a commodity not just in subjective-ideological terms (which was certainly solely the case with an unradicalised centre until after the war), but also in real terms, namely out of real non-contemporaneity [*realer Ungleichzeitigkeit*]. Impulses and reserves from pre-capitalist times and superstructures are then at work, genuine non-contemporaries therefore, which a sinking class revives or causes to be revived in its consciousness.[59]

Society is not permeated, therefore, by a single time that would prepare the playing field for a simple contradiction. In Bloch's view, Germany in particular is

---

57   Ibid.
58   Bloch 1990, p. 103.
59   Bloch 1990, pp. 105–6.

The classical land of non-contemporaneity [*klassische Land der Ung-leichzeitigkeit*], i.e. of unsurmounted remnants of an older economic being and consciousness... [In] Germany the victory of the bourgeoisie did not even develop to the same extent [as France and England] eco-nomically, let alone politically and ideologically. The 'unequal rate of development', which Marx assigns in the introduction to the 'Critique of Political Economy' to material production compared with the artistic kind for instance, equally existed here for long enough in material terms alone and thus prevented the clearly dominating influence of capitalist thinking...[60]

Hence, the Marxist revolution not only finds opposition in capitalistic contem-poraneity, but also in the non-contemporaneity whose roots run deeply into the material structure of society. Based on this analysis, Bloch distinguishes between subjectively and objectively non-contemporaneous contradiction:

As a merely muffled non-desire for the Now, this contradictory element is *subjectively* non-contemporaneous, as an existing remnant of earlier times in the present one *objectively* non-contemporaneous... The non-contemporaneous contradiction, and its content, has released itself only in the vicinity of capitalist antagonisms and is almost an accidental, or at least warped otherness there; so that between the non-contemporaneous contradiction and capitalism there exists a hiatus, a rift which can be consoled or filled with mist.[61]

To master this conception of contradiction, Bloch develops a theory of the 'multi-layered dialectic': social development is not understandable through the famous dialectic presented by Marx in his *Preface* of 1859 between forces of production and relations of production, a simple dialectic which presupposes the contemporaneity of the society to itself and a linear development of his-torical time. Rather, it requires a dialectic which 'make[s] the turbulent Now broader':

The subjectively non-contemporaneous contradiction is accumulated rage, the objectively non-contemporaneous one unfinished past; the sub-jectively contemporaneous one is the free revolutionary action of the proletariat, the objectively contemporaneous one the prevented future

---

60   Bloch 1990, p. 106.
61   Bloch 1990, pp. 108–10.

contained in the Now, the prevented technological blessing, the prevented new society with which the old one is pregnant in its forces of production.[62]

In opposition to the dialectic founded on simple contradiction, Bloch proposes a 'multi-temporal and multi-spatial dialectic', which must take into account polyrhythm and counterpoint. And yet he fails to push this proposal to the limit when he conceives of this complexity as temporary and not structural. The plurality of rhythms is only apparent; there is, in any case, a fundamental time with reference to which contemporaneity and non-contemporaneity are defined. And this fundamental time runs inexorably in the direction of communism, no matter how many fragments from the past may be strewn across its path, temporarily impeding its regular course. The plurality of rhythms is a momentary condition, while waiting for the *praesens* – as Bloch says in *Experimentum mundi* – to make itself *praesentia*, so that it may finally be said: 'Stay a while, how beautiful you are'![63]

In this sense, it is a matter of correcting Bloch using Althusser, of attempting to think of the non-contemporaneous as the unalterable structure of time itself, rather than as a temporary condition that will yield its place to a time that is full, to a present as *parousia*. In this sense, the introduction of the concept of 'overdetermination' in *For Marx* that Althusser uses to trace out a line of demarcation between Hegelian and Marxist contradiction is a fundamental point of passage. While the Hegelian contradiction is the development of a simple unit in which its *telos* is written *ab origine*, the Marxist contradiction is always 'overdetermined' inasmuch as it develops internally to an entire social complex that is structured in dominance. Turning to Mao's essay on contradiction, Althusser asserts that a distinction must be made in a historical process between the principle and secondary contradictions, and between the principle and secondary aspect of the contradiction, and that one must grasp its uneven development.[64] Althusser goes a step further:

---

62   Bloch 1990, p. 113.
63   Bloch 1975, vol. 15, pp. 81–114.
64   Mao writes: 'Hence, if in any process there are a number of contradictions, one of them must be the principal contradiction playing the leading and decisive role, while the rest occupy a second and subordinate position. Therefore, in studying any complex process in which there are two or more contradictions, we must devote every effort to finding its principal contradiction. Once this principal contradiction is grasped, all problems can be readily solved...' (Tse-Tung 2007, p. 88).

THE MANY TIMES OF THE MULTITUDE

If every contradiction is a contradiction in a complex whole structured in dominance, this complex whole cannot be envisaged without its contradictions, without their basically uneven relations. In other words, each contradiction, each essential articulation of the structure, and the general relation of the articulations in the structure in dominance, constitute so many conditions of the existence of the complex whole itself. This proposition is of the first importance. For it means that the structure of the whole and therefore the 'difference' of the essential contradictions and their structure in dominance, is the very existence of the whole; that the 'difference' of the contradictions (that there is a principal contradiction, etc.; and that every contradiction has a principal aspect) is identical to the conditions of the existence of the complex whole. In plain terms this position implies that the 'secondary' contradictions are not the pure phenomena of the 'principal' contradiction, that the principal is not the essence and the secondaries so many of its phenomena...On the contrary, it implies that the secondary contradictions are essential even to the existence of the principal contradiction, that they really constitute its condition of existence, just as the principal contradiction constitutes their condition of existence. As an example, take the complex structured whole that is society.[65]

According to Althusser, the conditions of existence spoken about in the classics of Marxism are not, therefore, the context in which contradiction develops but the mode in which the complex social whole exists, which is no different, in its turn, from its contradictions:

But if the conditions are no more than the current existence of the complex whole, they are its very contradictions, each reflecting in itself the organic relation it has with the others in the structure in dominance of the complex whole.[66]

The contradiction, then, Althusser concludes, is always 'complexly-structurally-unevenly determined. I must admit, I preferred a shorter term: overdetermined'.[67] In a theoretical horizon of this sort, the play of opposites does not admit a simple contemporaneity, not even in the eschatological

---

65   Althusser 1969, pp. 204–5.
66   Althusser 1969, p. 207.
67   Althusser 1969, p. 209.

perspective of a *praesentia* that finally resolves the complexity of the temporal planes by unravelling the tangle in a time that is completely full.

The question is explicitly addressed from the perspective of a theory of temporality in a paragraph from *Reading Capital*, in the 'Outline of a Concept of Historical Time'. As in Bloch (although even more patently), Hegel is once again used as a 'pertinent counter-example', in reference to a philosophy of history distinguished by a conception of time that is marked by two essential traits:

1) a homogenous continuity of time;
2) contemporaneity or the category of the historical present.

These two characteristics are none other than the two coordinates of the Idea in its sensory form, succession and simultaneity. Of the two, the most important by far according to Althusser is simultaneity, in which 'we find Hegel's central thought'. Indeed, the category of contemporaneity precisely expresses the structure of the historical existence of the social totality:

> The contemporaneity of time, or the category of the historical present. This second category is the condition of possibility of the first one, and in it we find Hegel's central thought. If historical time is the existence of the social totality we must be precise about the structure of this existence. The fact that the relation between the social totality and its historical existence is a relation with an immediate existence implies that this relation is itself immediate. In other words: the structure of historical existence is such that all the elements of the whole always co-exist in one and the same time, one and the same present, and are therefore contemporaneous with one another in one and the same present. This means that the structure of the historical existence of the Hegelian social totality allows what I propose to call an 'essential section' [*coupe d'essence*], i.e., an intellectual operation in which a vertical break is made at any moment in historical time, a break in the present such that all the elements of the whole revealed by this section are in an immediate relationship with one another, a relationship that immediately expresses their internal essence.[68]

---

68   Althusser 1970, p. 94.

Althusser believes that it is the specific nature of this totality which allows 'essential section': its spiritual nature, which makes each part *a pars totalis* in the Leibnizian sense. The continuity of time is based precisely on the continuous succession of these contemporaneous horizons, whose unity is guaranteed by the omnipervasiveness of the concept. This is where the *moment* of the development of the Idea in Hegel derives its double meaning:

1) from the moment as the moment of development that must receive a periodisation;
2) from the moment as a moment of time, like the present.

This provides the backdrop to Hegel's famous saying in the *Philosophy of Right*:

> To comprehend *what is*, this is the task of philosophy, because *what is*, is reason. Whatever happens, every individual is a *child of his time*; so philosophy too is *its own time apprehended in thoughts* [*so ist auch die Philosophie, ihre Zeit in Gedanken erfasst*]. It is just as absurd to fancy that a philosophy can transcend its contemporary world as it is to fancy that an individual can overleap his own age, jump over Rhodes.[69]

For Hegel, the present is the absolute horizon of all knowing, because all knowing is nothing but the existence, in knowledge, of the internal principle of the whole. In this horizon, a knowledge of the future is impossible and therefore so is any political science, inasmuch as it is a 'knowing that deals with the future effects of present phenomena':[70] 'World-historical men neither perceive nor know the future: they divine it as a presentiment'.[71]

In this Hegelian theory of historical time that 'is borrowed from the most vulgar empiricism, the empiricism of the false obviousness of everyday practice which we find in a naïve form in most of the historians themselves, at any rate in all the historians known to Hegel',[72] Althusser views the model of a conception of history, in which the pair homogeneity/contemporaneity is translated into diachronic/synchronic, as widespread in structuralism as well: 'This distinction is based on a conception of historical time as continuous and homogeneous and contemporaneous with itself'.[73] The synchronic

---

69   Hegel 2008, p. 15.
70   Althusser 1970, p. 95.
71   Ibid.
72   Althusser 1970, p. 96.
73   Ibid.

is contemporaneity understood in the Hegelian sense, while the diachronic is none other than the becoming of this presence in the 'successive contingent presents in the time continuum'. And, contrary to what one might think, this ingenuous representation of historical time continues to appear even in the historiography of the Annales school. Certainly, the Annales historians assert that there are different times (short, medium and long durations) and they observe the interferences that result from the encounters between them, but the question of the structure of the whole which causes these variations is never posed in conceptual terms. They believe that these variants can be measured by referring to a continuous and homogenous time.[74]

According to Althusser, it is a matter of comparing the temporality of the complex, always-already given whole as it appears in Marx's thought in terms of how it differs from Hegel. What is the temporality of the social whole? It is not *contemporaneity*, Hegel's historical present, because this has an expressive centre that irradiates uniformly outward to every point in the circumference. It is not the *synchronic*, which according to Saussure's definition occupies 'a period of time of varying length, during which the sum total of changes occurring is minimal': the ontologisation of Saussurian linguistics in structuralism renders possible the tracing out in the synchronic of a sort of 'general grammar' of an epoch[75] whose paradigm is the Foucauldian notion of *episteme* in the *The Order of Things*. It is not a *multiplicity of times* from Annales historiography, because this multiplicity maintains an essential relationship with the homogenous passing of one time that is the measure of the others. What we want to understand is which form of temporality belongs to the present moment, to the concrete situation as it presents itself to our knowing. And to do this, we must 'construct the Marxist concept of historical time on the basis of the Marxist conception of the social totality'.[76] The Marxist social totality:

> is a whole whose unity, far from being the expressive or 'spiritual' unity of Leibniz's or Hegel's whole, is constituted by a certain type of *complexity*, the unity of a *structured whole* containing what can be called levels or instances which are distinct and 'relatively autonomous', and co-exist

---

74   On the relationship between the Althusserian theory of historical time and that of the Annales school, see Schöttler 1993.

75   Saussure 1986, p. 99.

76   Althusser 1970, p. 97.

within this complex structural unity, articulated with one another according to specific determinations, fixed in the last instance by the level or instance of the economy.[77]

The Marxist conception of the social totality is brought to light by Althusser in his comment on a passage in the *Introduction* of 1857 in which Marx states that 'In all forms of society there is one specific kind of production which predominates over the rest, whose relations thus assign rank and influence [*Rang und Einfluß*] to the others'.[78] The whole, for Marx, is an '*organic hierarchized whole*', a totality which decides, as he writes, on the hierarchy, rank, and influence of the various levels of society.

What is the temporality of this hierarchised social whole? Not Hegelian contemporaneity:

> The co-existence of the different structured levels, the economic, the political, the ideological, etc., and therefore of the economic structure, of the legal and political superstructure, of ideologies and theoretical formations (philosophy, sciences) can no longer be thought in the co-existence of the Hegelian present, of the ideological present in which temporal presence coincides with the presence of the essence with its phenomena.[79]

A time that is continuous and homogenous 'can no longer be regarded as the time of history'. In fact, 'the process of the development of the different levels of the whole' cannot even be thought '*in the same historical time*'; each level has 'a *peculiar* time, relatively autonomous and hence relatively independent, even in its dependence, of the "times" of the other levels'.[80]

Every social formation has a corresponding time and history: of the development of the forces of production, of the relations of production, of the political superstructure, of philosophy, and of artistic production. This is because 'each of these peculiar histories is punctuated with peculiar rhythms' and can be known only if the concept of the specificity of its temporality is defined, along with its continuous development, its revolutions, and its ruptures. Rather than independent sectors, what we have are relatively autonomous ones which enjoy a relative autonomy founded on a particular articulation of the whole, or

---

77   Ibid.
78   Marx 1973, p. 106.
79   Althusser 1970, p. 99.
80   Ibid.

on a particular type of dependence: 'The specificity of these times and histories is therefore differential, since it is based on the *differential* relations between the different levels within the whole':[81]

> we cannot be satisfied, as the best historians so often are today, by observing that *there are* [*il y a*] different times and rhythms, without relating them to the concept of their difference, i.e., to the typical dependence which establishes them in the articulation of the levels of the whole. It is not enough, therefore, to say, as modern historians do, that there are different periodizations for different times, that each time has its own rhythms, some short, some long; we must also think these differences in rhythm and punctuation in their foundation, in the type of articulation, displacement and torsion which harmonizes these different times with one another. To go even further, I should say that we cannot restrict ourselves to reflecting the existence of *visible* and measurable times in this way; we must, of absolute necessity, pose the question of the mode of existence of *invisible* times, of the invisible rhythms and punctuations concealed beneath the surface of each visible time.[82]

According to Althusser, Marx was particularly sensitive to this necessity: in *Capital* he shows that the time of economic production cannot be read in the continuous time of life or clocks; what we are dealing with is a *complex, nonlinear time*, a time of times that must be constructed starting from the structures of production, from the various rhythms that punctuate production, distribution and circulation. This time is essentially invisible, unreadable, and opaque, a 'complex "intersection" of the different times, rhythms, turnovers, etc.', a time that can be revealed only by means of its concept, which must therefore be constructed, in the same way that, for Freud, the time of the unconscious must be constructed in order to understand some aspects of biography. Althusser also emphasises that in the construction of this concept, the categories of *continuous* and *discontinuous*, 'which summarize the banal mystery of all history', are completely useless; it is a matter of constructing 'infinitely more complex categories specific to each type of history, categories in which new logics come into play'.[83]

---

81   Althusser 1970, p. 100.
82   Althusser 1970, pp. 100–1 (translation modified).
83   Althusser 1970, p. 105.

The *present moment* is thus a differential interweaving of times. What happens if we subject this moment to 'essential section'?

The co-existence discernible in the 'essential section', Althusser responds, does not denote any omnipresent essence that may be the present of each 'level'. The section that 'counts' for any given political or economic level, corresponding therefore to an 'essential section' at the political level, does not correspond to anything similar in the other ones – the economic, ideological, artistic, philosophical, or scientific levels – which take place in other times and are subject to other sections, rhythms, and punctuation. The presence of a level is the absence of another, so to speak, and this co-existence of a 'presence' and absences is nothing but the effect of the structure of the whole in its articulated decentring.

A social formation is thus *an interweaving of different times,* requiring reflection on the displacement and torsion created by the articulation of the different levels of the structure. What is the risk implicit to this theory of temporality? It is to conceive of the 'essential section' not in a linear way but in steps, thinking of the absence of a level with respect to the presence of another as forwardness or backwardness. Althusser writes: 'If we were to accept this, we should relapse, as even the best of our historians usually do, into the trap of the ideology of history in which forwardness and backwardness are merely variants of the reference continuity and not the effects of the structure of the whole'.[84] To do this, we must free ourselves from the obviousness of empirical history and create the concept of history. If the different temporalities refer to the same time, we have fallen back into the ideology of a homogenous time: 'This amounts to saying that if we cannot make an "essential section" in history, it is only in the specific unity of the complex structure of the whole that we can think the concept of these so-called backwardnesses, forwardnesses, survivals and unevennesses of development which co-exist in the structure of the real historical present: the present of the conjuncture'.[85]

To speak using the metaphors of forwardness and backwardness, we must conceive the place and function of that differential temporality in the whole, in other words, its overdetermination. A theory of the conjuncture is thus indispensable to a theory of history. This allows us to reach two conclusions:

1) the pair diachrony/synchrony disappears;
2) it is not possible to speak about history in general, only about forms of 'specific structures of historicity'.

---

84   Ibid.
85   Althusser 1970, p. 106.

It is precisely at the end of this construction of the concept of historical time that Althusser offers us an indication that allows us once again to pick up on the question of the temporality of the multitude. It provides a useful understanding of the term synchronic: the synchronic not as the temporality of the real object, but as the temporal presence of the object of knowledge.[86] Althusser writes: '*The synchronic is eternity in Spinoza's sense [Le synchronique, c'est l'éternité au sens spinoziste]*'.[87]

The hermeneutic circle has come full turn: Althusser's outline renders intelligible Spinoza's theory of temporality, while receiving an ontological foundation from this intelligibility in return. And yet, this circle is not a pure, zero-sum game of interpretation. The game creates a displacement; it creates a definitive distance from the theological temporality into which Spinoza's interpretation of eternity often relapses.

6.2   *The Level of the Imaginary*

We now turn to the question of multitemporality on the plane of the imaginary. Naturally, it is grounded on ontological temporality, since the imagination is nothing but the effect and inadequate knowledge of this interweaving of durations, transfigured into a time-line travelled by a subject who is the centre and end of nature. Now, since each individual is situated differently within the interweaving of times, each individual imagines it differently, since our imagination is the cognitive repercussion, so to speak, of our position. Leibnizian perspectivism immediately comes to mind here, of course: the difference from Leibniz once again consists in the fact that in Spinoza representations (the imaginary) implicate the interweaving of times but do not explicate it. The representations register the interweaving and at the same time transfigure it according to the grammar of a centred 'I' and a single time (doubled in the play of mirrors of the finalistic prejudice of a transcendent God and an eternity that contains that same time contracted. Hence, there is

---

86   'What the synchrony aims at has nothing to do with the *temporal* presence of the object as a *real object*, but on the contrary, concerns a different type of presence, and the presence of a different object: not the temporal presence of the concrete object, not the historical time of the historical presence of the historical object, but the presence (or the "time") *of the object of knowledge of the theoretical analysis itself*, the presence *of knowledge*. The synchronic is then nothing but the *conception* of the specific relations that exist between the different elements and the different structures of the structure of the whole, it is the *knowledge* of the relations of dependence and articulation which make it an organic whole, a system' (Althusser 1970, p. 107).

87   Ibid.

no reciprocal expression of the monads as in Leibniz, no presence of everything in everything, but rather, a plurality of fragmentary and inadequate representations of the interweaving of durations, each of which is meant to be a
repository of the measure, or more, of the secret of time.[88]

As we have said, the imagination is the effect of the relation between the
body and the environment (understood in its widest sense as the biological,
social and historical environment); it implies both, but does not explicate
them.[89] It implicates them differently depending on the differences between
the bodies and the environments. The place where Spinoza provides us with a
proper map for reading these differences is the second chapter of the
Theological-Political Treatise dedicated to the prophetic imagination. Here
Spinoza writes that

> I shall show that prophecy varied not only with the imagination and the
> temperament of each prophet but also with the beliefs in which they had
> been brought up [*revelatio variabat... in unoquoque Propheta pro disposi-
> tione temperamenti corporis, imaginationis, & pro ratione opinionum quas
> antea amplexus fuerat*].[90]

Spinoza asserts therefore that the prophetic *revelatio* depends in the first place
on the *dispositio et temperamentum corporis* of the prophet, literally, on the
particular position of the body (*dis-ponere*) and on the mix of its elements, on
their proportion, and hence on the particular rhythm of the prophet's body
(*temperare* has a clear semantic tie with *tempus*), which provides the dominant passional note in each individual prophet. It depends in the second place
on the imaginative structure, whose articulation includes the theme of prophetic style, symbolic figurations [*hieroglyphica*] and perspicuity; and finally,
on the opinions of an age, namely, on the prejudices with which the prophet
himself is interwoven, based on the etymological meaning of the verb *plectere*.[91]

---

88   See Morfino 2002b.
89   What I mean by environment is not something given, naturally, but a changing system of
      relations. On this point, see chapter four of this volume, 'The Primacy of the Encounter
      Over Form'.
90   Spinoza 2002, *Theologico-Political Treatise*, II, p. 405.
91   The question of *perspicuitas* is extremely interesting. It should not be translated as 'clarity
      [chiarezza]', as Droetto does (Spinoza 1972, p. 53), since this calls up the Cartesian lan-
      guage of 'clear and evident', but rather as 'transparency' (that which allows us to *per-
      spicere*, see through), whose opposite is not 'obscurity' but rather 'opacity'. On the theme
      of the greater or lesser *perspicuitas* of the prophecies, Althusser writes: 'The prophets

Spinoza's analysis of prophetic revelation is in reality an analysis of the imagination *tout court* (and of its existence *between* the body understood biologically and society considered historically) inasmuch as all qualitative differences between the prophet and the common man are elided: the only difference lies in the *potentia vividius imaginandi* of the prophet, but not in the structure of his imagination.[92] The *potentia* and the *modus imaginandi* of each individual are determined by a complex interweaving of physiological, psychological, social, and historical factors: naturally, these factors are implicated and not explicated by the knowledge of the individual, by his imagination. These factors enter into the qualitative determination of the imaginary temporality that, *per se*, would be nothing other than the empty line constructed on the base of the absolutisation of a regular duration. This gives rise to imagined pasts, presents, and futures, both in the religious dimension of prophecy and in the secularised dimension of philosophy of history (and if what Löwith has shown is true, that every philosophy of history is founded on the secularisation of the prophetic Hebraic-Christian tradition, it must be noted that Spinoza's materialist criticism of prophecy provides the tools for deconstructing every subsequent philosophy of history *ante litteram*).[93]

I spoke about multitemporality on the plane of the imaginary precisely because the multitemporality on the ontological plane, the complex interweave of the durations with no full present which permeates the multitude with itself, gives rise to a plurality of representations of time whose difference is given by the variation in the point of intersection between the *ingenium* of the individual and the *ingenium* of the people[94] (neither exist outside the relation,

---

have not understood anything that God has said to them: it is explained to them carefully, and then generally they understand the message of God; except that imbecile Daniel who knew how to interpret dreams but who not only understood nothing of the message received from God (it was, however, the common lot of all) but, what is worse, would never comprehend any of the explanations the people gave him of the messages he had received! I saw in Daniel the prodigious proof of the stubborn resistance of every ideology to its clarification (and that against the naive theory that was to be the Enlightenment's)' (Althusser 1998, pp. 134–5).

92 For an analytical demonstration, see Bostrenghi 1996, pp. 107–33.

93 See Löwith 1989. In relation to Spinoza, see also Chaui 2003, pp. 63–80.

94 I am taking up the metaphor of Giulio Preti, who took it in his turn from Simmel, although I intend the intersection in an ontological sense and not a sociologistic (and therefore, ultimately, a classificatory) one: 'In a sufficiently evolved society, there are a lot of groups or classes or, generally, "social circles" that work and live together; and each individual, already from the fact that he or she belongs to a family and has a certain age, gender, and possibly profession, belongs simultaneously to various circles of these circles – thereby constituting a particular intersection' (Preti 1957, pp. 141–2).

they are nothing but common notions, and yet it is important to underline that there is no expressive relation between the two).[95] Such a conception allows us to avoid the double Hegelian trap of the prophet as expression of the substance of the community or the prophet as the conscience of the community.

From this perspective, Chapter XVII of the *Theological-Political Treatise*, dedicated to the history of the Jews, is of fundamental importance. At first Spinoza appears to describe the constitution of the Jewish state through the contractualistic model:

> For after their liberation from the intolerable oppression of the Egyptians, being bound by no covenant to any mortal man they regained their natural right over everything that lay within their power, and every man could decide afresh whether to retain it or to surrender it and transfer it to another. Finding themselves thus placed in this state of nature, they hearkened to Moses, in whom they all placed the greatest confidence, and resolved to transfer their right not to any mortal man, but to God alone. Without much hesitation they all promised, equally and with one voice, to obey God absolutely in all his commands and to acknowledge no other law but that which he should proclaim as such by prophetic revelation. Now this promise, or transference of right to God, was made in the same way as we have previously conceived it to be made in the case of an ordinary community when men decide to surrender their natural right.[96]

Advised by Moses, '*uno clamore promiserunt Deo, ad omnia ejus mandata absolute obtemperare, nec aliud jus agnoscere, nisi quod ipse revelatione Prophetica ut jus statueret*'. The Jewish state is thus erected on a covenant between the people and God which gives rise to a *Regnum Dei*, in which God was considered the *Rex Hebraeorum*, enemies of the state were the *hostes Dei*, usurpers were *rei lesae divinae Majestati*, and the *jura denique imperii jura et mandata Dei*. Spinoza describes in these terms the political form that '*Theocratica vocari potuit*':

---

95   As Simondon rightly says, 'Society is not the product of the reciprocal presence of many individuals; but neither is it a substantial reality to be superimposed over individual beings, almost as if it were independent of them' (Simondon 1989, p. 177).

96   Spinoza 2002, *Theologico-Political Treatise*, XVII, p. 539.

So in this state civil law and religion – which we have shown to consist only in obedience to God – were one and the same thing; the tenets of religion were not just teachings but laws and commands; piety [*pietas*] was looked upon as justice, impiety [*impietas*] as crime and injustice. He who forsook his religion ceased to be a citizen and by that alone became an enemy, and he who died for his religion was regarded as having died for his country. In short, there was considered to be no difference whatsoever between civil law and religion.[97]

Given this description, however, Spinoza makes a comment that catches us completely off guard: 'all this is matter of theory rather than fact [*Verum enim vero haec omnia opinione magis quam re constabant*]'. In actuality, the Jews entirely preserved their *jus imperii*, they did not transfer their natural right to others; rather, everybody surrendered it at the same time, just as they do in a democratic society. They gave up their natural right with the promise *uno clamore* to obey God:

> It follows that this covenant left them all completely equal, and they all had an equal right to consult God, to receive and interpret his laws; in short, they all shared equally in the government of the state. It was for this reason, then, that on the first occasion they all approached God on equal terms to hear what he wished to command. But on this first appearance before God they were so terrified and so thunderstruck at hearing God speak that they thought their last hour had come. So, overwhelmed with fear they went to Moses again, saying, 'Behold, we have heard God speaking in the midst of the fire; now therefore why should we die? For this great fire will surely consume us; if again we are to hear the voice of God, we shall surely die. Go thou near therefore, and hear all that our God shall say. And speak thou (not God) to us. All that God shall speak unto thee, we shall hear and do (Exodus 20:18).[98]

In the first covenant every *cives* could interpret God. The people decided not to exercise this right and they surrendered it to Moses, who received the power to:

1)   consult God and interpret His commands;
2)   constrain the subjects to put them into practice.

---

97   Spinoza 2002, *Theologico-Political Treatise*, XVII, p. 540.
98   Ibid.

Why did the people surrender their right? The answer lies hidden in the verb *interpretari*: the *interpres* is the prophet. The structure of the prophetic imagination is determined, as we have seen, by differences in temperament, style, symbolic figurations, perspicuity, and prejudices. The voice of God in the midst of the fire that will devour the people is not the echo of the power [*potentia*] of the multitude, but rather the deafening roar of a crowd that imagines God in a thousand different ways. For this reason Moses remained the only *lator* (promulgator) and *interpres*: as a consequence, he became '*etiam supremus judex*' and '*solus apud Hebraeos vicem Dei, hoc est, supremam majestatem habuit*':[99]

> Here we should observe that although the people chose Moses, they had no right to choose his successor. For as soon as they transferred to Moses their right to consult God and promised without reservation to regard him as the divine oracle, they completely lost all their right and were bound to accept as chosen by God whichever successor Moses should choose. Now if Moses had chosen a successor to have, like himself, complete control over the state, that is, the right to consult God alone in his tent, and consequently the authority to make and repeal laws, to make decisions on war and peace, to send envoys, to appoint judges, to choose a successor, in short, to exercise all the functions of a sovereign, the state would have become simply a monarchy. There would have been no difference but this, that ordinarily a monarchy is ruled in accordance with a decree of God which is hidden even from the monarch, whereas the Hebrew state would be, or should have been, ruled in a definite way by God's decree revealed to the monarch alone. This difference does not diminish the monarch's dominion and right over all his subjects; on the contrary, it increases it. As for the people, in both cases they are equally subject and equally ignorant of God's decree, for in both cases they are dependent on what the monarch says, understanding from him alone what is right and what is wrong. And by believing that the monarch issues commands only in accordance with God's decree as revealed to him, the people would in fact be more, not less, under the monarch's dominion. However, Moses appointed no such successor, but left the state to be so governed by those who came after him that it could be called neither a democracy nor an aristocracy nor a monarchy, but a theocracy. While the right to interpret the laws and to promulgate God's answers was vested in one man, the right and power to govern the state in accordance

---

99   Spinoza 1925, vol. 3, p. 207.

with laws thus expounded and answers thus made known was vested in another.[100]

To sum up Spinoza's argument: the Jewish state was not a theocracy in the sense of a direct government of God interpreted through one voice by the entire people (a sort of direct democracy of prophets – a concept that for Spinoza is a contradiction). It was not a democracy, it was not an aristocracy, and it was not even a monarchy (even if we make some concessions compared to the classical form of monarchy). It was a theocracy, in the sense of a division of powers between interpretation and command.

Spinoza's text does not explain, however, how Moses was able to impose his interpretation, his own prophecy, in other words. Stefano Visentin believes that the prophet is a sort of catalyser in the historical process of instituting a society:[101] this perspective rightly places the social dimension of the imaginary – or ideology, to use a Marxist term – at the centre of politics. However, it seems at the same time to negate another fundamental element of politics: violence. Spinoza, a careful reader of Machiavelli, certainly could not have been unaware of this famous passage from Book VI of *The Prince*:

> [T]he people are by nature variable; to convince them of a thing is easy; to hold them to that conviction is hard. Therefore a prophet must be ready, when they no longer believe, to make them believe by force. Moses, Cyrus, Theseus, and Romulus could not have gained long-continued observance for their constitutions if they had been unarmed. In our times, Fra Girolamo Savonarola was unarmed; hence he was destroyed amid his institutions when they were still new, as soon as the multitude ceased to believe in him.[102]

Moses was certainly not an unarmed prophet, something Machiavelli knew very well, as he shows in a passage from the *Discourses*:

---

100   Spinoza 2002, *Theologico-Political Treatise*, XVII, p. 541.

101   See Visentin 2001, pp. 125–47. Negri and Hardt also maintain something of this sort when they write: 'Perhaps we need to reinvent the notion of the materialist teleology that Spinoza proclaimed at the dawn of modernity when he claimed that the prophet produces its own people' (Negri and Hardt 2000, p. 75).

102   Machiavelli 1965, vol. 1, pp. 26–7.

He who reads the Bible intelligently sees that if Moses was to put his laws and regulations into effect, he was forced to kill countless men who, moved by nothing else than envy, were opposed to his plans.[103]

The real structure of the Jewish state, the Jewish theocracy, far from being an imaginary democracy of prophets, did not even arise from Moses's simple plan, from his prophecy (conscience of the community or expression of the substance of the community, as it may be); rather, it was the consequence of the people's adoration of a golden calf. Here, one prophecy is played against another, one imaginary temporality against another. This event led Moses to exclude the first-born sons from the sacred ministry to hand them over to the tribe of the Levites. The Biblical text openly states that the passage from one model to another was not the effect of an option offered by Moses; it was a genuine massacre, an unleashing of unprecedented violence that established a new power relation in the society:

Then Moses stood in the gate of the camp, and said, Who is on the LORD's side? let him come unto me. And all the sons of Levi gathered themselves together unto him. And he said unto them, Thus saith the LORD God of Israel, Put every man his sword by his side, and go in and out from gate to gate throughout the camp, and slay every man his brother, and every man his companion, and every man his neighbour. And the children of Levi did according to the word of Moses: and there fell of the people that day about three thousand men. For Moses had said, Consecrate yourselves today to the LORD, even every man upon his son, and upon his brother; that he may bestow upon you a blessing this day.[104]

Spinoza does not explicitly refer to this passage from *Exodus*. Instead, he cites Numbers 37, 21. But is it unrealistic to believe that he was unfamiliar with it and that he – of all people – did not know how to 'read the Bible intelligently'?

---

103 Machiavelli 1965, vol. 1, p. 496. For more on this point, see Del Lucchese 2006, pp. 9–31.
104 Exodus 32: 26–9. On the use of this passage during the English revolution, see Walzer 1985, p. 56.

7   Conclusion

What conclusion does this theory of temporality offer regarding the political sphere?

We can start with what it excludes:

1)   In the first place, this theory renders unthinkable the two great models that are founded on continuity and discontinuity: politics as the outcome of a philosophy of history (Hegel, Marx, Engels) and politics as the eruption of a full, qualitative moment into the homogenous, empty course of time (Benjamin).

2)   In the second place, this complex temporality renders unthinkable the Hobbesian *fiat* that gives rise to the constitution of the great Leviathan (but also to the decisional void theorised by Schmitt), just as it renders unthinkable the figure of the omnipotent legislator, lord of time.

3)   It renders unthinkable both the transfiguration of the multitude into the people as the subject of popular sovereignty, and its being subject in the person of the constituent power, as Antonio Negri intends it.[105]

And the *pars construens*? The weave of multitemporality that constitutes the being of the multitude renders ineffective all political action conceived as a transitive action that does not take this complexity into account. In this sense, to be equal to multitemporality, action must be strategic rather than instrumental; it must be complex action articulated in the complexity of the conjuncture.

This is the sense of the famous passage in Spinoza on Machiavelli:

In the case of a prince whose sole motive is lust for power, the means he must employ to strengthen and preserve his state [*imperium*] have been described at length by that keen observer, Machiavelli, but with what purpose remains uncertain. If he did have some good purpose in mind, as

105   I am referring in particular to Paolo Cristofolini's interpretation in his Spinoza lexicon, who writes: 'In agreement with Droetto we translate *multitudo* as "the people" rather than "the multitude", as the majority do: that which from whose *potentia* power emanates, in the language of modern constitutions, is indeed the people (one need only think of the concept of popular sovereignty)' (Spinoza 1999, p. 245).

one should believe of so wise a man, it must have been to show how fool-ish are the attempts so often made to get rid of a tyrant while yet the causes that have made the prince a tyrant cannot be removed; on the contrary, they become more firmly established as the prince is given more grounds for fear. This comes about when a people has made an example of its prince and glories in regicide as in a wonderful exploit. Perhaps he also wished to show how wary a free people should be of entrusting its welfare absolutely to one man who, unless in his vanity he thinks he can enjoy universal popularity, must go in daily fear of plots. Thus he is compelled to look more to his own defence and in his turn to plot against the people rather than to look to their interests. I am more inclined to take this view of that wise statesman because he is well known to be an advocate of freedom [*pro libertate fuisse*], and he has given some very sound advice as to how it should be safeguarded.[106]

Spinoza's view of the English revolution is well known. But does this mean, perhaps, that Spinoza did not approve of revolutions? After having long read Spinoza as a partisan of the revolution, symbolised by the self-portrait in which Spinoza would have painted himself in the guise of Masaniello, it has become fashionable to say that Spinoza was opposed to revolutions. In my view the problem is more complex and has its roots precisely in the multitemporality of the multitude. Political action must take this plurality into account, this com-plexity, this structural non-contemporaneity on the plane of the real and the imaginary (which is also real, of course) and it must provide itself with a com-plex strategy, one which will nevertheless remain forever fragile, forever sub-ject to the attacks of fortune.

Translated by Zakiya Hanafi

---

106   Spinoza 2002, *Political Treatise*, V, 7, p. 700.

Bibliography

Adorno, Theodor 1969, 'Einleitung', in *Der Positivismusstreit in der deutschen Soziologie*, Berlin: Herman Luchterhand Verlag.

Althusser, Louis 1969, *For Marx*, translated by Ben Brewster, London: Allen Lane.

——— 1974, *Philosophie et philosophie spontanée des savants*, Paris: Maspero.

——— 1976, *Essays in Self-Criticism*, translated by Grahame Lock, London: NLB.

——— 1994a, *Sur la philosophie*, Paris: Gallimard.

——— 1994b, *Écrits philosophiques et politiques*, Vol. 1, Paris: Stock/IMEC.

——— 1998, 'The Only Materialist Tradition', in *The New Spinoza*, edited by Warren Montag and Ted Stolze, Minneapolis: University of Minnesota Press.

——— 2006, *Philosophy of the Encounter: Later Writings, 1978–87*, translated by G.M. Goshgarian, London: Verso.

——— 2011, 'On Genesis', translated by Jason E. Smith, *Décalages*, 1, 2.

Althusser, Louis and Étienne Balibar 1970, *Reading Capital*, translated by Ben Brewster, London: NLB.

Aristotle 1984, *The Complete Works of Aristotle, The Revised Oxford Translation*, edited by Jonathan Barnes, Princeton: Princeton University Press.

——— 1995, *Fisica. Libri I and II*, translated by F.F. Repellini, Milano: Bruno Mondadori.

Augustine 2006, *Confessions*, translated by F.J. Sheed, Indianapolis: Hackett.

Avicenna 1977, *Liber de Philosophia Prima sive Scientia Divina I–IV*, Louvain-Leiden: E. Peters.

Balibar, Étienne 1982, *Spinoza et la politique*, PUF: Paris.

——— 1984, '"Ideologia" e "concezione del mondo" in Engels', in *Paradigmi*, 2, 5.

——— 1997, 'Spinoza: From Individuality to Transindividuality', *Mededelingen vanwege het Spinoza-huis*, Delft: Eburon.

——— 2009, 'Une rencontre en Romagne', in Louis Althusser, *Machiavel et nous*, Paris: Editions Tallandier.

Belaval, Yvon 1976, *Etudes leibniziennes*, Paris: Gallimard.

Benjamin, Walter 1997, *Über den Begriff der Geschichte*, in *Sul concetto di storia*, Torino: Einaudi.

Biard, Jacques et al. 1983, *Introduction à la lecture de la* Science de la logique *de Hegel*, Paris: Aubier Montaigne.

Bloch, Ernst 1971, *Gesamtausgabe*, Frankfurt: Suhrkamp.

——— 1975, *Werkausgabe*, Frankfurt: Suhrkamp.

——— 1986, *The Principle of Hope*, Vol. 2, translated by Neville Plaice, Stephen Plaice, and Paul Knight, Cambridge: MIT.

——— 1990, *Heritage of Our Times*, translated by Neville Plaice and Stephen Plaice, Berkeley, CA: University of California Press.

Bodei, Remo 1979, *Multiversum, Tempo e storia in Ernst Bloch*, Naples: Bibliopolis.

Bostrenghi, Daniela 1996, *Forme e virtù dell'immaginazione in Spinoza*, Naples: Bibliopolis.

Bove, Laurent 1994, 'Epicureisme et spinozisme: l'éthique', *Archives de Philosophie*, 57, 471–84.

Breton, Stanislas 1993, 'Althusser aujord'hui', *Archives de Philosophie*, 56: 417–30.

Canguilhem, Georges 2008, *Knowledge of Life*, translated by Stefanos Geroulanos and Daniela Ginsburg, New York: Fordham University Press.

Chaui, Marilena 2003, *Política em Espinosa*, São Paulo: Companhia das Letras.

Conry, Yvette (ed.) 1983, *De Darwin au darwinisme*, Paris: Vrin.

D'Anna, Giuseppe 2002, *Uno intuitu videre, Sull'ultimo genere di conoscenza in Spinoza*, Milan: Ghibli.

Darwin, Charles 1988, *The Works of Charles Darwin*, London: William Pickering.

Del Lucchese, Filippo 2006, 'Sedizione e modernità', *Quaderni materialisti*, 5.

Derrida, Jacques 1993, *Spectres de Marx*, Paris: Galilée.

Descartes, René 1985, *The Philosophical Writings of Descartes*, translated by John Cottingham et al., Cambridge: Cambridge University Press.

Dietzgen, Joseph 1984, *The Nature of Human Brainwork*, translated by E. Untermann, Vancouver: Red Lion Press.

Doz, André 1987, *La logiques de Hegel et les problèmes traditionnels de l'ontologie*, Paris: Vrin.

Epicurus 1994, *The Epicurus Reader*, edited by Brad Inwood and L.P. Gerson, Indianapolis: Hackett.

Fichte, Johann Gottlieb 1847, *The Vocation of the Scholar*, translated by William Smith, London: John Chapman.

—— 1968, *Gesamtausgabe*, Stuttgart: Frommann.

Findlay, John 1958, *Hegel, a Re-examination*, London: George Allen.

Fleishmann, Eugene 1964, 'Die Wirklichkeit in Hegels Logik, Ideengeschichtliche Beziehungen zu Spinoza', *Zeitschrift für philosophische Forschung*, 18.

—— 1968, *La science universelle ou la Logique de Hegel*, Paris: Librairie Plon.

Gerbier, Laurent 1999, *Histoire, médecine et politique. Les figures du temps dans le* Prince *et les* Discours *de Machiavel*, doctoral thesis under the direction of B. Pinchard.

Häckel, Ernst 1883, *The History of Creation*, translated by E. Lankester, London: Kegan Paul.

Harris, Errol 1987, *Lire la logique de Hegel*, Lausanne: L'Age de l'homme.

Hegel, Georg Wilhelm Friedrich 1911–44, *Sämtliche Werke*, edited by Georg Lasson, Leipzig: Meiner.

—— 1968, *Gesammelte Werke*, edited by Nordrhein-Westfälischen Akademie der Wissenschaften, Hamburg: Meiner.

—— 1977, *Phenomenology of Spirit*, translated by A.V. Miller, Oxford: Oxford University Press.

—— 1989, *Hegel's Science of Logic*, translated by A.V. Miller, Atlantic Highlands, NJ: Humanities Press International.

―――― 2008, *Outlines of the Philosophy of Right*, translated by T.M. Knox, Oxford: Oxford University Press.

Heidegger, Martin 1977, *Sein und Zeit*, in *Gesamtausgabe*, Vol. 2, Frankfurt: Klostermann.

Henninger, Mark 1989, *Relations*, Oxford: Clarendon Press.

Husserl, Edmund 1950, *Cartesian Meditations*, Boston: Kluwer.

Kant, Immanuel 1996, *Critique of Pure Reason*, translated by Werner Pluhar, Indianapolis: Hackett Publishers.

Kojève, Alexandre 1969, *Introduction to the Reading of Hegel*, edited by Allan Bloom, New York: Basic Books.

Knebel, Sven 2001, 'Intrinsic and extrinsic denomination: what makes Leibniz's departure from schoolmen so bewildering?', in *Nihil sine ratione*, edited by Hans Poser, Hannover: Gottfried-Wilhelm-Leibniz-Gesellschaft.

Jankélévitch, Vladimir 1980, *Le Je-ne-sais-quoi et le Presque-rien I, La manière et l'occasion*, Paris: Editions du Seuil.

Inwood, Michael 1992, *A Hegel Dictionary*, Oxford: Blackwell.

Lakebrink, Bernhard 1979, *Kommentar zu Hegels* Logik *in seiner* Enzyclopädie *von 1830, Vol. 1 Sein und Wesen*, Freiburg-München: Alber.

Lecourt, Dominique 1983, 'Marx au crible de Darwin', in *De Darwin au darwinisme*, Conry, Yvette 1983.

Leibniz, Gottfried 1960, *Die philosophischen Schriften*, edited by C.I. Gerhardt, Hildesheim: Georg Olms.

―――― 1970, *Philosophical Papers and Letters*, translated by Leroy E. Loemker, Dordrecht: D. Reidel.

―――― 1981, *New Essays on Human Understanding*, translated by Peter Remnant and Jonathan Bennett, Cambridge: Cambridge University Press.

Lenin, Vladimir Ilyich 2004, *Revolution at the Gates: A Selection of Writings from February to October 1917*, edited by Slavoj Žižek, London: Verso.

Léonard, André 1974, *Commentaire littéral de la logique de Hegel*, Paris: Vrin.

Locke, John 1975, *An Essay Concerning Human Understanding*, edited by Peter H. Nidditch, Oxford: Clarendon Press.

Longuenesse, Béatrice 1981, *Hegel et la critique de la métaphysique*, Paris: Vrin.

Löwith, Karl 1949, *Meaning in History*, Chicago: The University of Chicago Press.

Macherey, Pierre 1979, *Hegel ou Spinoza*, Paris: Maspero.

―――― 1992a, 'Action et opération: sur la signification éthique du De Deo', in *Avec Spinoza. Etudes sur la doctrine et l'histoire du spinozisme*, Paris: PUF.

―――― 1992b, 'L'actualité philosophique de Spinoza (Heidegger, Adorno, Foucault)', in *Avec Spinoza*, Paris: PUF.

Machiavelli, Niccolò 1965, *The Chief Works and Others*, translated by Allan Gilbert, Durham, NC: Duke University Press.

Mao Tse-Tung 2007, *On Practice and Contradiction*, London: Verso.

Marion, Jean-Luc 1999, *On Descartes' Metaphysical Prism*, translated by Jeffrey L. Kosky, Chicago: University of Chicago Press.

Marx, Karl 1973, *Grundrisse*, translated by Martin Nicolaus, London: Penguin.

Marx, Karl and Friedrich Engels 1975–2005, *Collected Works*, London: Lawrence and Wishart.

Monod, Jacques 1970, *Le hasard et la nécessité. Essai sur la philosophie naturelle de la biologie*, Paris: Editions du Seuil.

Montag, Warren 2005, 'Who's Afraid of the Multitude?', *South Atlantic Quarterly*, 104, 4: 655–73.

Moreau, Pierre-François 1989, 'Métaphysique de la substance et métaphysique de la form', in *Méthode et métaphysique*, Paris: Presses Universitaires de France.

—— 1994, 'Epicurus et Spinoza: la physique', *Archives de Philosophie*, 57: 541–58.

Morfino, Vittorio 1997, *Substantia sive Organismus. Immagine e funzione teorica di Spinoza negli scritti jenesi di Hegel*, Milano: Guerini.

—— 1999, 'L'evoluzione della categoria di causalità in Spinoza', *Rivista di storia della filosofia*, 2: 239–54.

—— 2002a, *Il tempo e l'occasione. L'incontro Spinoza Machiavelli*, Milano: LED.

—— 2002b, 'L'epoca dell'immagine del mondo: evidenza o adeguazione', *Oltrecorrente*, 5.

—— 2002c, *Incursioni Spinoziste*, Milano: Mimesis.

—— 2005, 'An Althusserian Lexicon', *Borderlands*, 4, 2.

—— 2007, 'Retour sur l'enjeu du vide', in *Pascal et Spinoza*, edited by Laurent Bove, Gérard Bras, Erich Méchoulan, Paris: Editions Amsterdam.

—— 2010, 'Escatologia à la cantonade. Althusser oltre Derrida', *Décalages*, 1, 1.

Morfino, Vittorio and Luca Pinzolo 2000, 'Introduzione', in Louis Althusser, *Sul materialismo aleatorio*, Milano: Unicopli.

—— 2005, 'Le primat de la rencontre sur la forme. Le dernier Althusser entre nature et histoire', *Multitudes*, 21: 149–58.

Mugnai, Massimo 1976, *Astrazione e Realtà. Saggio su Leibniz*, Milan: Feltrinelli.

Nancy, Jean-Luc 1996, *Être singulier pluriel*, Paris: Galilée.

—— 2000, *Being Singular Plural*, translated by Robert D. Richardson and Anne E. O'Byrne, Stanford, CA.: Stanford University Press.

Negri, Antonio 1991, *The Savage Anomaly*, Minneapolis: University of Minnesota Press.

—— 1999, *Insurgencies. Constituent Power and the Modern State*, Minneapolis: University of Minnesota Press.

—— 2008, *Reflections on Empire*, translated by Ed Emery, Cambridge: Polity.

Negri, Antonio and Michael Hardt 2000, *Empire*, London: Harvard University Press.

Opiela, Stanislas 1983, *Le réel dans la logique de Hegel, Dévelopment et auto-determination*, Paris: Beauchesne.

Paci, Enzo 1959, *Dall'esistenzialismo al relazionismo*, Messina-Firenze: D'Anna.

Plekhanov, George 1969, *Fundamental Problems of Marxism*, New York: International.

Plato 1961, *The Collected Dialogues*, edited by Edith Hamilton and Huntington Cairns, Princeton: Princeton University Press.

Plotinus 1962, *The Enneads*, translated by Stephen MacKenna, London: Faber and Faber.

Preti Giulio 1957, *Praxis ed empirismo*, Turin: Einaudi.

Robinet, André et al. 1977, *Spinoza Ethica. Concordances, Index, Liste des fréquences, Tables comparatives*, Louvain-la-Neuve: Université de Louvain.

Russell, Bertrand 1900, *A Critical Exposition of the Philosophy of Leibniz*, London: Allen and Unwin.

Saussure, Ferdinand 1986, *Course in General Linguistics*, translated by Roy Harris, Chicago: Open Court, 1986.

Serres, Michel 1977, *La naissance de la physique dans le texte de Lucrèce*, Paris: Les Editions de Minuit.

Schelling, Friedrich Wilhelm Joseph 1978, *System of Transcendental Idealism*, translated by Peter Heath, Charlottesville: University Press Virginia.

Schopenhauer, Arthur 1999, *Prize Essay on the Freedom of the Will*, Cambridge: Cambridge University Press.

Schöttler, Peter 1993, 'Althusser and Annales Historiography. An Impossible Dialogue?', in *The Althusserian Legacy*, edited by E.A. Kaplan and M. Sprinker, London: Verso.

Sextus Empiricus 2000, *Outlines of Scepticism*, edited by Julia Annas and Jonathan Barnes, Cambridge: Cambridge University Press.

Simondon, Gilbert 1989, *L'individuation psychique et collective à la lumière des notions de Forme, Potentiel et Métastabilité*, Paris: Edition Aubier.

Sini, Carlo 1991, *La verità pubblica e Spinoza*, Milan: CUEM.

Spinoza, Baruch 1925, *Opera*, edited by C. Gebhardt, Heidelberg: Carl Winters.

——— 1972, *Trattato teologico-politico*, translated by A. Droetto and E. Giancotti, Turin: Einaudi.

——— 1999, *Tractatus politicus/Trattato politico*, translated by Paolo Cristofolini, Pisa: ETS.

——— 2000, *Tractatus Theologico-politicus/Traité théologique-politique*, translated by J. Lagrée and P.F. Moreau, Paris: PUF.

——— 2002, *Complete Works*, edited by Michael Morgan, Indianapolis: Hackett.

Timpanaro, Sebastiano 1972, *Sul materialismo*, Pisa: Nistri-Lischi.

Thomas Aquinas 1912, *Summa Theologica*, translated by Fathers of the English Dominican Province, London: Washbourne, 1912.

Tosel, André 1993, 'Des usages "marxistes" de Spinoza', in *Spinoza au XXᵉ siècle*, edited by O. Bloch, Paris: PUF.

Vergani, Mario 2004, 'La lecture husserlienne de Leibniz et l'idée de monadologie', *Les études philosophiques*, 4, 71.

Virno, Paolo 2004, *A Grammar of the Multitude*, translated by Isabella Berti et al., Los Angeles, CA: Semiotext[e].

Visentin, Stefano 2001, *La libertà necessaria. Teoria e pratica della democrazia in Spinoza*, Pisa: ETS.

Walzer, Michael 1985, *Exodus and Revolution*, New York: Basic Books.

Wieland, Wolfgang 1962, *Die aristotelische Physik. Untersuchungen über die Grundlegung der Naturwissenschaft und die sprachlichen Bedingungen der Prinzipienforschung bei Aristoteles*, Göttingen: Vandenhoeck & Ruprecht.

Yamane, Tomoyuki 1983, *Wirklichkeit. Interpretation eines Kapitels aus Hegels Wissenschaft der Logik*, Frankfurt: Peter Lang.

Index of Names

Index of Subjects

Time forms and Social Domination